*If you really want to hurt your parents,
and you don't have the nerve to be a homosexual,
the least you can do is go into the arts.*
                                          —Kurt Vonnegut

THE GREATEST MYTH OF ROCK & ROLL

Created by Eric Segalstad and Josh Hunter

Samadhi Creations
Berkeley Lake

Published by Samadhi Creations
Berkeley Lake

First printing, October 27, 2008
10 9 8 7 6 5 4 3 2 1

ISBN 978-0-615-18964-2
Library of Congress Control Number: 2008908637

The 27s: The Greatest Myth of Rock & Roll
Created by Eric Segalstad and Josh Hunter.
Proofread and copy edited by Ashley Ess.

Printed in Canada by Transcontinental

ALEXANDRE LEVY
b. Nov. 10, 1864
São Paulo, Brazil
d. Jan. 17, 1892
São Paulo, Brazil

LOUIS CHAUVIN
b. Mar. 13, 1881
St. Louis, Missouri
d. Mar. 26, 1908
Chicago, Illinois

ROBERT JOHNSON
b. May 8, 1911
Hazelhurst, Mississippi
d. Aug. 16, 1938
Greenwood, Mississippi

MALCOLM HALE
b. May 17, 1941
Butte, Montana
d. Oct. 30, 1968
Chicago, Illinois

BRIAN JONES
b. Feb. 28, 1942
Cheltenham,
Gloucestershire, England
d. July 3, 1969
Hartfield, Sussex, England

ALAN WILSON
b. July 4, 1943
Boston, Massachusetts
d. Sep. 3, 1970
LA, California

JIM MORRISON
b. Dec. 8, 1943
Melbourne, Florida
d. July 3, 1971
Paris, France

RON McKERNAN
b. Sep. 8, 1945
San Bruno, California
d. Mar. 8, 1973
Corte Madero, California

ROGER LEE DURHAM
b. Feb. 14, 1946
Kansas City, Missouri
d. July 27, 1973

NAT JAFFE
b. Jan. 1, 1918
NYC, New York
d. Aug. 5, 1945
NYC, New York

JESSE BELVIN
b. Dec. 15, 1932
San Antonio, Texas
D. Feb. 6, 1960
Hope, Arkansas

RUDY LEWIS
b. Aug. 23, 1936

d. May 20, 1964

JIMI HENDRIX
b. Nov. 27, 1942
Seattle, Washington
d. Sep. 18, 1970
London, England

JANIS JOPLIN
b. Jan. 9, 1943
Port Arthur, Texas
D. Oct. 4, 1970
LA, California

ARLESTER CHRISTIAN
b. June. 13, 1943
Buffalo, New York
d. Mar. 13, 1971
Phoenix, Arizona

WALLACE YOHN
b. Jan. 12, 1947

d. Aug. 12, 1974
Jackson, Minnesota

DAVID MICHAEL ALEXANDER
b. June 3, 1947
Whitmore Lake, Michigan
d. Feb. 10, 1975
Ann Arbor, Michigan

PETE HAM
b. Apr. 27, 1947
Swansea, Wales
d. Apr. 23, 1975
Surrey, England

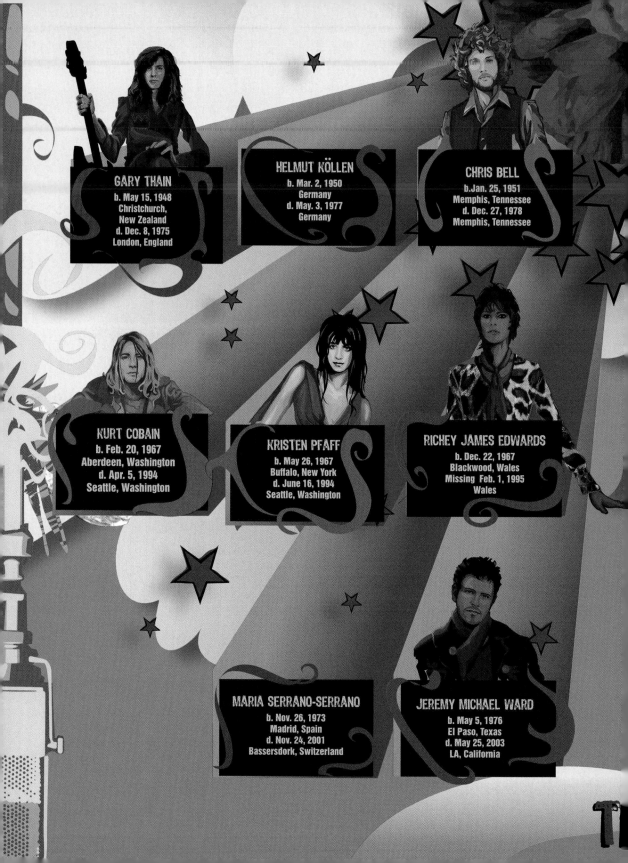

GARY THAIN
b. May 15, 1948
Christchurch,
New Zealand
d. Dec. 8, 1975
London, England

HELMUT KÖLLEN
b. Mar. 2, 1950
Germany
d. May. 3, 1977
Germany

CHRIS BELL
b.Jan. 25, 1951
Memphis, Tennessee
d. Dec. 27, 1978
Memphis, Tennessee

KURT COBAIN
b. Feb. 20, 1967
Aberdeen, Washington
d. Apr. 5, 1994
Seattle, Washington

KRISTEN PFAFF
b. May 26, 1967
Buffalo, New York
d. June 16, 1994
Seattle, Washington

RICHEY JAMES EDWARDS
b. Dec. 22, 1967
Blackwood, Wales
Missing Feb. 1, 1995
Wales

MARIA SERRANO-SERRANO
b. Nov. 26, 1973
Madrid, Spain
d. Nov. 24, 2001
Bassersdork, Switzerland

JEREMY MICHAEL WARD
b. May 5, 1976
El Paso, Texas
d. May 25, 2003
LA, California

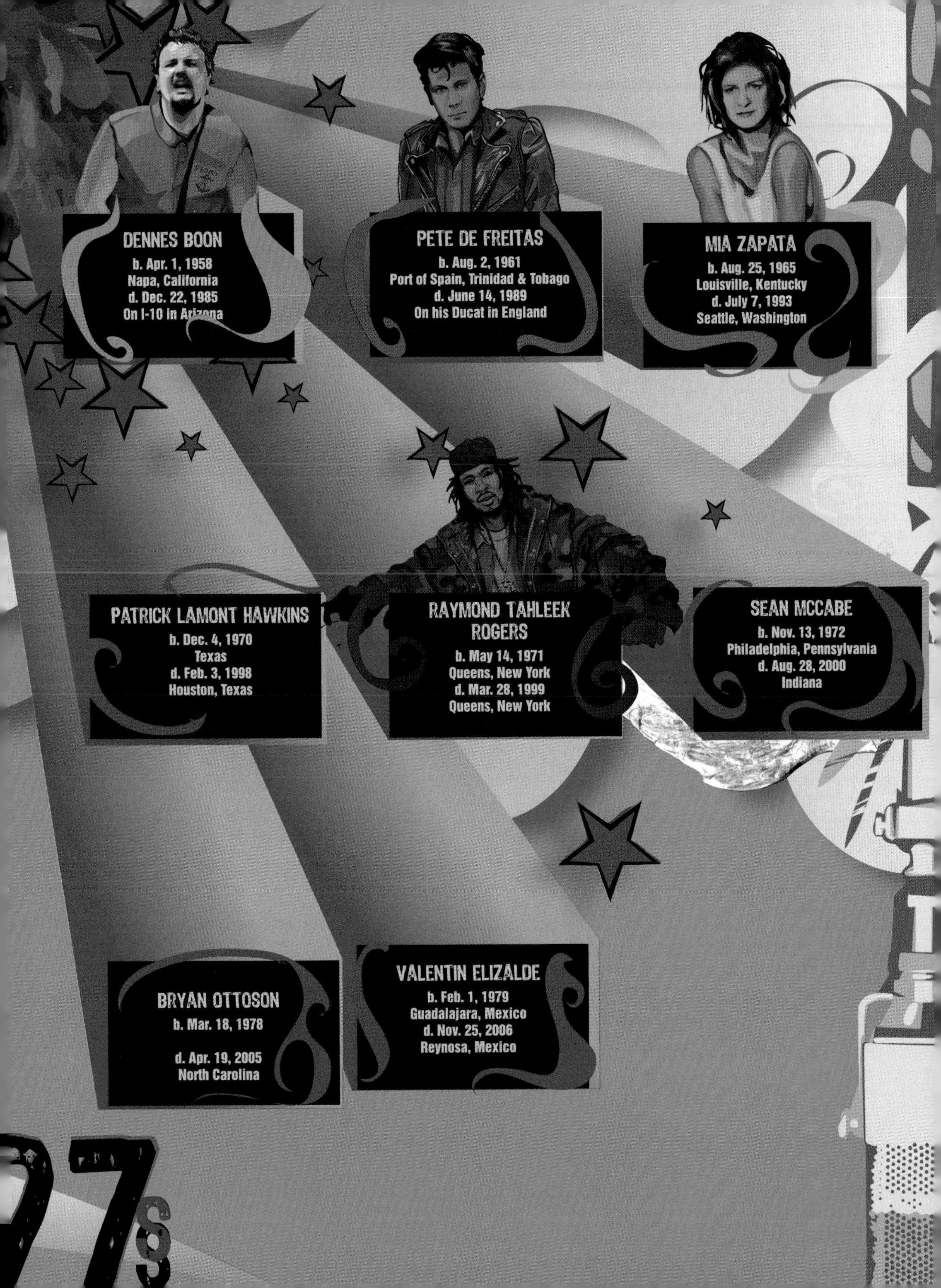

DENNES BOON
b. Apr. 1, 1958
Napa, California
d. Dec. 22, 1985
On I-10 in Arizona

PETE DE FREITAS
b. Aug. 2, 1961
Port of Spain, Trinidad & Tobago
d. June 14, 1989
On his Ducat in England

MIA ZAPATA
b. Aug. 25, 1965
Louisville, Kentucky
d. July 7, 1993
Seattle, Washington

PATRICK LAMONT HAWKINS
b. Dec. 4, 1970
Texas
d. Feb. 3, 1998
Houston, Texas

RAYMOND TAHLEEK ROGERS
b. May 14, 1971
Queens, New York
d. Mar. 28, 1999
Queens, New York

SEAN MCCABE
b. Nov. 13, 1972
Philadelphia, Pennsylvania
d. Aug. 28, 2000
Indiana

BRYAN OTTOSON
b. Mar. 18, 1978

d. Apr. 19, 2005
North Carolina

VALENTIN ELIZALDE
b. Feb. 1, 1979
Guadalajara, Mexico
d. Nov. 25, 2006
Reynosa, Mexico

27s

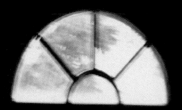

"He'd come to install an alarm system. The irony
is that long before electrician Gary Smith found
Kurt Cobain's body, it was clear that what Nirvana's
singer really needed protection from was himself. Cobain
wasn't identified for hours, but his mother, Wendy O'Connor,
didn't need anyone to tell her that it was her son who was found with
a shotgun and a suicide note that reportedly ended, "I love you, I love you."
The singer had been missing, and his mother had feared that the most troubled
and talented rock star of his generation would go the way of Jim Morrison and
Jimi Hendrix. "Now he's gone and joined that stupid club," she told the Associated
Press. "I told him not to join that stupid club."
—Jeff Giles for *Newsweek*, April 18, 1994

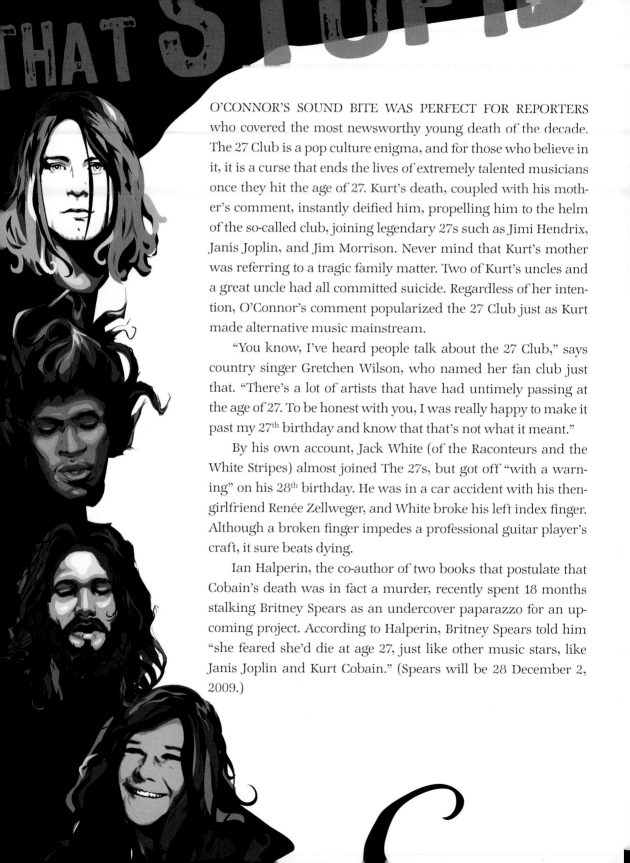

O'CONNOR'S SOUND BITE WAS PERFECT FOR REPORTERS who covered the most newsworthy young death of the decade. The 27 Club is a pop culture enigma, and for those who believe in it, it is a curse that ends the lives of extremely talented musicians once they hit the age of 27. Kurt's death, coupled with his mother's comment, instantly deified him, propelling him to the helm of the so-called club, joining legendary 27s such as Jimi Hendrix, Janis Joplin, and Jim Morrison. Never mind that Kurt's mother was referring to a tragic family matter. Two of Kurt's uncles and a great uncle had all committed suicide. Regardless of her intention, O'Connor's comment popularized the 27 Club just as Kurt made alternative music mainstream.

"You know, I've heard people talk about the 27 Club," says country singer Gretchen Wilson, who named her fan club just that. "There's a lot of artists that have had untimely passing at the age of 27. To be honest with you, I was really happy to make it past my 27th birthday and know that that's not what it meant."

By his own account, Jack White (of the Raconteurs and the White Stripes) almost joined The 27s, but got off "with a warning" on his 28th birthday. He was in a car accident with his then-girlfriend Renée Zellweger, and White broke his left index finger. Although a broken finger impedes a professional guitar player's craft, it sure beats dying.

Ian Halperin, the co-author of two books that postulate that Cobain's death was in fact a murder, recently spent 18 months stalking Britney Spears as an undercover paparazzo for an upcoming project. According to Halperin, Britney Spears told him "she feared she'd die at age 27, just like other music stars, like Janis Joplin and Kurt Cobain." (Spears will be 28 December 2, 2009.)

Musicians aren't alone with this fear and fascination, of course. Astrologers at the Astrological Lodge of London have reconstructed the most famous 27s' natal charts in an attempt to understand why they died when they did. Teenagers, college kids, and bloggers increasingly discuss The 27-phenomenon as well.

Wikipedia has featured an entry on The 27s since 2005, but even after more than four hundred revisions, the article still includes musicians who didn't die at 27 and excludes others who did.

Regardless, the *idea* of The 27s is seeping into our pop cultural consciousness, and it's being addressed in film, literature, and on the theater stage.

The 27 Club premiered at the 2008 Tribeca Film Festival in New York, but contrary to what you'd expect, it's not a biopic about these notorious musicians. The title lingers like a contextual backdrop for the fictional death of rocker Tom Wallace. The plot takes his bandmate on the long road from Los Angeles to New York on an errand to deliver a message left on a Post-It note to Wallace's authoritarian father.

NIRVANA
HOLE
BADFINGER
ECHO & THE B
BIG STAR
MINUTEMEN
THE MARS VO
THE ROLLING S
THE DOORS
DYKE & THE B
JIMI HENDRIX
GRATEFUL DEA
CANNED HEAT
JANIS JOPLIN
THE GITS
LOST BOYZ
THE DRIFTERS
THE STOOGES
URIAH HEEP
JESSE BELVIN
INK & DAGGER
AMERICAN HE
TRIUMVIRAT

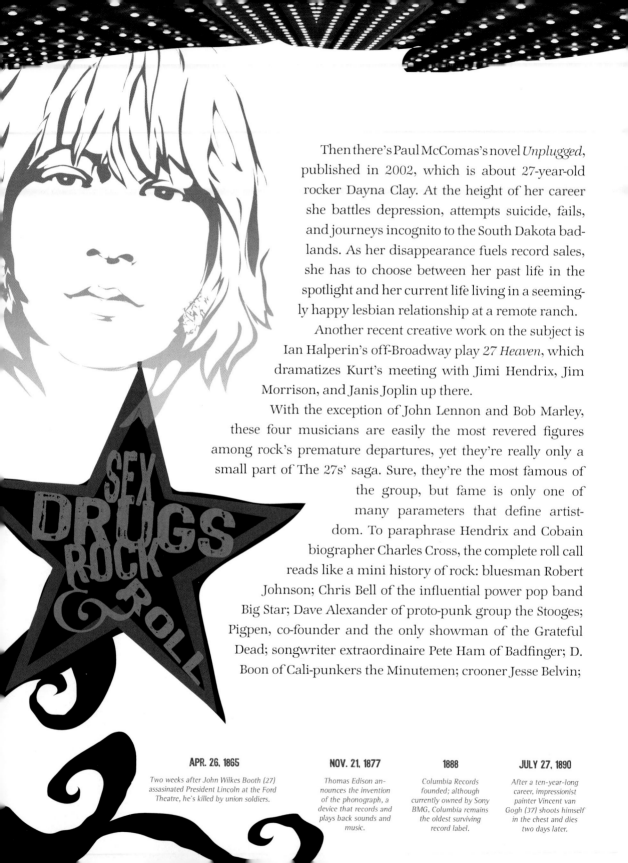

Then there's Paul McComas's novel *Unplugged*, published in 2002, which is about 27-year-old rocker Dayna Clay. At the height of her career she battles depression, attempts suicide, fails, and journeys incognito to the South Dakota badlands. As her disappearance fuels record sales, she has to choose between her past life in the spotlight and her current life living in a seemingly happy lesbian relationship at a remote ranch.

Another recent creative work on the subject is Ian Halperin's off-Broadway play *27 Heaven*, which dramatizes Kurt's meeting with Jimi Hendrix, Jim Morrison, and Janis Joplin up there.

With the exception of John Lennon and Bob Marley, these four musicians are easily the most revered figures among rock's premature departures, yet they're really only a small part of The 27s' saga. Sure, they're the most famous of the group, but fame is only one of many parameters that define artist-dom. To paraphrase Hendrix and Cobain biographer Charles Cross, the complete roll call reads like a mini history of rock: bluesman Robert Johnson; Chris Bell of the influential power pop band Big Star; Dave Alexander of proto-punk group the Stooges; Pigpen, co-founder and the only showman of the Grateful Dead; songwriter extraordinaire Pete Ham of Badfinger; D. Boon of Cali-punkers the Minutemen; crooner Jesse Belvin;

APR. 26, 1865

Two weeks after John Wilkes Booth (27) assasinated President Lincoln at the Ford Theatre, he's killed by union soldiers.

NOV. 21, 1877

Thomas Edison announces the invention of the phonograph, a device that records and plays back sounds and music.

1888

Columbia Records founded; although currently owned by Sony BMG, Columbia remains the oldest surviving record label.

JULY 27, 1890

After a ten-year-long career, impressionist painter Vincent van Gogh (37) shoots himself in the chest and dies two days later.

Hole's Kristin Pfaff; sound creator Jeremy Ward of The Mars Volta—and the list continues. Not all hover as important musical icons, but every one of them is a first-rate exponent of their style, whose influence lingers on today.

The 27s permeate across genres that have defined western music over the last century. Their lives and legacies are woven into the fabric of pop culture. Together, The 27s form the veins and arteries of rock & roll in all its beauty, tragedy, ugliness, glamour, stupidity, addiction, and diversity. Music would've sounded very different without their musical contributions, yet rock continues without their physical presence. This is the story of The 27s.

MAY 27, 1891

French poet Arthur Rimbaud's leg amputated; he dies six months later.

1898

Bayer markets heroin as a non-addictive alternative to morphine.

1903

The National League and the American League organize Major League Baseball.

SEP. 27, 1908

Henry Ford's first Model T rolls out of the factory.

American musicians who would later shape rock spent the early 1960s playing mostly white folk music (with some blues and bluegrass thrown in for good measure), while their British counterparts were hard-core blues fans. British schoolboys peered almost exclusively through dusty 78s at the record shop and went home listening closely for inspiration through the static. As a teen, Brian Jones was one such budding musician, and he founded the Rolling Stones to play the music he loved—music that was, at the time, at least thirty years old.

In the 1920s, "the blues" was Delta-slang for sadness, short for having a fit of the blue devils. The color itself connotes injury—black and blue, the color of a bruise—but being down isn't necessarily coupled with out. A blue sky signifies opportunity, a chance to create something from nothing, which is what the early blues purveyors did on street corners and in lumber mills and roadhouses. The venues scattered throughout the Delta, over in Texas, and up the Atlantic Coast were collectively known as the Chitlin' Circuit. The name stemmed from a dish often served at the same places: boiled, stewed, or fried pig intestines known as chitlins.

Life as a traveling musician obliterated the chains of incessant farm work and with it century-old bonds of slavery. But existence was still filled with suffering, which the lyrics reflected.

CHARLIE PATTON
1891-1934

is often credited as the first bluesman, and his style was mimicked and refined by artists like Lonnie Johnson, Blind Lemon Jefferson, Tommy Johnson, Skip James, Leadbelly, Blind Willie McTell, Son House, and Willie Brown. Patton was an accomplished composer, performer, and showman who played guitar behind his back, behind his head, and on his knees forty years before Jimi Hendrix dazzled white audiences with the same tricks.

The blues came to represent life's dichotomy, its highs and lows, freedom and agony, and were sung mixing humor and fatalism, the predecessor to hip-hop lyrics of today.

The heart of blues country was the impoverished Mississippi Delta—a place where sharecropping, old world feudalism, and lynching were still commonplace. It was here that a teenager named Robert Johnson first heard the tantalizing sounds of the blues. He'd often sneak out on Saturday nights and listen to Son House and Willie Brown whip the crowd into frenzy at the local juke joint. While people drank and danced, young Robert sat mesmerized at the musicians' feet. At set break he pestered his heroes until they'd let him play. Unfortunately, Robert's chops sagged the audience, so the guitar was taken away from him. He was still better at playing the Jew-harp.

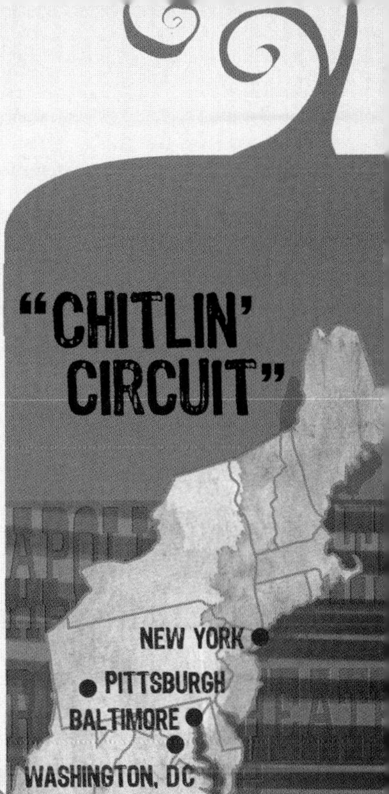

"CHITLIN' CIRCUIT"

NEW YORK
PITTSBURGH
BALTIMORE
WASHINGTON, DC
LOUISVILLE
RALEIGH
CHARLOTTE
COLUMBIA
LITTLE ROCK
ATLANTA
BIRMINGHAM
MACON
SHREVEPORT
JACKSON
ALBANY
JACKSONVILLE
AUSTIN
NEW ORLEANS

Johnson's first instrument was an unusual three-string version of the Diddley Bow—usually a one-string instrument made by stretching wire between nails on the side of a clapboard house. Tuned with a brick jammed at one end, the player changed the pitch with a glass bottle and used a firm stick to whip notes into the thick air.

By the time he pestered Son and Willie for a chance to play, he had picked up a cheapo second-hand guitar that only came with four strings. Robert had to save pennies to buy the last two strings, which cost him ten cents.

At nineteen he married a sixteen-year-old girl who lived further down in the Delta. Johnson's playing improved, and he gigged juke joints and lumber camps with the harmonica and the guitar. When his wife died in labor, Johnson "the family man" died with her. The young bluesman transformed into a rootless gypsy.

Slinging the guitar across his back, Robert Johnson headed back north. One night he walked into a juke joint where Son House was playing. Robert asked if he could play, but it took some convincing before the wizened Son budged. "And when that boy started playing and when he got through, all our mouths were standing open," Son reminisced a few decades later. "He was awful moufy—a terrible big chatterbox—proud as a peafowl."

During the depression Johnson hopped trains from place to place with drifters and hobos. Johnny Shines, a fellow musician and travel partner, recollected that even after a day of dusty travel Robert would appear neat and clean.

Robert Johnson lived and died in relative obscurity compared to his more famous peers. He was a restless, sly, street-smart, whisky-drinking hobo with a guitar and a gifted ability to pick up and

JULY 4, 1910	JUNE 28, 1914	AUG. 10, 1915	1917
Boxer Jack Johnson knocks out James Jeffries, sparking race riots across the US.	*World War I kicks off when a gunshot kills Austrian Archduke Franz Ferdinand in Sarajevo.*	*The periodic table's organizer, physicist Henry Moseley (27), bows to a bullet in the trenches.*	*Lev Sergeivitch Termen, a Russian cellist and engineer, invents the world's first electric instrument: the Theremin.*

synthesize the music he heard in juke joints, from records, and on the radio.

"Robert just picked songs out of the air," Shines said. "You could have the radio on, and he'd be talking to you and you'd have no idea that he'd be thinking of it, because he'd just go right on talking, but later he'd play that song note for note."

His repertoire wasn't comprised of just blues numbers, but as Shines tells it, "all kinds of songs. Hillbilly, blues, and all the rest."

The highlight of Robert Johnson's career was cutting tracks in Texas. The first session took place at the Gunter Hotel in San Antonio in November 1936. Producer Don Law says he had to bail out Johnson on a vagrancy charge after he had been out walking. A few hours later, Law received a phone call from the hotel. It was Johnson asking for money. "I'm lonesome and there's a lady here," he said. "She wants fifty cents and I lacks a nickel."

During the sessions, Robert Johnson played facing the corner of the room. Some say that the professional street performer was shy; others claim that he played to the corner for improved acoustics. He was known to hide his spidery fingers from onlooking musicians (which was after all how he had studied Son and Willie), so there's a chance facing the corner was a way to conceal his licks from the white suit-clad producer and recording engineer.

Johnson recorded sixteen tracks over the course of three days and approached recordings differently than most blues entertainers of his day. Robert's songs were tidy, well-rehearsed, and short enough to fit the single format. He avoided using floating verses, as championed by Son House, but focused instead on communicating specific messages, both metaphorical and real.

JAN. 16, 1920

The US Prohibition enacted, beginning an era of moonshine stills and underground mobster clubs to quench the thirsty.

JUNE 26, 1926

27-year-old Ernest Hemingway debuts with The Sun Also Rises, which many consider his best novel.

AUG. 4, 1927

Jimmie Rodgers, the father of country music, records his first tracks.

1928

Bluesman Tommy Johnson records "Canned Heat Blues."

He left November 27 with a few hundred dollars for his efforts, which was probably more money than he had ever seen. A few months later "Terra Plane Blues" was released as a single and sold fairly well for a new artist. About 5,000 copies were fed to jukeboxes scattered throughout the Delta.

Nobody knew what Robert Johnson looked like of course, but from time to time he'd be busking and somebody would request "Terra Plane Blues." He'd light up and proudly say, "I wrote that!"

A second session took place seven months later at a warehouse in Dallas. He cut thirteen more takes, including a fast-swinging ditty titled "They're Red Hot" that sounds like a guaranteed success on the dance floor even by contemporary standards.

Robert's main contributions to the blues was-assimilating a legacy of songs that are now considered classics, as well as transposing the boogie shuffle from the piano to the guitar.

"Sweet Home Chicago" is a prime example of both. It's a reworked Kokomo Arnold hit, but Johnson's arrangement is the definitive version. Just listen to the bass shuffle that's driving the song: that riff of boogie triplets *is* the blues.

"Some of the things that Robert did with the guitar affected the way everybody played," Shines said. "In the early thirties, boogie was rare on the guitar, something to be heard. Because of Robert, people learned to complement theirselves, carrying their own bass as well as their own lead with this one instrument." Nevertheless, it took a few decades until Robert Johnson's brilliant style really came into play.

AUG. 2, 1937	DEC. 23-24, 1938	SEP. 1, 1939	APR. 16, 1943
The US Marihuana Tax Act criminalizes the sale of this useful plant. Hollywood follows up with movies such as Reefer Madness.	John Hammond's "From Spirituals to Swing" introduces black music to Carnegie Hall.	Germany invades Poland, which marks the start of World War II.	Albert Hofmann accidentally discovers the psychedelic effects of LSD.

EARTH ANGEL

Countless artists have recorded "Earth Angel" since its release. Most significant are Elvis Presley, the Platters, Buddy Holly, Ritchie Valens, New Edition, and Bella Morte.

As a youngster, avant-garde rocker Frank Zappa frequented DJ Art Laboe's rock & roll shows (which featured a great deal of doo-wop) at El Monte Legion Stadium in LA. In 1961 Zappa wrote and produced a pastiche of doo-wop songs that he called "Memories of El Monte." The tribute includes parts of "Earth Angel" sung by Clive Duncan, one of the vocalists that recorded the original.

In 1968 Zappa followed with *Cruising with Ruben and the Jets*, an LP tribute to '50s rock and doo-wop. "It's always been my contention that the music that was happening during the fifties has been one of the finest things that ever happened to American music, and I loved it," he said later.

It's also worth mentioning that during the high school dance in *Back to the Future* Marvin Berry and the Starlighters play "Earth Angel," and that Death Cab For Cutie recorded it in 2005 for the video game *Stubbs the Zombie: Rebel Without a Pulse.*

BY THE 1950's THE ACOUSTIC BLUES WAS MARGINALIZED, but the Chitlin' Circuit lived on, connected by the American highway and African-American culture. Soul and electric blues were still popular, but a new and exciting vocal-based rhythm & blues that rose from urban centers in New York, Philadelphia, Chicago, and Los Angeles soon overtook both styles commercially.

Inner city youth who couldn't afford expensive instruments lined up on street corners and performed a cappella. Sensing hit material, record producers brought many of these adolescent groups to the studio, often adding basic backup tracks.

Doo-wop's most popular groups were the Flamingos, the Ravens, the Platters, and the Penguins. The latter took its name from the cartoon penguin in the *Kool* menthol cigarette ads and enjoyed a hit that *Rolling Stone* magazine ranks 151st on its list of the 500 Greatest Songs of All Time. "Earth Angel (Will You Be Mine)" was a low-budget recording by an independent record company, but local airplay in Los Angeles paved the way for a fantastic hit.

The song debuted on the national R&B charts in December 1954. From there it made an unprecedented migration to the pop charts, where it competed with white versions of the same song by The Crew-Cuts and Gloria Mann. The original soared higher

AUG. 5, 1945	1947	1950	1952
NYC jazz pianist Nat Jaffe dies at age 27.	Ahmet Ertegün and Herb Abrahamson found Atlantic Records, which becomes an important independent label for rock, blues, and jazz.	Chess Records founded in Chicago.	Gibson introduces the Les Paul Goldtop, its first solid-body electric guitar, to compete with Fender's Esquire (Telecaster).

DooWop

when it reached number eight the following month. At the time, music was segregated like the rest of American society, so African-American hits from the R&B charts were typically re-recorded by white groups and introduced to the pop charts. "Earth Angel" was one of the first singles to break that barrier, and when it did, a few people took notice.

Much like Delta blues, doo-wop was a style built from phrases and patterns that were recycled or at best slightly modified from song to song. After a lawsuit, the courts ruled that the song's lyrics plagiarized Jesse Belvin's "I'm Only A Fool" and "Dream Girl," a hit Belvin co-wrote with Marvin Phillips in 1953. Consequently, Belvin was awarded one third of the composer credits to "Earth Angel."

Jesse Belvin was a prolific songwriter in the 1950s, and he often used his gift as a fast way to raise cash. He was known to write a song on the car ride to the studio and sell the rights when he got there. He completed producer George Mottola's "Goodnight My Love" by adding a bridge and sold his part for $400. Belvin recorded it later under his own name, and his version climbed to number seven on the R&B charts, which helped cement his reputation firmly in place at the top of Los Angeles's many crooners. DJ Alan Freed used it for years as the outro theme to his immensely popular rock & roll radio show, which was syndicated in major markets across the country.

DJ ALAN FREED

Disc Jockey Alan Freed is credited with coining the term "rock & roll" to describe the groovy records that he played on his radio show starting in 1951. Freed fell from grace during the payola scandal in the early sixties, but he contended that he only played records he liked on his show, not ones he was paid to play. He died a broken man in 1965 and was inducted into the Rock and Roll Hall of Fame in 1986.

APR. 13, 1953	DEC. 30, 1953	1954	OCT. 27, 1955	MAY 13, 1957
CIA's MKULTRA program starts feeding unknown subjects with LSD in search for a mind-controlling serum.	The Wild One, starring Marlon Brando, takes the world by storm; it's banned in the UK from its release until 1968.	Leo Fender unveils the Fender Stratocaster, a guitar that becomes synonymous with rock after Hendrix uses it as his main axe.	Rebel Without A Cause, starring James Dean, hit the theaters.	A Life magazine article by R. Gordon Wasson describes the religious use of psilocybin mushrooms in Mexico.

In 1958 Belvin enjoyed another hit with a vocal quintet he formed named The Shields. Even though "You Cheated" reached the Top 20, Belvin quickly lost interest, preferring to work in the background. He helped a slew of groups cut tracks and did so often using assumed names.

After Belvin's wife Jo Ann started to manage his career, she worked out a deal with RCA Records. "Guess Who" was his first hit for the label, and it was followed by *Just Jesse Belvin*, his only full-length album.

Unusual for his time, Jesse's repertoire and vocal style reached mature white audiences without pushing away his younger African-American fans. He developed a strong stage presence and earned the nickname "Mr. Easy" from the many ballads that made up his set.

Jesse toured the South in early 1960. He performed for non-segregated audiences at a few gigs and received several death threats as a result. His mom, who was used to hearing from him every couple of weeks, received two nervous calls in three days.

On February 6, 1960, Belvin played the 2,600-seat Robinson Auditorium in Little Rock, Arkansas, with Jackie Wilson, Marv Johnson, Bobby Lewis, and a few other acts. It was the city's first show for a racially mixed audience, and white supremacists that shouted racial epithets managed to halt the show twice.

After the show Jesse and Jo Ann Belvin loaded up in the back-seat of a black Cadillac. Another band member rode shotgun while driver Charles Shackleford, who had recently been fired by Ray Charles for swerving, steered the vehicle southwest. The ride ended a hundred miles down Route 67 in a head-on collision near the town of Hope.

A state trooper on the scene stated that the rear tires had "ob-viously been tampered with." Belvin and Shackleford died short-ly after the accident, while Jo Ann died later at the hospital. The third passenger survived but never gave any interviews about what really went down that night.

Other acts on the bill had their tires slashed as well, but why did it take so long before the tires on Jesse's limo gave out? Ray Charles wrote in his autobiography *Brother Ray* that Shackleford liked to hang around during the show instead of catching sleep at the hotel. If he kept up his bad old habits he could've been driv-ing under the influence of sleep deprivation, alcohol, speed or some other drug. It's not unlikely, but we'll never know the truth. Regardless of what happened, Jesse's accident has always been considered an act of racism.

Belvin was one of the defining songwriters of his time and a groundbreaking artist able to woo both black and white audienc-es. Ray Charles wrote, "I was kind of thinking that Jesse would take Nat "King" Cole's place in the balladeer category."

ARKANSAS

LITTLE ROCK

HOPE

1957	SEP. 25, 1957	JAN. 12, 1959
Jack Kerouac's On The Road published; the Beat masterpiece becomes an inspiration for the hippie movement of the 1960s.	Troops called in to escort nine African-American students to an all-white high school in Little Rock, Arkansas.	Motown Records forms in Detroit, Michigan.

"I was surrounded by talented boys—Richard [Berry], Eugene [Church], Alex [Hodge], Gaynel [Hodge]. But I do believe the most gifted of them all was Jesse Belvin," Etta James said in *Rage To Survive*. "He lived one block over on 32nd Street. Jesse was something else—the golden boy, everyone's idol. He was five or six years older than me and a legend in our neighborhood. **Even now I consider him the greatest singer of my generation—rhythm and blues, rock and roll, crooner—you name it. He was going to be bigger than Sam Cooke, bigger than Nat Cole."** Even Marvin Gaye cited Jesse as an early influence.

Belvin wasn't the only doo-wop singer who died at 27. Rudy Lewis, who took over as The Drifters' lead singer in 1960, was found dead in his apartment four years later, the day of a recording session. Cops on the scene suspected a drug overdose, but his friends and bandmates swore Rudy's only vice was binge eating before bedtime. One thing is clear: In May 1964, Rudy Lewis choked to death in his sleep at 27, a feat Jimi Hendrix replicated six years later, although under very different circumstances.

Rudy Lewis's death will forever remain a mystery, but his stint with the Drifters garnered him an early induction to the Rock and Roll Hall of Fame in 1988.

THE DRIFTERS

The Drifters, one of the oldest groups still performing, was ranked 81st on *Rolling Stone* magazine's 2004 list of the 100 Greatest Artists of All Time.

Founded by Clyde McPhatter in 1953, the group's first hit was "Money Honey."

Legendary songwriters Jerry Lieber and Mike Stoller began working with the group in the mid-fifties and helped write and produce a string of hits starting with "I Gotta Get Myself A Woman." Low salaries ensured a revolving cast of members, but the group lived on.

Rudy Lewis's entrance launched the Drifters into its second golden age. He led the group on hits such as "Up On the Roof," "Please Stay," and "Some Kind Of Wonderful." Lewis died the day before the group was due to record "Under the Boardwalk." The studio session went on more or less as planned, but Johnny Moore sang lead in Lewis's place. The single charted and became a classic hit for this long-lived vocal-based group.

FEB. 3, 1959	1959	1960	APR. 17, 1960
The Day the Music Died: The Big Bopper (29), Buddy Holly (22), Ritchie Valens (17), and pilot Roger Peterson crash to their deaths in an Iowa cornfield.	*Ken Kesey voluntarily tests psychoactive drugs for a government research program. Next up: One Flew Over the Cuckoo's Nest.*	*The inaugural Newport Folk Festival takes place.*	*Rockabilly guitarist Eddie Cochran (21) dies in a car accident in England.*

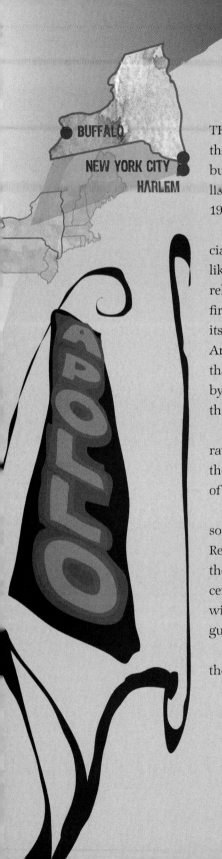

THE CORONATING VENUE OF THE CHITLIN' CIRCUIT WAS the Apollo Theatre in New York City's Harlem. The theater was built in 1913 as a venue for burlesque shows but was reestablished as the country's premier African American concert hall in 1934.

In 1962, James Brown was one of the most successful musicians on the Chitlin' Circuit, but he wasn't yet a household name like, say, Louis Armstrong. He recorded a show at the Apollo and released it the following year on LP. *Live at the Apollo* was the first record by a pure R&B artist to become a top-five album, and its crossover indirectly introduced the Chitlin' Circuit to white America. Few white Americans listened to black music other than jazz. They heard recycled versions of black hits performed by white groups, but suddenly James Brown's soul sensualism thumped through the ether on white radio stations.

Doo-wop was still popular with both audiences, but soul's raw, rhythm-based sound attracted a grinding party crowd on the Chitlin' Circuit, and it was this sound that altered the future of popular music.

James Brown was only one of many artists dispensing hard soul for the working masses. Little Richard, Wilson Pickett, Otis Redding, Sam & Dave, and Don Covay were equally famous, and they were supported by minions of contracted musicians who received little pay and no credit for the privilege of riding the Circuit with the stars. One of those subordinates was a shy and lanky guitar player from Seattle by the name of James Hendrix.

Although he would later call himself Jimi Hendrix, he rode the Circuit from '63 thru '66 and played juke joints and taverns from Virginia to Florida, in Texas, New York City and the Delta like thousands of other musicians who are long forgotten.

Biographer Charles Cross writes that Hendrix faked a crush on a fellow soldier to be discharged from the 101st Airborne at Fort Campell in Kentucky. As soon as Jimi left the barracks he traveled the South working on his music career. The guitar was already a fifth limb he seldom left behind, and he earned the nickname Marbles because people joked he had lost all his marbles from incessant practicing. He played on the way to the show, during set break, after the gig—pretty much every waking hour, which were kept long thanks to diet pills that contained speedy amphetamines.

Hendrix was a musical cannibal, always devouring what other guitarists were playing or figuring out how they made a certain sound. He once asked blues great Albert King how to get good. Albert didn't feel threatened by the young man in rags, so he divulged a couple of his secrets.

Hendrix's chops and knowledge of the R&B hits of the day eventually led to backup gigs for Ike and Tina Turner, Little Richard, and many others, but he was frequently fired for playing too "flashy," outshining the star. He didn't yet have a tone of his own—his style was pretty much based on B.B. King licks with frequent lapses to Curtis Mayfield, Steve Cropper, and others. It was a hard living. Road sex and glamorous moments on stage were quickly replaced by the road's brutish reality.

POPSIE

In 2006, Cliff Malloy went through the late, renowned New York City photographer William "PoPsie" Randolph's archive and stumbled on an unexpected treat.

PoPsie was Atlantic Records' main photographer for a long time, and in early May 1966 he shot a Percy Sledge release party. "When a Man Loves a Woman" was blowing up, so Sledge was hot shit. Sledge, Esther Phillips, Don Covay, and Wilson Pickett performed, and the backup band was King Curtis and the Kingpins with frequent member James Hendrix. PoPsie captured smiling moments of a tux-wearing Hendrix backing up Wilson "Wicked" Pickett with a white Fender Jazzmaster.

See the B&W stills PoPsie captured at this great soul night as well as candid moments with the Rolling Stones, The Doors, and others at popsiephotos.com or in the book *Popsie N.Y.—Popular Music Through the Camera Lens of William "PoPsie" Randolph.*

Otis Burke traded Jimi to Otis Redding for two horn players. He was fired a week later and left on the side of the highway, but the penniless guitarist simply hitched a ride to the nearest town and waited till another tour would take him on.

Although it was far from easy street, paying dues on the circuit primed Hendrix for his path. He did non-credited session work for a few R&B and soul artists. The most memorable of the lot are his guitar parts on Don Covay's "Mercy, Mercy," and The Isley Brothers' "Testify."

Jimi eventually decided to try his luck in New York City. He played for Curtis Knight, whose primary occupation was pimping. Not exactly a stranger to flash, Knight was more than happy to let Jimmy James, as he called himself, be as flashy as he wished during the many solo spots he granted the guitar player.

But glitzy side gigs weren't enough for Hendrix. The budding star assembled his own band, the eponymous Jimmy James and the Blue Flames. After nearly four years with backing jobs he was finally in the spotlight, but his guitar reverberated nightly across a near-empty room at the Cheetah Club. He had no way of knowing that he was on the verge of an unprecedented leap from a struggling black backup musician to become one of white rock's de facto superstars.

WHILE HENDRIX THRIVED IN A LIMELIGHT BEYOND HIS wildest dreams, another musician from the Chitlin' Circuit named Arlester "Dyke" Christian pushed soul in a harder and more syncopated direction.

Arlester grew up on the rough streets of Buffalo, New York, and his former bandmates say he lived like he had a rep to uphold. "He was a no BS-type guy," says Rich Cason, the original organist for Dyke and the Blazers. "He was a true leader, always in control on stage."

Dyke played bass for the O'Jays, but he was left stranded with half the band in Phoenix while on tour. With no money to make it home to Buffalo, Dyke and the others merged with a local group of young musicians that performed as Art Laroue and his Crew. Dyke dropped the bass and switched from backup vocals to lead, his 6'3" frame towering over the stage. The new group played around Phoenix and soon landed a steady gig at the Elks Club, where they churned bebop tunes for a Friday night audience.

Bored with playing standards, Dyke wrote a rap about his grimy Phoenix hood. This original, named "Funky Broadway," borrowed heavily from James Brown's soul, but with a stripped-down horn section, lyrics that were talked more than sung, and loose, syncopated rhythms, the group stumbled on a new sound. "It came out raw since we didn't know music the way James Brown's band did," Cason says.

When the Blazers performed "Funky Broadway" as a break from its standard set, the crowd went wild. A pair of local producers took notice and brought the group to the studio. The single was released in Phoenix in 1966, and legendary Los Angeles DJ Art Laboe dug it so much he funded a national release and hyped it on his syndicated radio show. Laboe's release entered the R&B charts in March 1967, where it remained for 27 weeks, peaking at eleven.

Funk was a word kept at bay from the airwaves and polite dinner conversations. The Blazers' single broke a barrier: It was the first recording to use *funk* in its title. Funk is old slang for "a stink," which is probably what Buddy Bolden alludes to in his 1907 jazz composition "Funky Butt."

With the record charging up the charts, the band ventured out of Phoenix and toured major Chitlin' venues in the South and on the East Coast, headlining most of the way. The band played to black audiences, with the exception of American Bandstand, where Dyke lip-synced the hit alone. "The record was so hot!" Cason says, "It was very exciting, but it all happened so fast."

The highlight of the Blazers' career was playing at the Apollo, where they supported headliner Joe Pecks. "We played three shows per day, and James Brown came by to chat in the dressing room," Cason says.

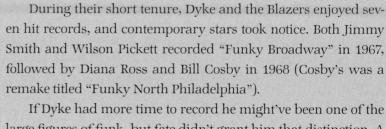

During their short tenure, Dyke and the Blazers enjoyed seven hit records, and contemporary stars took notice. Both Jimmy Smith and Wilson Pickett recorded "Funky Broadway" in 1967, followed by Diana Ross and Bill Cosby in 1968 (Cosby's was a remake titled "Funky North Philadelphia").

If Dyke had more time to record he might've been one of the large figures of funk, but fate didn't grant him that distinction. A character who went by the moniker One-Eyed Clancy owed Dyke money for heroin, so the two set up a meeting on the west side of Buckeye Road in downtown Phoenix. Dyke was waiting in his car when One-Eyed Clancy came up and fired several slugs from a handgun, killing Dyke. "He went to jail, but there was always speculation he was a snitch," Cason says. "See, the police was always suspicious of Dyke because of the drugs."

Dyke was only 27 when he was murdered in 1971, but he left a lasting albeit little known impact on music. Listen to James Brown before "Funky Broadway" and you hear upbeat soul with a big horn section. Then spin JB's "Cold Sweat," a song recorded after the Blazer hit. Hear that? Uh, now that's called funk! The hardest-working man in showbiz, god bless his soul, even quotes "funky, funky, Broadway" in that one.

And JB didn't forget the impact of Dyke and the Blazers. At a gig outside Phoenix three and a half months before his death in 2006 he said, "I met Dyke and the Blazers one time at the Apollo. Now that was one funky band." Unbeknownst to Brown, one of the Blazers was in the audience

IMMEDIATELY AFTER LANDING IN NYC FOR THE BAND'S
first US tour on February 7, 1964, the Beatles were met on the tar-
mac by screaming girls and rabid reporters. When asked what
they wanted to do while visiting, Paul McCartney said he wanted to see Muddy Waters. "Where's that?" the reporter wanted to
know. "You don't know who your own famous people are in this
country?" the Beatle responded.

Few in America realized that the Italian-American boy acts
groomed and marketed by Dick Clark on his bandstand were
merely the white reengineering of black R&B, which in turn was
rooted in the rural country blues of the Delta. But not everybody
was ignorant.

During the late fifties and early sixties, young, white adolescents who had grown up in post-war consumerism were pro-
actively searching for the roots of rock. Most blues musicians were
by now middle-aged and had either given up playing or were, like
Muddy Waters, struggling in Chicago's black club scene at night
and working in a factory during the day.

Blues is about life's suffering, a musical Buddhism that reso-
nates with rebellious souls. This largely forgotten art form's history was dark, musky, and exotic to the nascent musicians who
sought out records filed under *Folk Blues* or *Delta Blues*. The style
appeared like a lotus in a muddy backwater, blossoming with a
largely untapped cache of songs and techniques created by hard-
living musicians who had barely scraped by.

35

Someone at Columbia Records noticed the resurgent interest and released a compilation of Johnson's recordings in 1961 titled *King of the Delta Blues Singers*, and it was this disc that Brian Jones, Eric Clapton, Jimmy Page, Jeff Beck, and other future guitar aces listened to. Photographs of Robert Johnson didn't exist (one surfaced in 1986 and another in 1989), so the cover bore a painting of an anonymous black man hunched over his guitar, which only added to his mystique. Little was known about his life, but rumor had it he died from poisoned whisky in a roadhouse down south.

Researcher Mack McCormick's work brought him to two witnesses that, independently, were in agreement about what had really happened. Johnson and Honeyboy Edwards performed at a joint in Three Forks, Mississippi. It was a little dive out in the country, but enough people came around on Friday and Saturday nights to keep the two musicians employed.

Robert Johnson, always the womanizer, was sleeping with somebody's wife and the husband found out. In some stories it's the wife of the owner, in others she's married to somebody in the area. During the set Johnson supposedly sipped from an opened whisky bottle that was laced with strychnine. By one o'clock he felt sick but played on. An hour later he was delirious. Someone drove him the fifteen miles back to Greenwood, which was the nearest town. He died there a few days later. Word reached Robert Shines that Robert had "crawled on his hands and knees and barked like a dog before he died."

In the annals of the blues Robert Johnson was nothing more than a footnote. Few old blues aficionados knew his name since Johnson had been less successful and influential than, say, T-Bone Walker, Blind Lemon Jefferson, or Lonnie Johnson. But that was all set to change. **A quarter of a century after his death, Robert Johnson was like a rare artifact to the white bluesocologists who re-discovered him. Johnson epitomized not only the raw, rural style of the genre, but also the bluesman's way of life**

Robert Johnson's enigmatic persona, mysterious death, thrilling lyrics, and otherworldly voice and music were symptomatic of the classic Delta era. He was poor, charming, and a loner ultimately murdered in an act of jealousy.

Decades later, dropping the needle onto the thick vinyl transports the listener back in time. Robert Johnson sounds primal and sings with authenticity about waiting at the crossroads, loving in vain, and hellhounds on his trail. These powerful lyrics are whispered, cried, mourned, or sung in terror and he plays guitar with subtlety, reverence, and a distinct rhythm.

"I have never found anything more deeply soulful than Robert Johnson," Eric Clapton wrote in the liner notes to *Discovering Robert Johnson*. "His music remains the most powerful cry that I think you can find in the human voice."

Keith Richards heard Johnson play the blues for the first time in Brian Jones's crash pad. He asked who it was and upon hearing his name replied, "Yeah, but who's the other guy?" Keef heard not one, but two guitars.

In 1964, college student Dick Waterman and two of his buddies tracked down Son House in Rochester, New York. The man who had influenced Robert Johnson, Muddy Waters, and countless others was working for the railroad and boasted that he hadn't touched a guitar in twenty years. Unabashed, Waterman roped in twenty-one year-old Alan Wilson to re-teach the old master how to play his old slide licks. After successfully completing Wilson's refresher course, House entered the coffeehouse

DICK WATERMAN

Dick Waterman's lifelong work as a blues scholar and promoter merited an induction to the Blues Hall of Fame in 2000. He is the only non-musician or record producer who's honored with that distinction.

SON HOUSE
1902-1988

circuit. Later that year, Son House invited Alan Wilson to play guitar and harmonica with him at the Newport Folk Festival and on a few of the sessions that became *The Legendary Son House: Father of Folk Blues* record.

By most accounts, Son House is the originator of the often-told myth of Robert Johnson selling his soul to the devil at the crossroads.

The idea of a deity protecting or watching the crossroads appears in mythology, religion, and folklore all over the world. It's found in Greek, Roman, Mayan, Hindu, Japanese, European, and African cultures. Delta bluesman Tommy Johnson (no relation to Robert) claimed he sought out the gift at the crossroads. His brother LeDell related Tommy's process to blues scholar David Evans:

"If you want to learn how to make songs yourself, you take your guitar and go to where the road crosses that way, where a crossroads is. Get there, be sure to get there just a little 'fore twelve that night so you know you'll be there. You have your guitar and be playing a piece there by yourself... A big black man will walk up there and take your guitar and he'll tune it. And then he'll play a piece and hand it back to you. That's the way I learned to play anything I want."

In the African-American hoodoo tradition the crossroads is the ideal spot for the ritual. Tommy never mentioned the devil, selling his soul, or making a pact, because neither is indigenous to the polytheistic tradition. These terms are used in the European Faust legend because they're the only terms that fit in the

monotheistic religion of Christianity. The Big Black man isn't the devil. He is Legba, an African door opener to the magic world.

Telling the story of Robert Johnson in the sixties, House could've either confused Tommy with Robert or simply told young blues aficionados what they wanted to hear. By all accounts except House's (and possibly Honeyboy Edwards's), Robert Johnson never claimed to have sold his soul to the devil. "Cross Road Blues" is about hitchhiking, which can of course be a metaphor for whatever you want. He asks the *Lord* for mercy and wants to flag a ride with the Greyhound bus, which at the time was a new, novel, and luxurious way of travel for a train hopping hobo. Lucifer isn't mentioned in any shape or form.

Nevertheless, it's the combination of mystery, great musicianship, and lack of biographic information that prompted white rockers to elevate Robert Johnson to the pantheon as an enigmatic folkloric hero. During his lifetime Robert was never King of the Delta—just a talented minstrel—but his influence on artists of the sixties and beyond makes him the grandfather of rock.

Howlin' Wolf and Muddy Waters and others followed the Mississippi migration and brought rural country blues with them to the Northern manufacturing centers. The city's noisy bars effectively exiled acoustic duos, so Muddy answered with a five-piece electric lineup, which consisted of vocals, harmonica, lead guitar, rhythm, bass, and drums.

In Britain a small tribe of musicians mixed electric blues covers with their jazzy skiffle. The music didn't sound nearly as good as that of authentic bluesmen such as B.B. or Albert King, but they were the first clumsy notes of a movement that soon swept across both Europe and North America.

One of these adolescent boys was Brian Jones who belonged to a burgeoning group of bluesers infringing on a scene

TOMMY JOHNSON
1896-1956

A character named Tommy Johnson appears in the movie *O Brother, Where Art Thou?* from 2000. In *The New York Times* review of the movie Tommy Johnson is described as a "reference ... to the real-life bluesman Robert Johnson." The writer was obviously not well versed in blues history.

1960	JUNE 10, 1960	JAN 20, 1961	FEB 9, 1961
Harper Lee's To Kill A Mockingbird published. The novel describes race relations in Alabama.	Johnny Kidd & the Pirates release "Shakin' All Over." It becomes the first British-composed rock hit.	John F. Kennedy sworn in as the President of the United States.	The Beatles debuts at Liverpool's Cavern.

dominated by suit-clad trad jazzers. Jones was capable of laying down decent jazz strums but habitually wandered off stage if the band switched to numbers he felt were a bit too trad. He was already a rebel.

Brian's boyhood in middle-class Cheltenham, England, was filled with altar service, depression, school pranks, chronic asthma, and various nervous disorders. His mother taught him piano and he practiced the clarinet at home, but listening to jazz and swing or playing other instruments was best done covertly, and away from the house. He picked up an acoustic guitar and became infatuated with rural bluesmen such as Blind Lemon Jefferson, Lightning Hopkins, the mysterious Robert Johnson, and Leadbelly, who would later become Kurt Cobain's favorite from that era.

When Muddy visited England in 1958 with a quartet, fans included a sixteen-year-old Brian Jones. The bluesman's Telecaster was the first electric Brian heard in concert; its sound mesmerized him. His heart was in the blues, a style he grasped better than most in the UK. He was already experimenting with open tunings and the harmonica, and was the first British musician to wield the slide on stage.

That same year Brian fathered his first child, Julian. The child's mother was a little younger than Brian, so the teenagers' parents worked out the details while Brian completely detached from the girl, their child, and the situation. The baby was quickly put up for adoption while Brian was sent abroad

AUG. 13, 1961	JULY 12, 1962	AUG. 5, 1962
Construction on the Berlin Wall commences. The Wall divides East and West Berlin for the next 28 years.	The Rolling Stones debuts at London's Marquee Club.	Anti-apartheid activist Nelson Mandela is jailed for the next five years.

for the summer under the pretext that his grades were so good—keeping the façade was important in Cheltenham.

His second child, also named Julian, was born two years later to a different girl, Pat Andrews. This time Brian cared for mother and child the best he could—at least in the beginning. When he left Cheltenham for London to jumpstart his career, the young family followed.

Brian Jones met Mick Jagger and Keith Richards in 1962 and recruited them to found a group. Brian named the band The Rolling Stones after a Muddy song and immediately aimed for success. He worked in a department store during the day so he could pay a bare minimum of bills.

The band's repertoire in the early days consisted of Chuck Berry numbers, Bo Diddley covers, and a selection of older blues songs penned by the likes of Elmore James, Howlin' Wolf, and Muddy Waters. Brian was the leader and without doubt the most accomplished musician. He chose cover songs, hustled gigs, signed contracts, and disbursed proceeds—always skimming a little extra as an unspoken management fee (the other members didn't take it lightly when they discovered Brian's modest financial acrobatics).

"Brian had more edge to him than any of the others then," said Alexis Korner, the musical godfather of the British blues scene, "He was the nasty one. He could be really evil on stage."

He liked to dance out to the end of the stage and snap the tambourine in some fan's face, stick his tongue out in a real fuck you manner, and move back before anyone had the time to punch him.

But women found the broad-shouldered sparkplug adorable—girls screamed in ecstatic cacophony whenever he looked

CRAWDADDY!

In 1966, seventeen-year-old Paul Williams launched the first rock & roll magazine out of his bedroom. He named it *Crawdaddy!* after the London club where the Rolling Stones gained their noteriety. Jann Wenner published the first issue of *Rolling Stone* two years later. Wenner's magazine and rock journalism in general are both molded on Williams's critiques.

The mag ariseth once again: check in at crawdaddy.wolfgangsvault.com.

JAN. 11, 1963	MAR. 21, 1963	NOV. 1, 1963	1963
Whisky A Go Go becomes the first disco in the US.	*Alcatraz Prison locks up and the last 27 prisoners are transferred elsewhere.*	*The Rolling Stones debuts the single "I Wanna Be Your Man."*	*The Mellotron is invented, an early electronic keyboard capable of playing taped samples.*

up from the guitar with those green beams. His charm lingered latently; he could be funny, jovial, and cordial, his husked voice softly lisping underneath his long blonde hair.

Just like the Beatles got comfortable playing for British audiences at Liverpool's Cavern, The Rolling Stones' embryonic mainstay was a London club called Craw Daddy, where the group held residency for most of '63. People stood in line for hours for an opportunity to sweat and shake in near-immobility at these early Stones shows. Girls with bouncing tops up front, gawking guys in the back. The Beatles, who had already garnered a reputation well beyond their Liverpool home stage, came to listen and were blown away. They invited the band to one of their concerts, talked them up to potential producers and the press, and gave them the ultimate honor: John and Paul wrote "I Wanna Be Your Man" for the Stones to record. Brian promptly dirtied it up with his slide and it became an early hit for his band.

Problem was that Brian Jones soon lost the reigns to his undisputed leadership. Stones manager Andrew Loog Oldham reprimanded him for bringing Pat and their infant son to a photo shoot. Showing that he was taken was bad publicity, Oldham argued. Regardless, it didn't take long for Brian to abandon his nascent family and pick the tempting fruits of stardom. The band's profile rose quickly, and Brian was treated like royalty.

In the early days Brian was the only *bad* Stone. He sculpted what a music celeb is all about, and although he personified the now stale cliché of sex, drugs, and rock & roll—and in that order, too—the blonde-haired Rolling Stone was rock & roll's proto bad-boy long before Keith, Mick, and others made it vogue. He basked with babes and fathered enough offspring to fill a soccer team. Perhaps the greatest love of his life was Anita Pallenberg—a Teutonic beauty who was his girlfriend for almost two years.

The couple shared an apartment on Courtfield Road that they decorated in an eclectic mix of tapestries and knick-knacks. **Anita made him forget about his deficiencies; he became more confident and thrived in his new role as the mysterious Stone.**

Mick Jagger's girlfriend Marianne Faithfull describes an episode that stunned her. Pat, their two-year-old son Julian, and her father were outside pleading for child support. Instead of letting them in, "Brian and Anita just peered down on them as if they were some inferior species. Foppish aristocrats in their finery jeering at the *sans culottes* below."

He had made it: his band was the counterpoint to the Beatles and his girlfriend was a movie-star blonde. Why would he care about anyone else? Brian's hedonistic lifestyle and thirst for celebrity quickly overshadowed his interest to develop the band from a cover-playing jukebox. Meanwhile Oldham urged Mick and Keith to work on crafting songs, which soon elevated the glitter twins' control of the Stones.

It wasn't that Brian was excluded from songwriting, it was just that he didn't get any songs together. Nobody remembers hearing a single completed Jones tune, and the few parts that he presented were based on intricate chord patterns that were far removed from the Stones' basic rock & roll. His bandmates' refusals fuelled Brian's paranoia. "One of the things Brian liked to do when he was high was to make tapes. He'd record all night long and then in the morning erase everything," Faithfull recalled in her autobiography.

"Brian made some desperate attempts to write songs, but they *were* desperate," one-time Stones keyboardist Ian Stewart says in *Blues in Britain*.

LIVERPOOL

CHELTENHAM

LONDON

Everything looked normal from the front of the stage of course; Brian was still the star, much to Mick and Oldham's chagrin. The group went on its first US tour a few months after the Beatles' maiden voyage, and although the Stones' visit was subject to far less media hoopla, the tour was another important front of the British Invasion, bringing rockin' blues back home.

In 1964 the Stones made an important pilgrimage to the epicenter of the blues: Chess Studios on Chicago's Michigan Avenue. They wanted to cut tracks with the same team that had produced all those hits for Bo Diddley, Howlin' Wolf, Chuck Berry, Muddy Waters, and countless others. The Brits were the first musicians allowed to use the front doors. Their experience peaked when Muddy happened to walk in during the recording of the bluesman's "I Can't Be Satisfied."

The band returned the next fall and recorded additional tracks at Chess, including Don Covay's "Mercy, Mercy." The Stones had no idea that the guitar player on the original was only one year away from changing music forever. The sound of rock, although revolutionary in the ears of kids and parents, was still in its infancy.

American artists that went on to conquer rock later in the decade grew up playing a combination of jug band, folk, blues, and country in the post-beat coffee house scene. These eager musicians made their own happenings and continued the creative burst long after the Beats—Jack Kerouac, Alan Ginsberg, Neal Cassidy, Gary Snyder, Peter Orlovsky, Bill Burroughs and others— drifted away to foreign locales, extreme alcoholism, or discovered new realities at the sharp end of a needle.

AUSTIN

PORT ARTHUR

HOUSTON

LOWELL
GEORGE

Lowell George, he later played in Frank
Zappa's Mothers of Invention and went on
to found Little Feat, first picked up the slide
after hearing Brian Jones's licks at a show
in LA.

The most famous folkies emerged from New York City's Greenwich Village—Bob Dylan got his start there of course—but San Francisco had its own scene and even Austin, Texas, was touched by the phenomenon. There, a feisty woman from Port Arthur, Texas, excited an audience with her soulful voice and freewheeling behavior. She was part of a small, bustling folk scene that sprung from a decrepit apartment building near the University of Texas campus known as the Ghetto. Philosophically freed from society's shackles, its inhabitants painted, drew, sang, played instruments, and experimented with speed, marijuana, and peyote in search of creative enlightenment. The native cactus revered by Indian shamans was still legal and available for ten cents from nearby Hudson's Cactus Gardens.

The Ghetto crew caravanned to perform with old time country and bluegrass musicians at a bar called Threadgill's on Wednesday nights, while Sunday afternoons brought them to the Union Building on the same errand.

An Austin trio known as the Waller Creek Boys featured the girl from Port Arthur: her name was Janis Joplin. She sang bluegrass with a shrill voice, roared the blues like Bessie Smith, and mellowed to a sweet purr for slow ballads. Old Mr. Threadgill took a fatherly liking to Janis, and his feelings were reciprocated.

It had only been two years since she stood on a stage for the first time, but it didn't take long for people to drive out to Threadgill's just to hear her sing. Janis's filthy appearance and demeanor ostracized her from her conservative hometown, so she found this modest group of fans especially thrilling.

JOPLIN'S JINGLE

Janis Joplin's first recording was a radio jingle for a bank set to the famous Woody Guthrie tune "This Land Is Your Land."

Janis had yet to bloom as an artist, but her personality was already in place: she could be shy about her voice and looks, yet loved being crude, loud, and drunk.

A skinny vagabond named Chet Helms felt the musical future lay in San Francisco and urged Janis to hitchhike out with him. Janis liked her life in Austin, but disturbed by her recent nomination at the University of Texas at Austin as the "ugliest man on campus," she decided to tag along.

Once there they sought out the North Beach folk scene that centered around two coffeehouses: Coffee and Confusion and the Coffee Gallery. It was the winter of '63, and people like David Crosby, Jerry Garcia, Nick Gravenites (later of Electric Flag), James Gurley (who later played with Janis in Big Brother), Marty Balin and Jorma Kaukonen (both of Jefferson Airplane), David

FROM THE GHETTO TO THE HAIGHT

The Austin chapter of bohemian derelicts was a tight-knit crew that possessed talent, drive, and vision that would in time sculpt the counterculture. Most of the collective eventually migrated to San Francisco where they became successful.

Gilbert Shelton created *The Fabulous Furry Freak Brothers* comic and co-founded Rip Off Press with fellow Austin artist and counterculture comics trailblazer Jack "Jaxon" Jackson. Travis Rivers managed a poster shop on Haight Street, while Powell St. John from the Waller Creek Boys played in Mother Earth (he also wrote "Bye, Bye Baby" that Janis made a hit).

Most famous of all was Chet Helms, who founded Denver's Family Dog, the Avalon Ballroom, and produced early light shows and free concerts in the Golden Gate Park. After he died in 2005 the *San Francisco Chronicle* lauded him a "towering figure in the 1960s Bay Area music scene."

SAN FRANCISCO

CALIFORNIA

ARIZONA

NEW MEXICO

TEXAS

AUSTIN

PORT ARTHUR

ROKY ERICKSON

The legendary Roky Erickson has commanded cult status since the 13th Floor Elevators released its debut, *The Psychedelic Sounds of the 13th Floor Elevators*, in 1966. Unfortunately, Erickson was diagnosed as a paranoid schizophrenic two years later. He received shock therapy while incarcerated at a Houston mental institution. Shortly after he was back on the streets he was arrested for the possession of a single joint. Facing ten long years, he pleaded insanity and ended up in another mental institution, this time at the Austin State Hospital. Shock therapy and Thorazine treatments, a fashionable liquid antipsychotic, ensued until 1972.

From then until his 2005 comeback, Roky played random and infrequent projects whenever he could muster. Erickson's 2007 tour brought him career-first performances in New York City, at Caliornia's Coachella music festival, and in European countries such as Finland and Norway.

Freiberg (of Quicksilver Messenger Service), and an older folkie named Billy Roberts (who composed what became Jimi Hendrix's breakthrough hit "Hey Joe") kicked around at these informal jams. The musicians in this loose group possessed extreme talent, and seeing the same in Janis they quickly accepted her into the fold.

Jorma Kaukonen often accompanied Janis Joplin on acoustic guitar, and their demos provided a look into her future. Chick folkies were supposed to sing ballads like the angelic Joan Baez or Judy Collins. Compare those to one of Janis's early songs titled "What Good Can Drinkin' Do."

"She juiced constantly," a friend recalled later. Janis even drank with the winos on the corner and was as big-mouthed and LOUD as she became famous for later. Once she cussed out a group of bikers at a bar, and they responded by beating the shit out of her.

Life as a starving musician was a full-time job, so she kept a schedule to fit it all in. "We walked right into a speed crowd," Helms said later. She panhandled, stole from grocery stores, and procured firewood from construction sites to get by. When she wasn't hustling she listened to blues and country stations and studied Leadbelly, Billie Holiday, and Bessie Smith. **Her days were filled with euphoric highs and disturbing lows, but she lived her life convinced that true artists live beautifully doomed existences.**

A side stage performance at the 1963 Monterey Folk Festival wasn't enough to convince Janis that she was breaking through. She left San Francisco and continued her speed-fuelled life in New York City, followed by a brief return to Port Arthur, up to Austin, and eventually back to San Fran the following fall.

FEB. 1, 1964	APR. 4, 1964	APR. 16, 1964
The Beatles conquers the US singles chart for the first time with "I Want to Hold Your Hand."	The Beatles control the first five spots on Billboard's Top 40.	The Rolling Stones' eponymous debut album is released.

The San Francisco scene was emerging, but Janis probably wasn't aware that Mother McCree's Uptown Jug Champions' Jerry Garcia, Bob Weir, and Ron "Pigpen" McKernan were in the process of regrouping. Singing had taken the back seat to doping, and Janis's sexual escapades now included both men and women. She shot methedrine, began dealing, and even tried heroin during a meth draught in '65. One day she took a look in the mirror and decided it was time to move back to Port Arthur, marry, and grow up.

Her choice was a con artist and speed freak named Michel Raymond (which was actually a pseudonym he used around that time) whom she started dating in San Francisco. They decided Janis would return home and plan the wedding. Once they were both clean they'd reunite in Texas in anticipation of their big day.

Michel seemed like a good catch to her. He wore suits, shiny shoes, and had impeccable manners that would impress her parents. Back in Port Arthur Janis tried to blend in. She wore dresses, brushed her hair, registered for classes at the community college, and went shopping with her younger sister Laura, who was appalled that Janis didn't wear—or own—underwear.

For the better part of the year Janis strived to live in normalcy. When word reached that Michel was already married and that he had women scattered around the country, Janis chose not to believe it. She held on to the belief that she was going to marry and leave her bohemian life behind. She went to counseling for her habit and spent evenings at home crafting a Texas Star quilt. If old Janis was a fun-loving honky-tonk gal, the reformed Janis took it to the other extreme. She didn't drink, and even her straight hometown friends found her endlessly boring. When it finally sunk in that Michel would never marry her, she picked herself up and went back to Austin.

She considered joining Roky Erickson's 13th Floor Elevators, but Chet Helms had other plans for her in San Francisco. Helms sent mutual friend Travis Rivers to recruit her for a rock group called Big Brother and the Holding Company.

San Francisco had changed in a major way during Janis's yearlong absence. Spurred by Dylan's switch to electric and the popularity of the Stones (the Beatles played pop, which was a *faux pas* by most Bay Area musicians), the folkies formed electric bands and played free concerts for LSD-dropping longhairs.

One of the early enthusiasts was Ron McKernan, who saw a future in electric blues, and on his suggestion, Mother McCree's Uptown Jug Champions re-formed as the Warlocks in late '64.

The new band was modeled on Ron's favorite group at the time, the Rolling Stones, and the following year they had found their ideal lineup and perfect name: the Grateful Dead.

Known to the band and fans as Pigpen, Ron was a key ingredient of the Dead's early career. The band was leaderless during its embryonic phase, but since Pig's musical knowledge vastly dwarfed the rest of the crew's, he *was* the Grateful Dead.

"I tend to think of the Grateful Dead's existence in terms of Pigpen-as-center period and then the more self-sufficient, growing-out time that came when we got used to playing without him," Jerry Garcia told David Gans many years later. "It's not a question of better or worse—it's just different."

During Ron's childhood his dad worked as an R&B disc jockey for a black radio station, so the young boy knew the arcane moss-covered Delta, St. Louis, and Chicago blues by heart. Ron was an astute student of the blues, but instead of idolizing one or two musicians, Pigpen loved the *style* more than anything.

Ron wore dirty tees and greasy pants, a bike chain welded around his wrist, and perpetually unkempt hair. He looked so filthy that he wasn't allowed to swim in the local pool. Expelled from high school, Ron spent his time living like an outlaw and frequenting black blues dives. He looked like a mean biker, drank bourbon, and smoked unfiltered cigarettes, but his rough exterior was the yin to the yang of his kind soul. As a self-described alcoholic at thirteen, it seemed that he learned to cherish his addiction as an inseparable part of his persona.

The Grateful Dead spent the summer of '66 living away from the city in the town of Legunitas at a former youth camp. Big Brother and the Holding Company lived only five minutes away with their new chick singer.

BOBBY BLAND

Bobby Bland, born January 27, 1930, recorded a string of hits in the late fifties and early sixties and Pigpen is only one of many Bland fans. Van Morrison performed "Turn On Your Love Light" with Them, and Jerry Lee Lewis, Stevie Wonder, Aretha Franklin, Susan Tedeschi, Kenny Rogers, Marvin Gaye, the Isley Brothers, Eric Clapton, and Jay-Z have all covered this oft-forgotten Rock and Roll Hall of Famer.

55

JULY 1965

Ken Kesey hosts the first acid test. Attendees include The Warlocks, the Merry Pranksters, the Hells Angels, and Hunter S. Thompson.

JULY 25, 1965

Folksinger Bob Dylan goes electric at the Newport Folk Festival.

AUG. 11, 1965

The arrest of a black man for drunken driving ignites the Watts Riots in Los Angeles.

The two bands hung out quite a bit, and it didn't take long for Pigpen and Janis to get acquainted. Pig introduced her to Southern Comfort, and the two fell into the habit of swimming in the on-site pool, followed by noisy romps, and singing and playing by the piano.

During these early days Pigpen selected covers—some that endured the band's thirty-year-long career—and was busy crafting songs.

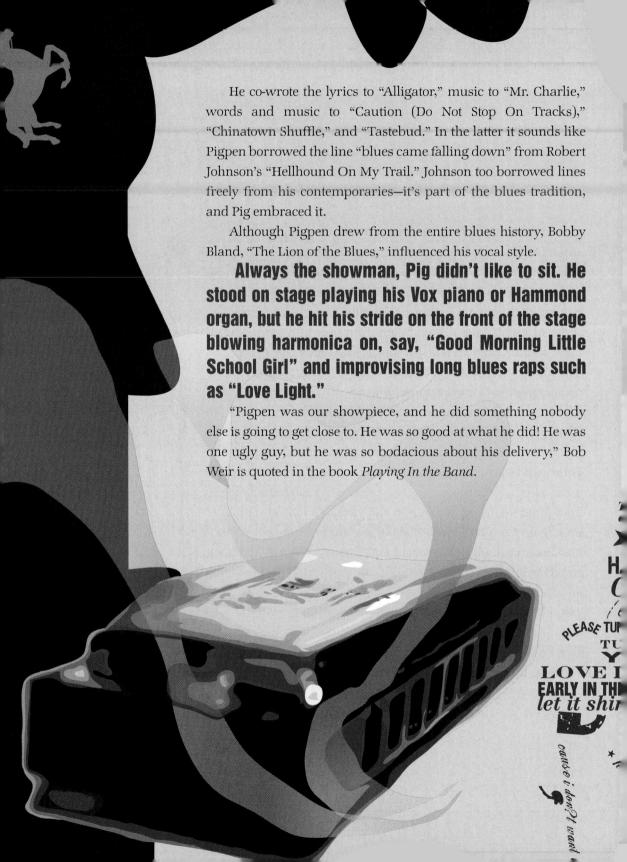

He co-wrote the lyrics to "Alligator," music to "Mr. Charlie," words and music to "Caution (Do Not Stop On Tracks)," "Chinatown Shuffle," and "Tastebud." In the latter it sounds like Pigpen borrowed the line "blues came falling down" from Robert Johnson's "Hellhound On My Trail." Johnson too borrowed lines freely from his contemporaries—it's part of the blues tradition, and Pig embraced it.

Although Pigpen drew from the entire blues history, Bobby Bland, "The Lion of the Blues," influenced his vocal style.

Always the showman, Pig didn't like to sit. He stood on stage playing his Vox piano or Hammond organ, but he hit his stride on the front of the stage blowing harmonica on, say, "Good Morning Little School Girl" and improvising long blues raps such as "Love Light."

"Pigpen was our showpiece, and he did something nobody else is going to get close to. He was so good at what he did! He was one ugly guy, but he was so bodacious about his delivery," Bob Weir is quoted in the book *Playing In the Band*.

Hey Pigpen, tell 'em about the bear!

The BEAR WHEW, WELL YOU ALL KNOW *about the* BEAR

HA! He's kind OF WHEN HE BEGIN to move, you know. he comes, haayree HIS CHOPS KINDA OPEN UP JUST A TOUCH YOU KNOW, SNEAKIN' SO WIN he DOWS AROUND them *young* ladies ON HIS MIND *late in the evenin time,* HE'S GOT SOMETHING *scrabblin your know,* may JUST COME UP KINDA SCREETCHIN' AND A UP AROUND YER WINDOW YOU KNOW SCRATCHIN' on yer wall AND HE *Young Ladies* F OF YOU feel any kinda NOSES somethin, MIGHT THERE'S *got* KINDA GO SOME IN THE THIS EVENIN some GROWL SNORT SNORT GUY AUDIENCE STANDING CLOSE ideas *a little bit or* SO AROUND YOU WHO'S on his YOU THAT MAKES YOU HUNGRY. BUT YOU KNOW *mind* KNOW HERE QUIET IN THE THAT OLD STEPPIN ALL AROUND BEAR HE COME EVENIN' TIME he just a YER OUT OF *snifflin',* WINDOWS THE HILLS JUST & *snufflin'* AND AND BACKDOORS KINDA HE'S BIG HAIRY YER SO YOU GIRLS *that ole bear is* CAUSE YOU GOT A PIE BETTER WATCH OUT HUNGRY, *always* UT THERE ONE YOUR WINDOWSILL COOLIN' OFF HE JUST CAN'T DO WITHOUT HE BE COMIN' *kind of pie at night time when it gets cooled* OF SOMETHIN' UP ON YOUR WAS HAIRY HE'S LOOKIN' FOR DOWN A LITTLE BIT WINDOW SILL n't got to worry WELL scuffling AROUND HA! YOUR out no BEAR YOU OUGHTA SEE MY OLD LADY, I TOLD YOU WINDOWS IDDLE OF THE NIGHT & A DOZEN OF 'EM. WELL I GET A LITTLE LONELY she can whip ON baby I need you darlin EVERYTHING'S ALRIGHT a little n baby) for BABY PLEASE (baby I'M BEGGIN' YOU BABY On R LIGHT your (I'm beggin' you baby) CAUSE I'M ON MY KNEES my light) Let it SHINE ON ME (LET IT SHINE ON ME) Let it shine on knees) (turn on your love light) LET IT SHINE ON ME) SHIIINE LET IT SHINE m ne, Let it shine on me) LET IT LATE on me! hu LET IT SHINE ON ME IN THE EVENING let it BIT shine it's LET IT SHINE ON ME need it's all I need, I NEED i all JUST WANT A LITTLE your light II NEED YOUR LOVIN' STONE ROLLING come on NEED YOUR let it shine KISSIN NEED YOUR RIDIN i need your SHINE ON ME

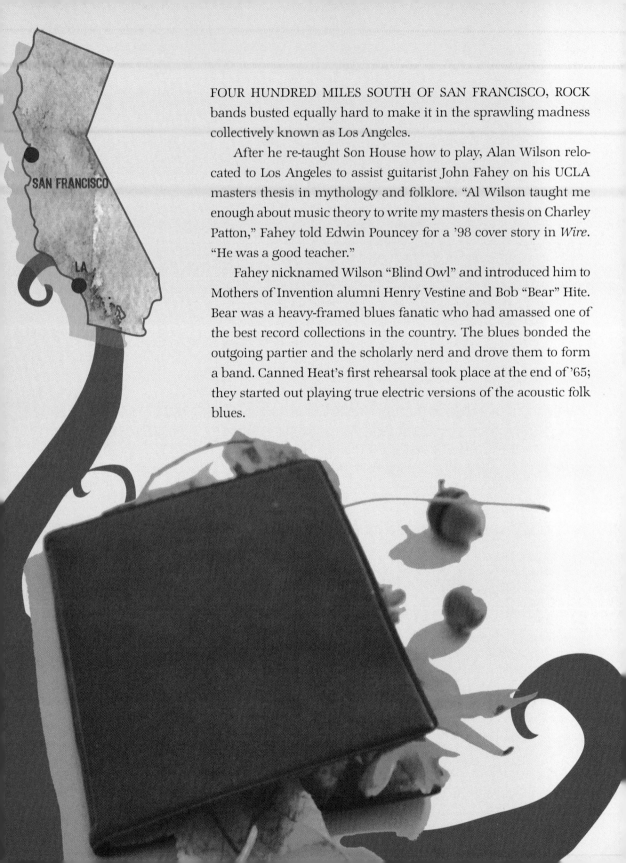

FOUR HUNDRED MILES SOUTH OF SAN FRANCISCO, ROCK bands busted equally hard to make it in the sprawling madness collectively known as Los Angeles.

After he re-taught Son House how to play, Alan Wilson relocated to Los Angeles to assist guitarist John Fahey on his UCLA masters thesis in mythology and folklore. "Al Wilson taught me enough about music theory to write my masters thesis on Charley Patton," Fahey told Edwin Pouncey for a '98 cover story in *Wire*. "He was a good teacher."

Fahey nicknamed Wilson "Blind Owl" and introduced him to Mothers of Invention alumni Henry Vestine and Bob "Bear" Hite. Bear was a heavy-framed blues fanatic who had amassed one of the best record collections in the country. The blues bonded the outgoing partier and the scholarly nerd and drove them to form a band. Canned Heat's first rehearsal took place at the end of '65; they started out playing true electric versions of the acoustic folk blues.

The band name came by the way of a Tommy Johnson song. Canned Heat is a brand of jellied alcohol meant for use with camping stoves. Drunks who were desperate enough to wring this toxic alcohol through a rag for consumption definitely had the blues.

Early on the group struggled to find gigs, went through numerous personnel, and even had to disband. "[I]n Los Angeles at least, there was no interest in blues, and an actual fear of blues music by club owners. We hardly got any work whatsoever and folded up," Wilson told *Down Beat*.

Four months later the band regrouped; John Hartmann and Skip Taylor signed on as management. In two short years Taylor had transformed from a suit and tie wearing record scout to a freewheeling hippie. He was looking for a band to break and believed Canned Heat was it.

"Their musicianship and knowledge of what they were playing was so far beyond any group I'd ever been around," Skip Taylor says today.

Larry Taylor (no relation to Skip) brought his bass to the mix as the band closed in on its golden lineup. The Mole, as he was known, was a seasoned session musician who at age sixteen laid down grooves with Jerry Lee Lewis and had recorded pop hits with The Monkees.

Blind Owl was academic, über-nerdy, suffered from a frail psyche, and craved inner peace. He knew all shades of blues guitar and blew the harp better than most old bluesmen. Owl also played Indian

BUSTED!

In 1967 Denver's anti-drug detective John Grey promised to rid the city of all its longhairs. His mission went into overdrive after Chet Helms opened the Family Dog. Unfortunately for Grey, Helms ran the place by the book, so he decided to bust one of the hippie bands that played there instead. A dispatched slimeball who happened to be a childhood friend of Bear stopped by Canned Heat's hotel room, hung out for a bit, and left. Minutes later the cops busted the down the door and discovered a little grass hidden where Bear's "buddy" had just sat.

The band was hauled to jail, minus Alan Wilson, who wasn't present.

Manager Skip Taylor, desperate for bail money, ended up selling the group's publishing rights for $10,000 to the president of Liberty Records. To this day, the band members (or their estates) still don't receive a dime for their classic tunes, which keep popping up in movies and commercials.

AUG. 29, 1966

The Beatles's final concert takes place in San Francisco's Candlestick Park.

OCT. 6, 1966

California bans LSD; the psychedelic becomes illegal in the rest of the country the following year.

OCT. 7, 1966

Fredrick Heath (30), a.k.a. Johnny Kidd, dies in a car accident.

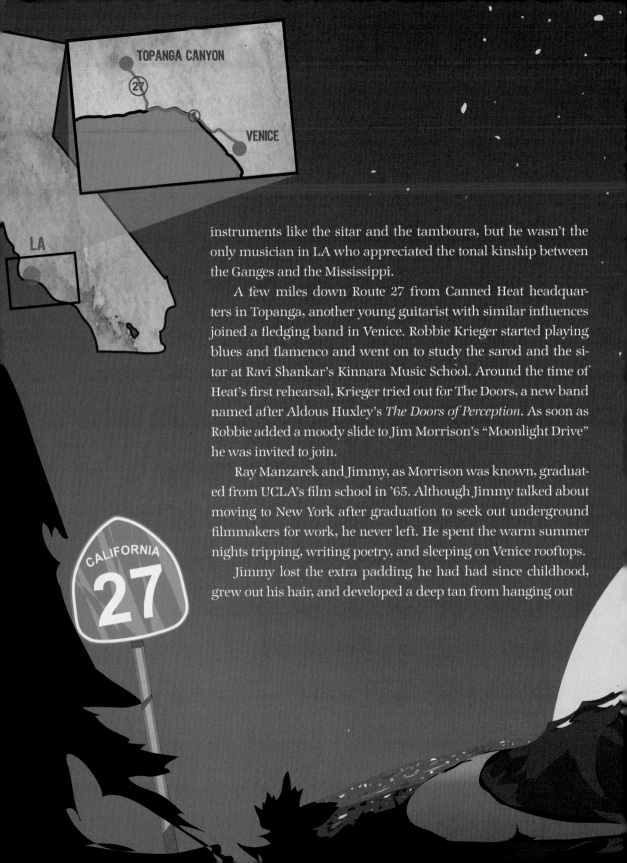

instruments like the sitar and the tamboura, but he wasn't the only musician in LA who appreciated the tonal kinship between the Ganges and the Mississippi.

A few miles down Route 27 from Canned Heat headquarters in Topanga, another young guitarist with similar influences joined a fledgling band in Venice. Robbie Krieger started playing blues and flamenco and went on to study the sarod and the sitar at Ravi Shankar's Kinnara Music School. Around the time of Heat's first rehearsal, Krieger tried out for The Doors, a new band named after Aldous Huxley's *The Doors of Perception*. As soon as Robbie added a moody slide to Jim Morrison's "Moonlight Drive" he was invited to join.

Ray Manzarek and Jimmy, as Morrison was known, graduated from UCLA's film school in '65. Although Jimmy talked about moving to New York after graduation to seek out underground filmmakers for work, he never left. He spent the warm summer nights tripping, writing poetry, and sleeping on Venice rooftops.

Jimmy lost the extra padding he had had since childhood, grew out his hair, and developed a deep tan from hanging out on the beach with his notebook. He later told *Rolling Stone* that he knew his calling after he heard an entire concert in his head and saw a large audience in front of him. "Those first five or six songs I wrote, I was just taking notes at a fantastic rock concert that was going on inside my head. And once I'd written the songs, I had to sing them," he said.

Ray Manzarek chanced upon Jimmy Morrison one day at the beach. "I'm working on some songs," Jimmy admitted and Ray, who played keyboards in a cover band with his brothers, asked to hear them. Encouraged by Ray, shy Jimmy sang "Moonlight Drive," "My Eyes Have Seen You," and "Summer's Almost Gone." Ray recognized Jim's talents—the deep baritone, Rimbaudesque

lyrics, sense of harmony, and beautiful features—and said Jim could move in with him and his girlfriend while they tried to start a band together.

A few months of rehearsals yielded a collection of original songs for the new quartet. By October they had a six-track acetate demo to shop around to every record company in LA. The demo was anything but bland. "A Little Game" with its lyrics "Crawl back in my brain ... go insane" struck a dissonant chord with the conservative record execs, one of whom responded with *"Take this record and get out! You guys are sick!"*

Lou Adler was the hippest in the biz, at least in California. He was the executive producer for The Mamas and the Papas' "California Dreamin'" and Barry McGuires's "Eve of Destruction." Even Stones manager Andrew Loog-Oldham dug Adler enough to give him a shout-out in the liner notes to the Stones' stark *December's Children*.

After a lot of legwork and a little luck Jim and Ray were granted a sit-down with Adler in his office. They handed him the acetate, and the producer listened to the first seconds of each track. "Nope, sorry. Nothing here I can use," he said and smiled. "That's okay man, we don't wanna be used anyway," Jim retorted and walked out.

Finally Billy James at Columbia Records bought into their sound and Morrison's lyrics. "'Go insane'—That's an option we hadn't considered in rock and roll," he says in Jac Holzman's *Follow the Music*. But James's promise didn't result in an offer, so the band played on.

BARRY McGUIRE

"Eve of Destruction" burned up the charts in the early fall of '65, but although Barry McGuire continued to write quality songs, he never sang a bigger hit. "It's just as well I didn't get another hit tune," he writes on his website. "I would have gone the way of Jim Morrison, Hendrix, or Joplin. I say 'Thank God' and I do thank God for that too, because I wouldn't have survived."

The Doors scored a residency engagement at the London Fog, a club next door to the hip Whisky A Go Go where big groups like Buffalo Springfield, the Byrds, and Love played.

On the last night of their residency, the booker at the Whisky walked in the door and fell for Jim. She offered them the house band slot, and Jim responded, "I'm not so sure. Give me a call tomorrow and we'll see." They were dying to play there, but he didn't want to appear over-anxious. The Doors accepted, of course, and supported headliners such as Captain Beefheart, Frank Zappa's Mothers of Invention, boogieman John Lee Hooker, the Byrds, Van Morrison's Them, Otis Redding, and many others.

The Stones spent part of the summer relaxing in LA and returned in August to record "Let's Spend the Night Together" and "Yesterday's Papers," but Brian Jones opted to hit up the night clubs instead. He stopped by the Whisky with Anita Pallenberg one night the Doors were playing. He liked the band, but didn't stick around to chat.

Another night, Elektra-band Love was playing at the Whisky when label prez Jac Holzman came by to listen. Love frontman and self-proclaimed original black hippie Arthur Lee insisted that Holzman should stay and check out the Doors' late night set, which he did, but Holzman wasn't immediately taken. "Perhaps I was thinking too conventionally, but their music had none of the rococo ornamentation with which a lot of rock and roll was being embellished—remember, this was still the era of the Beatles and Revolver, circa 1966. Yet, some inner voice whispered that there was more to them than I was seeing or hearing, so I kept returning to the club," he recalls. Finally he offered them a contract for three records and a little cash.

With a signed deal, Jim blew off one of the gigs at the Whisky and dropped acid instead. After the first set Ray and Robbie scrambled over to the Alta Cienega Motel in search of their missing singer.

The two find Jim in his room completely zonked out. They get him to the gig in time for the second set and start playing. But Jim's only half there. He sings with his back turned to the audience, mumbles into the microphone, and the crowd grows restless. Mid-set he insists on performing "The End," which is always reserved as the closer, but they get into it and Jim sings beautifully. They find that hypnotic groove in the middle for Jim's improvisational rant. Ray's organ swells roll like lazy waves, and Krieger plays hypnotic raga fills on his Gibson SG while Densmore adds tension with offbeat spurts on the snare drum. "The killer awoke before dawn [*cack-tha-cack*] ...he put his boots on [*cack-cack*] ...he took a face from the ancient gallery ...and he walked on down the hall..."

It's a première of perfect cadences—not even the band has heard them. Transfixed, John, Ray, and Robbie play on. "He paid a visit to his brother and then he..." Jim mesmerizes: the chatter dies down, the dancers stop dancing, nobody's taking drink orders, and he commands the full attention of every single soul in the bar. "Father? Yes, son? I want to kill you! Mother? I WANT TO FUCK YOOOU!" The band erupts like a volcano, waking everybody up, in Ray's words, "from this state of hypnosis to an absolute primal primordial scream shock of volume."

JAN. 27, 1967	AUG. 4, 1967
Elektra Records releases The Doors' eponymous album.	Arthur Penn's Bonnie & Clyde debuts; the film is ranked #27 on the American Film Institute's "100 Years, 100 Movies."

There it is, Sophocles' Oedipus Rex reared its twenty-five-hundred-year-old ugly face, brought to life by "the wild, crazy poet who's free of all the chains."

The Doors left the stage to deafening ovations, but the owner reprimanded the group backstage. "You filthy foulmouth, Morrison, you guys are fired!" The Doors' mix of rock and theatre was everything art should be: intelligent, perverse, and shocking.

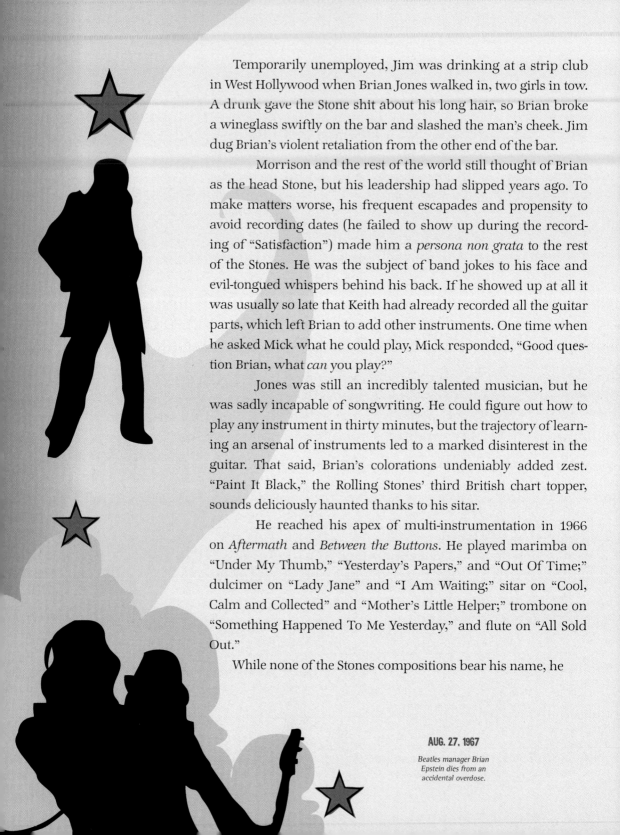

Temporarily unemployed, Jim was drinking at a strip club in West Hollywood when Brian Jones walked in, two girls in tow. A drunk gave the Stone shit about his long hair, so Brian broke a wineglass swiftly on the bar and slashed the man's cheek. Jim dug Brian's violent retaliation from the other end of the bar.

Morrison and the rest of the world still thought of Brian as the head Stone, but his leadership had slipped years ago. To make matters worse, his frequent escapades and propensity to avoid recording dates (he failed to show up during the recording of "Satisfaction") made him a *persona non grata* to the rest of the Stones. He was the subject of band jokes to his face and evil-tongued whispers behind his back. If he showed up at all it was usually so late that Keith had already recorded all the guitar parts, which left Brian to add other instruments. One time when he asked Mick what he could play, Mick responded, "Good question Brian, what *can* you play?"

Jones was still an incredibly talented musician, but he was sadly incapable of songwriting. He could figure out how to play any instrument in thirty minutes, but the trajectory of learning an arsenal of instruments led to a marked disinterest in the guitar. That said, Brian's colorations undeniably added zest. "Paint It Black," the Rolling Stones' third British chart topper, sounds deliciously haunted thanks to his sitar.

He reached his apex of multi-instrumentation in 1966 on *Aftermath* and *Between the Buttons*. He played marimba on "Under My Thumb," "Yesterday's Papers," and "Out Of Time;" dulcimer on "Lady Jane" and "I Am Waiting;" sitar on "Cool, Calm and Collected" and "Mother's Little Helper;" trombone on "Something Happened To Me Yesterday," and flute on "All Sold Out."

While none of the Stones compositions bear his name, he

AUG. 27, 1967

Beatles manager Brian Epstein dies from an accidental overdose.

scored *Mord und Totschlag (A Degree of Murder)*, a German movie from '67 that stared Jones's girlfriend Anita Pallenberg. The soundtrack features a pre-Zeppelin Jimmy Page on guitar, Nicky Hopkins on piano—and Brian on organ, sitar, recorder, autoharp, dulcimer, harmonica, clarinet, banjo, and harpsichord. It was the first time a rock musician composed a score for a full-length movie, and Brian did it splendidly. The soundtrack has never been officially released, but bootlegs dubbed straight from the movie exist.

ONE EARLY SUMMER EVENING IN 1966, KEITH RICHARD'S girlfriend Linda Keith stopped by the Cheetah where Curtis Knight and the Squires were playing. The New York City club was nearly empty, but the reedy, wild-haired, and flashy musician with rapid-fire guitar licks who was performing on stage astounded her. The man's sound and showmanship was unlike anything she had ever heard, so at set break she invited Jimmy James to join her and her model friends at their table. Jimmy James wasn't used to compliments, especially not from a British model who dated Keith Richards and could talk about Robert Johnson.

NICKY HOPKINS

Nicky Hopkins was one of rock's busiest session men. Unfortunately he suffered from Crohn's, a terrible inflammatory bowel disease, which prevented him from incessant touring. Nevertheless his talents on the piano allowed him to play on The Who's debut *My Generation*, The Kinks' *The Kink Kontroversy*, The Beatles' "Revolution," a slew of classic Stones tracks including "Sympathy for the Devil," "Gimme Shelter," "No Expectations," "Tumbling Dice," "Torn and Frayed," and "Angie," as well as cuts by the Quicksilver Messenger Service, Jefferson Airplane (he supported them at Woodstock), John Lennon, George Harrison, Joe Cocker, The Move, Cat Stevens, Jeff Beck, and Lowell George to mention, eh, a few.

Hopkins toured with the Stones in the early seventies, and Jerry Garcia enlisted him for his eponymous solo band in 1975.

Nicky Hopkins died in 1999 after complications from an intestinal surgery.

OCT. 9, 1967	DEC. 10, 1967	JAN. 1968	JAN. 30, 1968
Marxist revolutionary Che Guevara is executed in Bolivia.	Otis Redding (26) and six members of his backup band dies in a plane crash near Madison, Wisconsin.	Pink Floyd announces the departure of Syd Barrett; Barrett's erratic solo career ended in 1973, when he was 27.	The Tet Offensive commences, a bloody three-phase military campaign launched by the Viet Cong and the North Vietnamese army.

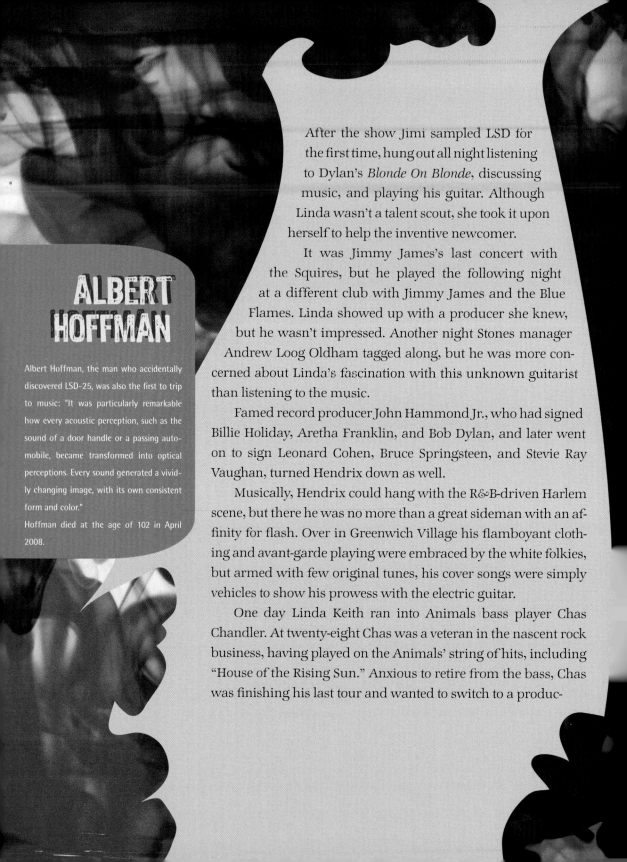

After the show Jimi sampled LSD for the first time, hung out all night listening to Dylan's *Blonde On Blonde*, discussing music, and playing his guitar. Although Linda wasn't a talent scout, she took it upon herself to help the inventive newcomer.

It was Jimmy James's last concert with the Squires, but he played the following night at a different club with Jimmy James and the Blue Flames. Linda showed up with a producer she knew, but he wasn't impressed. Another night Stones manager Andrew Loog Oldham tagged along, but he was more concerned about Linda's fascination with this unknown guitarist than listening to the music.

Famed record producer John Hammond Jr., who had signed Billie Holiday, Aretha Franklin, and Bob Dylan, and later went on to sign Leonard Cohen, Bruce Springsteen, and Stevie Ray Vaughan, turned Hendrix down as well.

Musically, Hendrix could hang with the R&B-driven Harlem scene, but there he was no more than a great sideman with an affinity for flash. Over in Greenwich Village his flamboyant clothing and avant-garde playing were embraced by the white folkies, but armed with few original tunes, his cover songs were simply vehicles to show his prowess with the electric guitar.

One day Linda Keith ran into Animals bass player Chas Chandler. At twenty-eight Chas was a veteran in the nascent rock business, having played on the Animals' string of hits, including "House of the Rising Sun." Anxious to retire from the bass, Chas was finishing his last tour and wanted to switch to a produc-

ALBERT HOFFMAN

Albert Hoffman, the man who accidentally discovered LSD-25, was also the first to trip to music: "It was particularly remarkable how every acoustic perception, such as the sound of a door handle or a passing automobile, became transformed into optical perceptions. Every sound generated a vividly changing image, with its own consistent form and color."
Hoffman died at the age of 102 in April 2008.

tion role. He saw the same potential in Hendrix that Linda Keith sensed and promised he'd come back after the tour to work out the details.

September 23 Hendrix flew first class to London. Chas Chandler wasted no time introducing him to swinging London's musical elite. **Within a week Hendrix upstaged Eric Clapton at a Cream concert and started dating Kathy Etchingham, who had previously been with Brian Jones and the Who's Keith Moon.**

The press dubbed him "the wild man of Borneo," and although it was a racist label, Hendrix cherished all the attention he was getting. Britain held a deep fascination with African-American bluesmen, so when Hendrix arrived with his wild guitantics he was welcomed as an amazing oddity.

Drummer Mitch Mitchell and guitarist Noel Redding (who was asked to switch to bass for the job) were quickly hired to form a trio dubbed the Jimi Hendrix Experience. Invited to support Johnny Hallyday, a popular French singer, the band became better acquainted during a two-week tour of the continent. Back in England the trio recorded their debut single: Billy Roberts's "Hey Joe." When Chas encouraged Jimi to write the b-side, he came up with "Stone Free," a quick autobiographical song about life as a traveling musician.

The band often played two gigs per evening and recorded during the graveyard shift when studio time was cheaper. "Purple Haze" and "The Wind Cries Mary" followed "Hey Joe;" all three charted top ten in the UK.

LEMMY KILMISTER

After a gig in Liverpool the road manager for the Experience gave his friend Lemmy Kilmister a ride back to London. Lemmy, who later founded Motörhead, ended up roadieing for the band for a good two weeks.

ROGER MAYER

In mid-January 1967, the Experience played a club gig packed with who's who in British music: Paul McCartney, Ringo Starr, Pete Townshend, Eric Clapton, Jeff Beck, John Entwistle, Jimmy Page, members of the Animals, the Hollies, and the Small Faces, Beatles' manager Brian Epstein, Hendrix's effects guru Roger Mayer, and many others.

Brian Jones, who was already a big fan of Hendrix and shared his flamboyant fashion sense, told singer Terry Reid that it was all wet up front from all the weeping guitar players.

After Jimi Hendrix received an advance copy of *Are You Experienced?* he and Brian Jones listened to the LP all night. Brian was impressed and suggested that he'd produce Jimi in the future, but the talk never materialized into an actual deal.

Shortly thereafter Brian flew to the Cannes Film Festival for the premiere of *A Degree of Murder*. The movie was supposed to be a coronation of his ability to stand on his own feet as a musician, but it didn't turn out that way. Anita Pallenberg—Brian's starlet, now ex-girlfriend—was there with Keith Richards.

Pallenberg was initially turned on by Brian's moodiness, but fifteen months of it had become a drag. Especially the violence. Like the time in Los Angeles when Brian hit a chair over her back and yelled "you fucking cunt." It was four a.m., and he continued to smash both the furniture and the TV. The noisy debacle was enough to rouse management, who was otherwise known for its discretion. Tour manager Michael Gruber muttered later that Brian and Anita's bungalow "looked demolished, like a truck had ran through it."

Keith was a different creature of course— confident, laid-back, and with a passive cool— the complete opposite of Brian.

Brian's final blow occurred a few months before Cannes during a road trip with Anita, Keith, Mick, and Marianne Faithfull. A severe asthma attack left Brian stranded at a hospital in Toulouse while Mick and Marianne, Keith and Anita continued en route to Morocco.

When Brian caught up with the rest in Marrakech, Morocco, he correctly sensed that Keith had hooked up with "his" bird. He beat up Anita for the last time that night. The following morning Keith and Anita flew home while Brian shopped for trinkets in the *souks*.

WARHOL'S FACTORY

The Factory, Andy Warhol's Midtown studio on East 47th Street, was a creative and social meeting point for hip artists, musicians, authors, photographers, drug dealers, porn stars, and drag queens.

During the day, a team of workers produced Warhol's famed two-dimensional silk screens, while the night offered drug-fuelled parties, concerts, and orgies in the tinfoil-lined loft.

Many such events were filmed, and Warhol even hired scribes to record taped conversations that took place inside the Factory.

Brian left *Festival de Cannes* early and headed back to the studio. The Stones recorded "No Expectations" sitting in a circle on the floor, and Brian's slide makes the song. "That was the last time I remember Brian really being totally involved in something that was really worth doing," Jagger recalled years later and added that the guitarist had "lost interest in everything." Days after the session the Scotland Yard knocked on the door of Jones's apartment and busted him for cannabis possession. Life went awry for the pop star, while his friend Jimi held the metaphorical torch high in the sky.

A few weeks after Brian's arrest, the Experience played two shows at the Saville Theatre, owned by Beatles manager Brian Epstein. It was June 4, 1967, and *Sgt. Pepper's Lonely Hearts Club Band* had been released just three days earlier. The record blocked *Are You Experienced?* from reaching number one, but newcomer Hendrix knew how to one-up the Beatles. Jimi showed up thirty minutes before the band was due on stage and announced to Noel and Mitch that they were opening with "Sgt. Pepper." "We thought he'd gone daft," Noel recalled to Charles Cross. They listened to the song on a portable record player while Jimi played through the chord changes and quickly rearranged the horn section to make it work on the guitar.

The Experience hit the stage in front of an audience that included Paul McCartney, George Harrison, Eric Clapton, Jack Bruce, and the rest of Britain's music cognoscenti. Opening with a Beatles cover three days after its release with members of the Beatles in the audience was an extremely cocky move, but the Experience pulled it off. Afterwards, the band headed to Epstein's après party, and Paul McCartney greeted Hendrix at the door with a huge joint and said, "That was fucking great, man."

Paul's endorsement was the best thing that could've happened for Hendrix's career at that stage. The Beatle was on the board for an upcoming festival in California, and he strongly recommended The Who and Jimi's Experience—he even suggested that the virtually unknown expat should be one of the headliners. A few weeks later Jimi left England for a strange mix of premiere and homecoming. **Only nine months had passed since he was a penniless sideman on the Chitlin' Circuit, but the changes in Jimi's life were more than most musicians could even dream. He returned from Britain leading a trio with a successful record, escorted by Brian Jones of the Rolling Stones.**

Jones skipped band duties to join Jimi on the other side of the Atlantic. When they stopped by New York City en route to Monterey, Jimi used the opportunity to check out what was happening in the city he had left behind. They went to The Scene where the Doors held residency.

NYC dug the Doors, and with "Light My Fire" burning up the charts, Jim found himself courted by the Warholites. Encouraged to drop by pop artist Andy Warhol's Factory any time, he scored pills from the hangers-on and head from the Siren-like Nico. Jim's loose relationship with Pamela Courson never precluded him from random affairs, but his times with Nico were more than a faceless fuck. The

NICO

Nico, nee Christa Päffgen (October 16, 1938–July 18, 1988), was a German fashion model and actress who modeled for *Elle, Vogue, Camera,* and *Tempo.* She starred in Federico Fellini's masterpiece *La Dolce Vita* (1959) and had the lead role in Jacques Poitrenaud's *Strip Tease* (1963).

Nico met Brian Jones in early 1965 and Bob Dylan that same summer in Paris; she had flings with both. Dylan's "I'll Keep It With Mine" is reportedly about her.

In the mid-sixties Nico split her time between Paris and New York, where she participated in Andy Warhol and Paul Morrissey's experimental films, including *Chelsea Girls.* She met Lou Reed and the Velvet Underground at Warhol's Factory and ended up singing three songs on the group's debut album *Velvet Underground and Nico* (1967).

At the end of the decade Nico followed Iggy Pop back to Michigan and hung out with The Stooges at their Funhouse. "She was the one who took me when I was a skinny little naïve brat and taught me how to eat pussy and all about the best German wines and French champagnes," Iggy told Nick Kent.

Teutonic actress was Jim's perfect partier in crime. Together they formed one dangerous duo—both felt the other was crazier, so there were no stops.

Unbeknownst to Jim, Brian was in the City to scoop Nico with him. Towards the end of the week, when Jim called to set up yet another debaucherous weekend, he was told she was in Monterey with his favorite rock star. Jealousy soon shifted to depression, and he spent the weekend drinking heavily—even by his own dejected standards—while the world's first real rock festival went down in the band's home state.

Although Woodstock '69 historically overshadows The Monterey International Pop Festival of '67, the latter was in many ways a more important event.

An estimated 35,000 people attended Monterey's three-day festival. It included the first major performances by Big Brother and the Holding Company, the Jimi Hendrix Experience, Canned Heat, the Grateful Dead, Otis Redding, the Steve Miller Band, Jefferson Airplane, and Ravi Shankar. The event catapulted most of them from local notoriety to instant stardom.

It was a ground-breaking show with acts in blues, pop, rock, and psychedelia, and the first time rock bands from LA, San Francisco, New York City, Memphis, and Chicago were on the same bill.

Brian Jones weaved through the crowd in full hippie regalia followed by curious fans—few had any idea who his lanky black friend was. Speaking at the festival's fortieth anniversary, Grateful Dead's Bob Weir remembered it as a weekend spent forging friendships between San Francisco and London. He recalled jamming on Saturday with "this black kid with a headband on" who turned out to be Jimi Hendrix.

Janis & Big Brother's performance blew both the press and the audience away. In fact, it was so good that Big Brother was asked to play again the following day. The star of Saturday night was without a doubt Otis Redding, and both Pigpen and Janis, who were still occasionally hooking up, tried to get a piece of the action.

After the show Pig macked on the African-American chicks from Redding's entourage, while Janis hit on the man himself. Pig didn't have any luck and went back to the grounds where he ended up jamming with Jimi Hendrix and Jefferson Airplane's Jorma Kaukonen and Jack Casady. Janis Joplin was out all night. When she made it back to her room early in the morning Pigpen was there waiting. "So does God have a big dick?" he asked, referring to Redding. "Only if you believe in him!" Janis replied.

Jimi Hendrix spent Sunday afternoon painting his red Stratocaster while Janis delivered another gripping performance. The slots for the British contingent, Hendrix and The Who, had yet to be decided. Both were hungry for a breakthrough that the countless journalists dispatched from all over the country could rave about; neither Jimi Hendrix nor Pete Townshend wanted to follow the other. A coin toss finally settled the lineup. The Who went on first and tore it up. The Dead followed with Pigpen in fine form on "Alligator," but the band failed to play a showstopping set like Canned Heat, Big Brother and the Holding Company, The Who, and Otis Redding.

As soon as the Dead cleared the stage Brian introduced Hendrix as a one of the most exciting stars he had ever heard. The Jimi Hendrix Experience launched the set with "Killing Floor." Jimi pulled out all the stops for his now-legendary performance: wrapped in a pink feather boa he rode the guitar, made it squeal, played behind his neck, between his legs, with his teeth, humped the amp, and lit his howling guitar on fire at the end of "Wild Thing." He egged on the flames with his hands, resembling a voodoo shaman.

BRIAN SPIRALS

Ten days after Monterey Brian flew to Rome where Anita Pallenberg was filming. It was a desperate attempt to win her back, and her refusal sent him further down the spiral.

Back in England he tried to check in at a mental clinic but was refused. Two days later he was accepted for a three-week stay at the Priory Nursing Home in Surrey.

Monterey was a defining weekend for the hippie movement and the apex of the so-called Summer of Love, which tipped downhill as soon as mainstream media advertised it as such. Eager journalists filed hundreds of articles on the subject along the lines of *Time* magazine's cover story titled "The Hippies: Philosophy of a Subculture" and *CBS News's* report "The Hippie Temptation." The press's scare about free love, drugs, and cool rock bands led to an influx of adolescents that descended on San Francisco with no place to stay and little money in their pockets. Community groups like the Diggers and the Haight Ashbury Free Clinic did their best to care for them, but their donation-driven systems were on the constant verge of breaking down. Cynical drug dealers replaced cool bros and pushed increasingly harder drugs. Tourists crammed tour buses to witness the zoo first-hand while cops tried to hold it all down.

By autumn many of the young pilgrims had left, but fearful of another invasion the following spring, the Diggers staged *The Death of Hippie* parade in October 1967. Mimicking a funeral procession, the participants carried a dummy resting on a stretcher that read "Hippie—Son of Media."

The bands still lived in the area, but not for much longer. Jefferson Airplane was at 2400 Fulton, Janis kept an apartment at 122 Lyon, and the Dead's communal digs were at 710 Ashbury. Pigpen's lair was behind the kitchen. He never opened the curtains, and kept a TV, an upright piano, a random selection of guitars, empty bottles of Southern Comfort, and crushed beer cans scattered around the room. If he wasn't playing music or entertaining guests in the kitchen, he read science fiction, English history, or the legends of King Arthur and the Knights of the Round Table.

When the Dead started to create original material, Pig found himself on the sidelines. Although his bandmates didn't eschew him, his story echoes Brian Jones's in a way. Pig didn't have the chops to play anything but blues and rock, had little interest for the rest of the band's spacey psychedelic jams, and hardly practiced. The other members were, to use Timothy Leary's words, "turned on" in a major way—the band's soundman and benefactor was the famous LSD alchemist Owsley "Bear" Stanley— but Pig refused to partake. He was dosed twice and broke down in nervous jitters on both occasions. At least he was calm and confident in his sober state, which wasn't the case at all with Canned Heat's Blind Owl.

BLIND OWL WASN'T GLAMOROUS LIKE JOPLIN, FLASHY LIKE Hendrix, or loud like Morrison. Pigpen didn't have the looks, but he commanded great showmanship. Poor Blind Owl lacked all the usual traits associated with stardom, but he made up for it with a true, gentle soul and masterful reinterpretations of the blues.

Wilson often slept outside instead of crashing in his hotel room, wore the same clothes for weeks, and refused to bathe. Even when Canned Heat was one of the hottest acts around, he found himself unable to bed otherwise star-obsessed groupies.

"Alan failed at finding a relationship with any gal," Skip Taylor says. "He definitely talked about it and was emotionally scarred by it. He had trouble relating to the world and people in general."

Blind Owl's many pains and disappointments made their way into his music. He describes his depression in "My Time Ain't Long" and laments being used by an ostensible groupie in "London Blues," but his lyrics weren't confined to internal struggles. "So Sad (the world is in a tangle)," "Future Blues," and "Poor

Moon" had clear environmental messages, which was a new lyrical direction in rock. Sure, Jim asked, '*What have they done to the earth?*' in a section of "When the Music's Over," but Canned Heat's prophesizing was more deliberate. Alan Wilson really hoped fans would latch on to his message.

Blind Owl's fear about the state of the planet came to full fruition on *Future Blues*. The LP included a gatefold plea penned by Alan C. Wilson titled "Grim Harvest." Only ninety percent of the original redwoods were still standing at the time of writing, and Blind Owl hoped his words would raise awareness about the majestic California forests. "At the current rate of *harvest* these remaining acres will be cleared within ten years," he wrote.

The LP cover was his idea as well. Decked out in spacesuits, the band members raise the American flag upside down in a cluster that resembles the famous Iwo Jima photograph. A polluted earth is suspended in the background. Superstores such as Sears and K-Mart found the cover provocative enough to merit a storewide ban. It was Alan's way of saying he was terrified that humans would pollute the moon.

Wilson's feelings didn't just manifest themselves through lyrics, of course. His solo in "So Sad" starts out as an odd-metered country blues lick, then he picks at his frustration through minor chords, throws a fit, and jumps into a mean and spunky blues solo.

The nerdy guitar player with the boyish face had sided with nature from an early age. As a young boy he complained that he heard the trees scream in pain under the weight of Boston's winter snow. Naturally the statement merited plenty of teasing from the other boys.

Owl truly found his place in Canned Heat. It was a musical brotherhood where he was encouraged to be himself. Blind Owl

APR. 4, 1968	APR. 5, 1968	APR. 5, 1968
Martin Luther King assassinated in Memphis, Tennessee.	*Jimi plays an hour-long instrumental in Dr. King's honor, moving members of his audience to tears.*	*James Brown urges the crowd in Boston to "make Dr. King's dream a reality," effectively preventing 80,000 people from rioting.*

hated fame's manifestations, diametrically opposite of, say, Janis. "Do you think they love me?" she asked compulsively, expecting affirmation from everybody within earshot.

Alan was so down to earth that he schlepped a huge botany book on tour that he stuffed with leaves, soil samples, and flowers he found along the way.

The band bought him a camping van so he could get out whenever he wanted. The problem was that Blind Owl didn't know how to drive, but as soon as Skip and Bear taught him, Owl went to Yosemite, Big Sur, or Northern California's redwood forests.

Once when Wilson was late for band practice he rolled in the driveway with a dented van. He apologized for arriving late and told his band brothers some disturbing news: "I was driving along the freeway and all of a sudden I just thought *'fuck it'* and drove off the road."

"REDS"

The barbiturate Seconal is often referred to as reds and was a common downer during the sixties and seventies. Famous casualties include Marilyn Monroe, who overdosed on reds in '62, followed by *Wizard of Oz* starlet Judy Garland seven years later. Jimi Hendrix swallowed nine German-made Secobarbital tablets before he choked to death in his sleep in 1970.

Seconal derivatives still work well enough to warrant frequent use in Oregon's physician-assisted suicides.

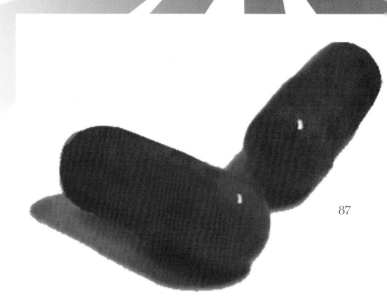

AUG. 26-29, 1968

The infamous Chicago Democratic Convention takes place.

JAN. 30, 1969

The Beatles' rooftop performance filmed at Apple Records.

MALCOLM HALE

Thanks to Spanky And Our Gang's '67 hits "Sunday Will Never Be The Same" and "Lazy Day," the group is remembered as a mid-sixties pop sensation in the same vein as The Mamas and the Papas, but that was only one of the many flavors this Chicago-based band could concoct. Our Gang was studio-polished yet put on an entertaining act in that old-timey way, all while dazzling audiences with its display of sublime musicianship.

Elaine "Spanky" McFarlane and Malcolm Hale, the group's principal members, spent 1962-64 as The New Wine Singers, a fantastic quintet that mixed jug band, folk, barbershop a capella, show tunes, and Irish standards. "We were eclectic as hell and loved every minute of it," Spanky says today. "We did anything we wanted and there was a lot of cornball comedy."

"Malcolm had charisma and a rubber face that never stopped, he was right in there," she adds.

The New Wine Singers put out a few LPs, including two live recordings, which capture the ensemble's entertaining live show. Once that band fizzled out they formed Spanky And Our Gang.

"Malcolm was such an integral part of the group," Spanky says. "Very talented, but totally underrated, well, almost not rated at all."

Malcolm Hale wrote and arranged most of the tunes, played lead

→

Another time, after he lost a bottle of pills known as reds, he complained, "Christ, I'm so fucked up I can't even kill myself right."

A shrink issued him a script for anti-depressants and instructed Bear to care for him. Heat's drummer Fito de la Parra describes the arrangement as "putting some berserk Viking in charge of little orphan Bambi."

The pills never did much good because the chronically disorganized Owl soon lost them somewhere on tour. A few weeks later he quit the band in an attempt to reach equilibrium. When he asked to rejoin two weeks later, the rest of the band just shrugged and welcomed him back in the fold.

Canned Heat was like a pack of outlaw bikers who had room for everybody, and they didn't cultivate a superficial image, unlike, say, Jimi's Experience, who looked like three psychedelic brothers with their matching bell-bottoms and two-foot afros; or Janis, the upscale honky-tonk acid queen with feathery boas; or the mysteriously androgynous Victorian decadent Stones.

Ready to shed the leather-clad Lizard King persona, Morrison loved Canned Heat for their laid-back attitudes, beards, worker's clothes, and updated blues covers. He even told Ray Manzarek that he felt the Doors should veer in a more bluesy direction a la the hard-hitting Heat.

These white middle class kids suddenly became rich and famous for playing black blues through a fuzz box. That irony wasn't lost on Muddy Waters. "There are some beautiful white bands," he said, but added that they lacked his Baptist-raised soul: "They can't deliver the message. They're playing the white folks' blues. I'm playing the real blues." The fiscals underlined Muddy Waters' problem with authenticity. "These young white kids get up and sing my stuff, and other people's stuff that I know, and the next thing is they're one of the biggest groups around and making real big money."

But Joplin's harshest critics weren't musicians—they worked in the press. By '68 Janis was in the crosshairs, struggling to pass for a real blues broad amidst her immense success. Big Brother was frequently pigeonholed for playing "out of time and out of tune," so Janis left them behind, but her new band wasn't shaping up to be what she or anybody else involved wanted.

guitar, trombone, and sang. Still, since Malcolm spent every sixth weekend with the Army Reserves, the rest of the group learned to play occasional gigs without him.

Over the course of 1967 and 1968 the group placed five singles on Billboard's Top 40 and made coveted TV appearances on the Tonight Show, the Dick Cavett Show, Hollywood Palace, and so on.

Spanky And Our Gang's most notorious gig was The Smothers Brothers Comedy Hour where they performed "Give A Damn," which was banned in several states for its un-kosher title

(never mind that the song had a positive message; to *give a damn* about "your fellow man").

CBS received a flood of complaints after the show, one of which purportedly came from Richard Nixon. See, "damn" was not an appropriate word during 1968's "family viewing hours."

That October Malcolm Hale failed to

→

show up for a gig in Boise, Idaho, but the band set up his guitar amplifier on stage; they figured he might show up a little later. Mid-set, the amp screeched uncontrollably, disrupting the song. As soon as the band walked off stage they learned that Malcolm Hale was dead.

The 27-year-old multi-instrumentalist had gone to bed drunk at a girlfriend's place in Chicago (Spanky says he was quite the multi-dater), and even though the band called her to rouse him up, she refused to do so. After 28 hours of "sleep" the girlfriend discovered that he was dead. Malcolm Hale died of monoxide poisoning due to a faulty space heater.

Spanky And Our Gang played the rest of the year to fulfill their obligations and called it quits. "I was devastated and cried every day for a year," Spanky says.

The group's hits keep popping up on various CD box sets, most recently on the three-disc *Summer of Love: The Hits of 1967*. To really figure them out you've gotta seek out their records. "It's not about the hits. It's about the album cuts and we had that going," McFarlane adds.

Rolling Stone's Jon Landau opinioned that Erma Franklin's "Piece of My Heart" had *soul* while Janis Joplin covered up her lack thereof by singing it with *balls*. And this distrust about authenticity wasn't reserved for caucasian musicians—it haunted African-American performers as well. The Supremes were accused of creating a style too polished and not "black" enough. Joplin wasn't one to leave smack-talk unanswered and wrestled the steer by its horns.

INSTEAD *of* SUFFERING FROM WHAT SHE CALLED *the* BLACK MAN'S BLUES: *not* HAVING $, BOOZE, BABY SHE SAID HERS CAME FROM *not digging* college, *holding a* job OR OWNING A CAR IN EFFECT JANIS DEFINED THE BLUES *as something* BEYOND RACIAL LINES OR FINANCIAL MEANS BLUES *was something* FELT IN A BRUISED soul A YEARNING TO OVERCOME DISPAIR

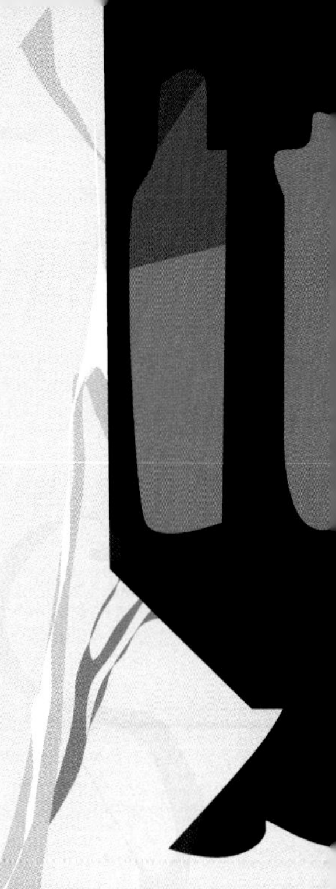

The mere presence of a rout about black versus white clearly indicated that blues was firmly assimilated into popular music and culture—a notion that hadn't fully sunk into opinioned minds. Luckily it's the open-minded and not critics or followers who further art. Brian Jones still got *that* and it led him on a musicological quest across the Gibraltar.

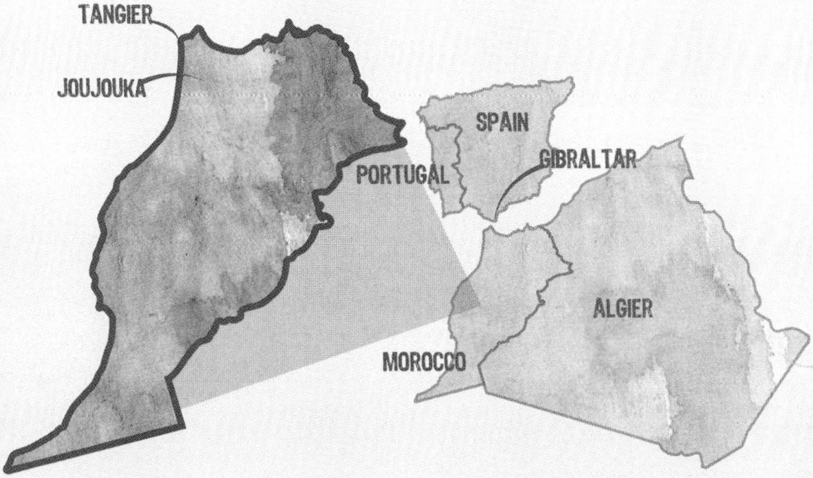

TANGIER

JOUJOUKA

SPAIN

GIBRALTAR

PORTUGAL

ALGIER

MOROCCO

During a vacation with Anita in '66, Brian heard about a group of magician musicians whose music William Burroughs and Brion Gysin described to him as the "primordial sounds of a 4,000 year-old rock & roll band." Moroccan painter Mohamed Hamri introduced painter and writer Gysin to the Master Musicians of Joujouka in 1950. Brian was hooked after listening to Gysin's field recordings.

The Joujouka musicians improvise with droning *ghaita* (an Arabic oboe), *lira* (a bamboo flute), and *gimbri* (a three-stringed lute) supported by complex percussion and accented by eerie chants. The music is considered a variation of an Islamic Sufi trance, but it might have a far older origin. After Gysin witnessed the annual *Äid el-Kebir* festival, he connected it to the ancient rites of Pan.

Pan is the goat-legged, divine pasturer of ancient Greece, a bearded creature of the night. He embodies both the androgynous and the phallic, dances with the nymphs and beds Dionysus' maenads.

Herders and common folk cherished Pan's free spirit and love of nature, but the rise of Christianity brought a new school of patriarchs that turned the natural order upside down. Under this new realm giving in to one's natural urges was a sinful act. It's probably no accident that Satan often looked and acted like Pan: black hair, horns, and goat's feet, capable of seducing even chaste women. The true Pan never died, and part of his rites survived in the small Moroccan village of Joujouka (also spelled Jajouka).

During the annual *Äid el-Kebir*, the music keeps the Pan-like goat man *Boujeloud* (whose name translates to "the one wearing skins") at bay until late in the night when he appears dancing with switches in front of a flickering bonfire. A group of

COBAIN BURROUGHS

Kurt Cobain put music to beat-author William Burroughs' "The Priest They Called Him" in 1992. The two sent tapes back and forth, but they never met face to face until the following year when Kurt drove out to see him in Kansas. After Kurt left Old Bill said, "There's something wrong with that boy; he frowns for no good reason."

JULY 4-5, 1969
The first Atlanta International Pop Festival features acts such as Janis Joplin, Canned Heat, Creedence Clearwater Revival, and Led Zeppelin.

JULY 14, 1969
Easy Rider debuts.

JULY 20, 1969
Neil Armstrong and Buzz Aldrin walks on the moon.

screaming women run out in front of him, and it's believed that whoever is struck with one of the branches will become pregnant before year-end.

Brian showed up unannounced with girlfriend Suki Poitier and soundman George Chkiantz at Gysin's doorstep in Tangier and told Gysin that he wanted to record the musicians. Guided by Hamri, the five set off for the Rif Mountains. With Gysin's introduction, the musicians gladly obliged their longhaired guest's request and played the night away while Brian grooved to the beats through a set of headphones.

The following afternoon, two villagers led a white sheep with tusks dangling above its eyes past the hut. The glint from a long-bladed knife warned Brian of what was about to happen, and he raced to his feet. "That's me," he uttered with a choked throat. Gysin too saw the resemblance between the longhaired rock star and the sheep to the slaughter. The symbolism wasn't lost on Brian, who paled like he had received an omen.

Curiously, Jimi Hendrix had a premonition in Morocco the following year. Biographer Charles Cross writes that Hendrix vacationed there with three women he had recently befriended in NYC. The nine-day trip was a much-needed break for Jimi, and his mood was unusually elated. That changed when a seer that worked for the King of Morocco read his tarot cards. The first card she dealt was the Star, and she told him that he would soon be surrounded by a large group of people (he played Woodstock later

AUG. 1969
Super group Blind Faith releases their eponymous debut album.

OCT. 31, 1969
Wal-Mart Stores incorporates in Arkansas.

SUFISM

Sufism is a mystic branch of Islam that professes a range of beliefs dedicated to cultivating pure love and devotion to God. Sufis believe the Divine lies within everybody's heart, and it's up to each of us to unlock and realize IT. Truth and knowledge of oneself is attained through the practice of poetry, art, and music.

In the West, the most famous Sufi is the thirteenth-century poet Jalalu'ddin Rumi, the best selling poet in America according to *Publisher's Weekly*.

that month). The second card changed the vibe: death. It didn't necessarily mean that he would soon die, she told him.

The death card could also mean rebirth, a warning that time is short, or that he was about to pass through some sort of a gateway, but her assurances didn't help. Jimi was visibly shaken, and the omen kept visiting him in his dreams over the next year. He told people he was soon going to die and that he wouldn't live to see thirty.

Turning thirty is a big deal. Many experience the last years of their twenties as a transitional phase between youth and matu-

BLUE CHAKRA

Followers of Southeast Asian religions may read another warning from Brian's choked throat.

The seven energy centers in the human body are known as *chakras*, and together they form the colors of the rainbow. The blue chakra sits in the throat and deals with personal expression through creativity, lack of authoritative respect, and addiction—all common traits in artists—and it bridges the physical and the spiritual world.

SOMETHING
COME T

rity. Thirty marks the real entry to adulthood—an age where most people have completed their university degrees, found their vocation, and are comfortably settled in a relationship—or not.

Renowned astrologer Rob Tillett, who spent the seventies as a touring rock & roller in his native Australia and now publishes the popular site Astrology On The Web, says that we spend the end of our twenties "clearing the decks of karmic debris for a clean course for the next cycle."

"Every twenty-nine years naturally presents us with the challenge to rise to new levels of awareness, or face the consequences of having failed to gain the wisdom required to do so," Tillett says. It's a phenomenon known in astrology as Saturn Return.

It takes the planet Saturn twenty-nine and a half years to return to the same position it occupied at the time we were born, a significant event as it marks the end of one cycle and the beginning of another.

Astrologers argue that Saturn Return is one of life's most important thresholds as it intensifies one's feelings of sadness, isolation, and purpose. In the words of Rob Hand, author of *Planets In Transit*, it's "a time of endings and new beginnings," a fitting characteristic for Saturnus, the Roman harvest god, the model for the grim reaper.

The Romans celebrated the god at Saturnalia. This festival commenced December 17 during winter solstice, the darkest night of the year. Saturnalia turned society's laws and customs upside down. Slaves became masters (or at least ate at the same table as their masters), gambling was permitted for all, and, in

MASTER MUSICIANS OF JOUJOUKA

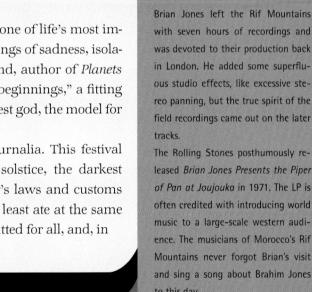

Brian Jones left the Rif Mountains with seven hours of recordings and was devoted to their production back in London. He added some superfluous studio effects, like excessive stereo panning, but the true spirit of the field recordings came out on the later tracks.

The Rolling Stones posthumously released *Brian Jones Presents the Piper of Pan at Joujouka* in 1971. The LP is often credited with introducing world music to a large-scale western audience. The musicians of Morocco's Rif Mountains never forgot Brian's visit and sing a song about Brahim Jones to this day.

In 1989, the Stones collaborated with the Master Musicians on *Steel Wheels'* "Continental Drift," as have Ornette Coleman, Marianne Faithfull, Sonic Youth's Lee Renaldo, the amazing Bill Laswell, and electronica artist Scanner.

IT'S IN THE STARS

The Western world's awareness of astrology has declined since the renaissance, when astronomy broke off as a separate and quantifiable science.

Unfortunately, the most pedestrian form of astrology is the most well known: the newspaper horoscope. There's a lot more to astrology than whether it's time to take charge at work or fix a personal relationship.

Some of Western culture's greatest thinkers were also astrologers—Pythagoras, Hippocrates, Nicolas Copernicus, Tycho Brahe, Francis Bacon, Galileo Galilei, Johannes Kepler, Gustav Holst, Isaac Newton, Carl Jung, and Benjamin Franklin.

For proof that planets can influence us here on earth, remember that the combination of our tiny moon's gravitational pull and the earth's centrifugal spin is great enough to shift the tide.

Historically, every great civilization studied the heavens to calculate time and to seek answers about earthly events.

Astrology, astronomy, and religion used to be one indistinguishable stew. It's quite astonishing to look at the fundamental similarities between Mayan, Egyptian, Chinese, Babylonian, Greek (western) and Vedic (read: Indian) study of planets and constellations. The link between the actual constellations and their Zodiac namesakes remains unbroken in the Vedic tradition, whereas the West's use of the tropical zodiac does not take into account that the constellations appear

the words of a Roman commentator from 50 AD, "loose reigns were given to public dissipation."

But Saturnalia meant more than a drunken carnival. It was a celebration of Rome's golden age, an era of peace and harmony that was supposed to have taken place under Saturn's rule. The Greek poet Hesiod wrote that it was the purest of all ages, a time of balmy weather, leisure, and no fear of death.

Thomas Paine, the American Revolution's ideological inspirator, noted that, "The supposed reign of Saturn was prior to that which is called the heathen mythology, and was so far a species of theism that it admitted the belief of only one God." So according to Paine, Saturn is the ur-God, the lone ruler of the vast, ancient universe. Saturn was Ninib to Babylonians and Cronus to the Greek—one of the seven Titans who ruled the world until Zeus kicked them off their galactic thrones.

SATURN IS KNOWN AS THE "GREATER MALEFIC," OR "THE killing planet," and it manifests itself in various ways. "Saturn demands resolution and restructuring," Tillett says. "Resolution of unfinished business and restructuring of our lives to move forward into the future."

The changes instigated by Saturn are really fantastic opportunities for those who are ready and capable of making major changes in their lives—harvesting what's been sown.

"Saturn rules the responsibilities, restrictions and limitations we are apt to encounter, and the lessons we must learn in life. He does not deny or diminish imagination, inspiration, spirituality, or good fortune, but he does demand that these things be given structure and meaning," Tillett explains.

The 27s died before their Saturn returned, and Tillett postulates that other astrological factors are involved. "The 27th year is an incredibly hefty one," he notes. "Astrologically, it's the

building up to Saturn Return, but other key factors are at work too."

Moving at less than one degree per month, it takes the moon 27 to 28 years to make it 360 degrees around the zodiac. At that point, the moon revisits its natal position: "The first progressed Lunar Return at age 27 marks the beginning of the difficult transition from the Phase of Youth to the Phase of Maturity," Tillett says. "The pace of our lives seems to accelerate, as we hurry to clear the decks of karmic debris, in preparation for the next grand stage of the great journey of life. This transitional phase lasts until the Saturn Return, which usually occurs within a year or two." (This process is repeated at age 56 when we experience another transition, from the Phase of Maturity to the Phase of Wisdom.)

Another strong effect occurs when the moon's pathway crosses the sun's course. These sensitive points are known as the moon's nodes (also called the dragon's head and tail). "A collision between the north and south nodes occurs during the 27th year, which often generates intense insecurities that lead to major transformations of the life-path," Tillett adds.

A fourth cause of difficulties is completing the 27-year cycle around the Pythagorean Triangle, a numerical and astrological concept that we'll explore later on.

For The 27s, Tillett theorizes, "Their energy is so heavily pushed into a particular channel (i.e. music) and when that channel dries up, they don't know how to move through the pathway."

With Tillett's perspective in mind, it's easy to see that their creativity waned, replaced with distractions (bad relationships, drugs, dwelling on missed opportunities, or fumbling for a "real" or "new" purpose) and a sense of out-of-focusness toward the end of their lives. At least that's the case for most of them.

Robert Johnson stuck his tongue in the honey pot and got stung; Jesse Belvin was caught up in things he couldn't control—be it hiring a party driver or becoming a victim to American

differently in our skies than they did for the Babylonians or the Greeks. The second diversion is the ancient Vedic use of 27 nakshatras as an additional ecliptic. Each nakshatra is a fixed point in the sky that the moon travels past on a given day, and it takes 27.322 such days to complete what's called a sidereal month. (Since the Earth orbits the sun, the moon must travel farther than 360 degrees to create the next new moon, which makes the lunar month—the month our calendar approximates—slightly longer: 29.531 days.)

Some astrologers worry that the moon's immense power is taken too lightly in the West, with its focus on sun sign astrology. "The moon is the most potent and powerful cosmic factor that affects our mental, emotional, and physical well-being on planet Earth," says astrologer Rob Tillett.

apartheidists; Brian Jones was a medicated mess for the latter part of his life; and as we shall see, Jimi Hendrix fumbled for a purpose; Janis Joplin chose to walk alone; Jim Morrison turned to destructive disgust. Ad nauseum.

Could it be that The 27s were too caught up in their youth and therefore unwilling, unable, or simply not ready to move across that threshold and face the responsibilities and expectations (theirs and/or others') that come with adulthood?

the sun rotates on its axis every 27 days

the moon completes a sideral month in 27 days

Mercury
Venus
Earth
Mars

Jupiter

Saturn

142 Million miles

484 Million miles

887 Million miles

1784 Million m

27°degrees

saturn rotates the sun every 29.47 years

Neptune

Pluto

2800 Million miles

3675 Million miles

JIM MORRISON, ROCK'S CEREMONIAL MASTER OF CHAOS, cut loose Saturnian's reigns at the Doors' most infamous show, which took place in 1969 at the deceivingly named Dinner Key Auditorium in Florida.

The Dinner Key Auditorium was nothing more than a musky old seaplane hangar rigged as a concert hall for the occasion. It was HOT and the promoters, a pair of brothers who owned a karate dojo, feared gatecrashers if they were to open the enormous sliding doors to let in fresh air. Thuggish promoters were abound in this early era of large rock shows, but this Miami duo were especially bad.

The day of the show, manager Bill Siddons realized that the 8,000-seater was oversold by at least 5,000 tickets. He threatened to call off the concert, but the brothers were unfazed. They said that if the group didn't play they'd keep the band's custom-made sound system and equipment in lieu, which were loaded on their trucks en route from the airport to the venue. Mr. Morrison was already drunk from a long day spent in airports and on planes, and he took to the scene like a bothered hornet.

In an effort to avoid confrontation the band went on stage, but Jim kept cutting songs short, swearing, yelling, and reciting from his poem "Rock is Dead." Pre-arranged, a guy brought a lamb to the stage and pleaded for people not to kill animals. Jim couldn't pass on an opportunity to hold it. "I'd fuck her," he announced over the PA, "but she's too young." The crowd roared.

Doors producer Paul Rothchild commented later on Jim's theatrics: "His talent was in creating dramatic situations with his voice and with his persona on stage, directing entire rock audiences into the drama in his mind. And he was very successful at it—more successful as a dramatic performer than he was as a singer, live, because his singing frequently failed him, but his sense of drama never did." In that light, the show in Miami was perhaps the most dramatic performance of his career.

After "Light My Fire," the requisite crowd pleaser, Jim urged the crowd to come up on stage. "Let's get on up here! No limits! No laws! Come on. COMMMME OOOON!" Dozens of people crawled up. Off mike he asked some of the kids if they wanted to see his cock. He unbuckled his belt while Ray, John, and Robbie watched in shock and fear.

The stage became rapidly tumultuous. Hundreds of camera flashes documented what ensued. Road manager Vince Treanor held up Morrison's pants by the waistband—he says the singer didn't attempt to pull the pants down. The promoters rushed to the stage; one of the brothers attempted to take the microphone, but Jim pushed him away; the other retaliated by flipping him into the audience. Not missing a beat, Jim led the crowd in a chaotic whirlpool around the dark, filthy hangar. "It was Dionysus calling forth the snakes," Ray Manzarek described years later, referring to a myth about the Greek god of wine and intoxication.

In the story, Dionysus sought passage to Naxos with a crew of sailors, but the sailors changed their minds during the voyage and decided to sell him as a slave instead. The god, who was notorious for shape shifting, turned the mast and oars into snakes and filled the ship with ivy and the sound of flutes. The sailors went mad and dove overboard where they turned into dolphins.

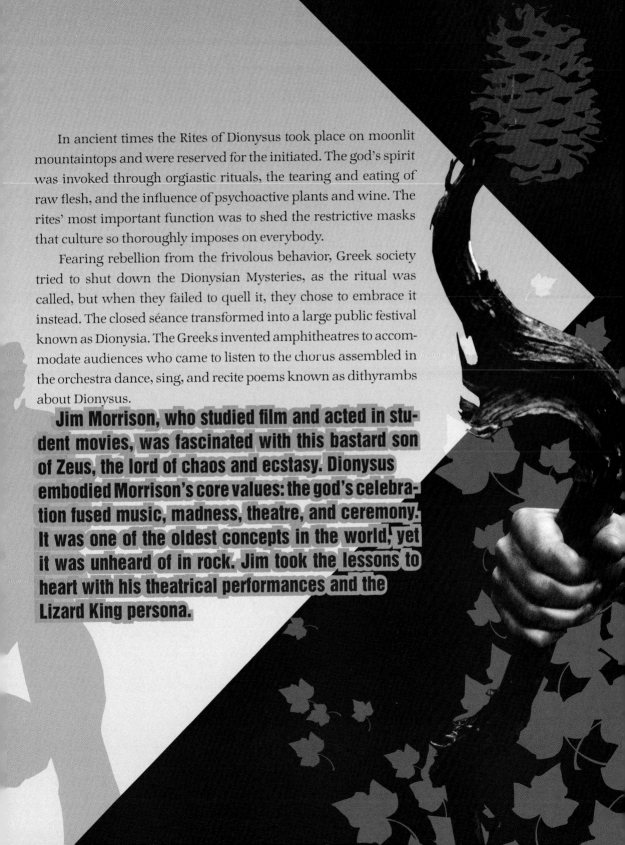

In ancient times the Rites of Dionysus took place on moonlit mountaintops and were reserved for the initiated. The god's spirit was invoked through orgiastic rituals, the tearing and eating of raw flesh, and the influence of psychoactive plants and wine. The rites' most important function was to shed the restrictive masks that culture so thoroughly imposes on everybody.

Fearing rebellion from the frivolous behavior, Greek society tried to shut down the Dionysian Mysteries, as the ritual was called, but when they failed to quell it, they chose to embrace it instead. The closed séance transformed into a large public festival known as Dionysia. The Greeks invented amphitheatres to accommodate audiences who came to listen to the chorus assembled in the orchestra dance, sing, and recite poems known as dithyrambs about Dionysus.

Jim Morrison, who studied film and acted in student movies, was fascinated with this bastard son of Zeus, the lord of chaos and ecstasy. Dionysus embodied Morrison's core values: the god's celebration fused music, madness, theatre, and ceremony. It was one of the oldest concepts in the world, yet it was unheard of in rock. Jim took the lessons to heart with his theatrical performances and the Lizard King persona.

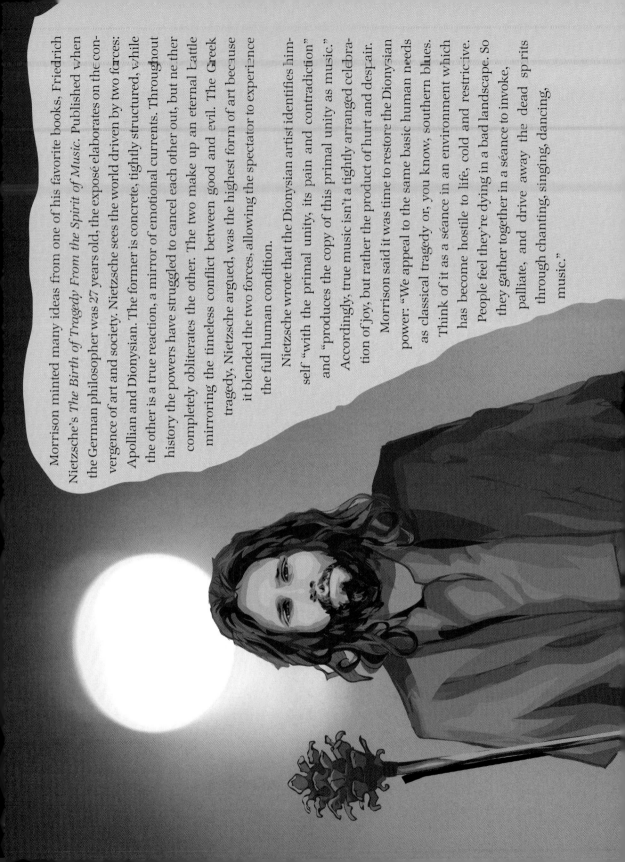

Morrison minted many ideas from one of his favorite books, Friedrich Nietzsche's *The Birth of Tragedy From the Spirit of Music*. Published when the German philosopher was 27 years old, the exposé elaborates on the convergence of art and society. Nietzsche sees the world driven by two forces: Apollian and Dionysian. The former is concrete, tightly structured, while the other is a true reaction, a mirror of emotional currents. Throughout history the powers have struggled to cancel each other out, but neither completely obliterates the other. The two make up an eternal battle mirroring the timeless conflict between good and evil. The Greek tragedy, Nietzsche argued, was the highest form of art because it blended the two forces, allowing the spectator to experience the full human condition.

Nietzsche wrote that the Dionysian artist identifies himself "with the primal unity, its pain and contradiction" and "produces the copy of this primal unity as music." Accordingly, true music isn't a tightly arranged celebration of joy, but rather the product of hurt and despair. Morrison said it was time to restore the Dionysian power: "We appeal to the same basic human needs as classical tragedy or, you know, southern blues. Think of it as a séance in an environment which has become hostile to life, cold and restrictive. People feel they're dying in a bad landscape. So they gather together in a séance to invoke, palliate, and drive away the dead spirits through chanting, singing, dancing, music."

A few days after the Doors' disastrous Miami show, a young reporter for the *Miami Herald* wrote an article about the concert that claimed Morrison had exposed himself and incited a riot. The reporter's vendetta gained momentum after he quizzed the city's police chief on what he planned to do about the rock star's sordid antics. Ignited by the inquiries, the chief summoned the troops, and the incident quickly reverberated.

*had enough
worses of cities
in the evening
in the sunlight
and forever*

Miami's self-styled moral protectors protested the Doors' performance with a "Rally for Indecency" that was attended by the city's archdiocese and comedian Jackie Gleason. President Nixon took the time to send a letter of support.

At the end of March '69, the FBI contacted Morrison's lawyer with a warrant signed by a federal judge for his arrest. Jim had left the state before any charges had been filed, yet the warrant cited interstate flight. Never mind that not one of the innumerable cameras that went off when Jim supposedly exposed himself actually captured anything indecent. Driven by lust for re-election and national notoriety, the Dade County prosecutor wanted to set an example, but Jim's lawyer knew what to do. By prior arrangement Jim was booked by the FBI office in Los Angeles and released a few minutes later on $5,000 bail.

Morrison faced a court case with a potentially dangerous outcome. Although he was disturbed by the prospects he devoted his time to poetry. He published a poem in an alternative newspaper and recorded others in the studio. The recordings captured rehearsed cadences, including three sung a cappella in his signature baritone.

Later that spring Jim Morrison debuted "An American Prayer" at a reading headlined by his friend, beat poet Michael McClure. McClure had his agent send a copy of Jim's poems entitled *The Lords/Notes On Film* to New York publisher Simon & Shuster, which scheduled publication the following year. **Jim wrote in a journal that it was the beginning of his real career—James Douglas Morrison the poet.**

108

1970
Bob Moog unleashes one of the earliest portable synthesizers: the Minimoog.

FEB. 18, 1970
The Chicago Seven found not guilty of inciting a riot at the 1968 Democratic National Convention.

MAY 9, 1970
100,000 people take to streets in Washington, DC, demonstrating against the Vietnam War.

With a new direction in life, Jim didn't worry too much about the non-legal repercussions from what supposedly happened in Florida—he left that to the rest of the Doors machinery. A flood of cancellations followed a dire warning by the Concert Halls Management Association. Radio stations dropped The Doors from airplay for the remainder of the year. Unfortunately the anti-Doors campaign affected other bands as well.

In mid-March, the Grateful Dead's management was informed that the group's upcoming show in Miami was cancelled because the local promoters believed the two bands were of the same ilk. A few months later Janis Joplin was busted for profanity in Tampa, Florida. During the show the police demanded that the audience sit still in their seats. When the request went unheeded a policeman walked up on stage and blew a foghorn during "Summertime." Janis flipped, and after the show she oozed with profanities toward a backstage cop. The blowout earned her two indictments for "vulgar and indecent language." The affair was eventually settled with a fine, but it had a negative impact on her bookings as well.

Girls could be pop singers of course, but America wasn't yet used to Janis, the rowdy female variety that commuted between sold-out shows, the studio, and debaucherous hotel parties in a trippy, swirl-painted Porsche.

Janis Joplin's idol was Bessie Smith, the most famous blues artist of the 1920s. Smith traveled in a private railroad car and toured theaters and tent shows (that era's summer festivals) all over the South and East. While Delta musicians like Robert

---

SEP. 9, 1970

Elvis Presley returns to touring for the first time since 1958.

NOV. 27, 1970

George Harrison's triple album All Things Must Pass released.

DEC. 31, 1970

Paul McCartney sues to cease The Beatles' contractual partnership.

I'M SICK OF THESE STINKY BOOTS

Johnson barely made enough to scrape by, Bessie made more than even well-known white performers. The press dubbed her the Empress of Blues, but Bessie fell from grace in the thirties when she tried to break into the popular swing craze. She died September 27, 1937, following a car crash and was buried in an unmarked grave.

Like her heroine, Janis Joplin felt she deserved a different treatment than her peers. On Janis's request, publicist (and later biographer) Myra Friedman pummeled Southern Comfort's headquarters with press clippings in which Joplin mentioned their liquor. It was a thinly veiled hint that the company owed her. Today it's not unusual for artists to have multi-million dollar deals with the likes of American Express and Volkswagen, but when Southern Comfort cut Janis a $2,500 check, corporate sponsorship of musicians was in its infancy. Elated, Janis spent the money on a lynx coat and bragged that getting paid for passing out for two years was her best hustle.

COTCHFORD FARM

EAST SUSSEX

she DIED TRAGICALLY *while all the others* PASSED AWAY CALMLY & BEAUTIFULLY *at a* RIPE OLD AGE

NIETZSCHE

The early summer of '69 didn't appear quite as bright over in England. Brian Jones had moved out of London to Cotchford Farm, an estate previously owned by *Winnie the Pooh* author A. A. Milne, and was put on a diet of tranquilizers. The broken Stone looked pale, grew tubbier, and was generally zonked from a combination of medicine, booze, depression, asthma, and frail nerves.

In addition, he struggled with a group of builders contracted by the Stones office to conduct renovations on the property. Some of Brian's belongings disappeared, and Frank Thorogood, the brutish foreman, was more interested in chasing after a local nurse than improving the situation.

In early June, Mick Jagger, Keith Richards, and Charlie Watts drove out to sever the ties between Brian Jones and the rest of the band. It was a sense of relief for both parties. Brian was promised a golden handshake equivalent to $1.7 million and an annual stipend for as long as the Stones existed.

July 2, 1969, was a hot day at Cotchford. The air was filled with pollen, but news about the check from the Stones organization lifted the allergic Brian's spirits. He drank heavily, sucked on his inhalator, and popped downers. Although he was hardly fit for stable movement on land, he decided to take a dip in the deep blue swimming pool that night. Nurse Janet Lawson suggested that it wasn't a good idea for him to swim but was brushed off. Anna Wohlin, Brian's Swedish girlfriend, and Frank joined the rock star, but they left after a little while to fetch cigarettes, leaving Brian alone.

He either felt a drowsy calmness while splashing alone in his pool or croaked in an epileptic fit, eventually sinking down to the tile-covered bottom, filling his lungs with chlorine water. Brian Jones was 27 years old. The coroner ruled the cause of death a "misadventure."

Brian was the first truly significant rock star to die. His death prompted elegies from a few of his peers. Pete Townshend of The Who published a poem titled "Brian Jones, the man who died every day," and Jimi Hendrix dedicated "Lover Man" to him on the Tonight Show.

Jim Morrison considered Brian one of rock's founders, and he asked an Elektra executive what he thought would happen to the Doors if he—Jim—died. Less than three weeks later in Los Angeles, attendees at a Doors show received printed copies of Jim's elegy to the fallen Stone. The dirge was titled "Ode to LA while thinking of Brian Jones, deceased." Many critics say it's Jim Morrison's strongest poem.

TOWNS ON BRI & JIM

Interviewed for a *Mojo* feature on Brian Jones in 1999, Pete Townshend said, "Brian should have been sectioned into a mental hospital like a street drunk, not allowed to flounder about in a heated swimming pool taking fucking downers. If I'm honest I suppose I was one of the friends who should have called the ambulance." Perhaps a little wiser Townshend says he took some responsibility after Brian Jones's death. "I told Jim Morrison he was turning into a fat drunk in 1971. I could tell from his stunned expression that until then no-one had indicated they might even care."

More than thirty-five years after Brian Jones's death, people are still wondering whether it was an accidental suicide or a murder. Claims of the latter are supported by at least five books, some of which are written by former friends and girlfriends. I'm not suggesting they are without merit, but why did Brian's friends wait twenty-five years or more before they published their sides of the story?

There is little doubt that additional investigation at the time of Brian Jones's death could've thwarted some of the suspicions, but unexpected deaths—be it accidents or questionable suicides—are frequently difficult to rationalize by those who are left behind. Asking questions that are hard or impossible to answer helps fill the void with something besides grief. Perhaps this urge is intensified when it concerns someone famous.

We know Jones was frequently intoxicated, yet many fans don't believe he could've been too messed up to swim. Similar questions come to mind: Did Jim Morrison just wander off? We knew Kurt Cobain wasn't happy, but how could he be *that* unhappy? Asking questions is important, but journalists who spin conspiracy theories from a short yarn speculate in the fans' desire to put the blame on someone besides their fallen hero.

In November 2005 *The Independent*, one of Britain's largest newspapers, printed a four-page article with new findings on Jones's death in its Sunday magazine. Stephen Woolley, director of the then-new movie *Stoned*, contends that Frank Thorogood accidentally killed Jones during an attempt to scare the rock star into paying him £8,000 that he was owed. Woolley referred to an unnamed witness who claimed Jones had just fired the builder, and as a result Thorogood was "out of control" the night of Jones's death. In support of that theory, the builder supposedly admitted responsibility on his deathbed in 1993. It's unclear why Woolley didn't produce the confession that would've set the record straight.

Then there's super-fan Trevor Hobley and abandoned lover Pat Andrews' 150-page dossier from 2005 that claims there was "some sort of cover up from a fairly high level." Based on their findings, a cold case team presented the Sussex Police with eight reasons why the coroner's verdict is not definite. They claim that exhuming Brian's body will solve the mystery.

The passing of time fertilizes afterthought, but the truth is when Brian died few people were surprised that he checked out. Fans and musicians paused to reflect, but the warm days of summer quickly evaporated the tears. *Easy Rider* premiered to great acclaim, Neil Armstrong walked on the moon, and Hollywood was in a state of shock and fear after a terrible mass murder. Actress Sharon Tate, coffee heiress Abigail Folger, Polish writer Wojciech Frykowski, and celebrity hairdresser Jay Sebring (who Jim Morrison had gone to in the past) were found murdered with more than one hundred stab wounds between them and *pig* scribbled in blood on the front door. Inspired by gross misinterpretations of the Beatles' "Revolution 9" Charlie Manson ordered his hodgepodge of followers to carry out the grisly slaughter.

EASY RIDER

Peter Fonda and Dennis Hopper's *Easy Rider* changed the movie biz profoundly. It was the first flick with a rock soundtrack (featuring "Born to be Wild" by Steppenwolf, "If 6 was 9" by Jimi Hendrix, Dylan songs performed by Roger McGuinn and more). Equally important, the movie helped big studios see the potential in lower budget movies. Executives started bankrolling artistic directors such as Francis Ford Coppola, Steven Spielberg, Martin Scorsese, and Brian De Palma.

The summer of 1969's counter-cultural highlight occurred in mid-August when 500,000 hippies descended on Bethel, New York, for a weekend of peace, love, and music. Thirty-two bands played during the four-day festival, and while quite a few of the bands are now considered legendary, many of the acts—even some big ones—are almost forgotten today.

Cue the *Woodstock* documentary: Canned Heat's "Going Up The Country" sets the mood. Alan's flute and lyrics about leaving the city is an undeniable zeitgeist for aging hippies who lived through this era. Heat was one of the festival's headliners, yet today's music fans can't tell you much about them. Drummer Fito de la Parra claims Woodstock's organizers cut them the third largest paycheck after Jimi Hendrix and Janis Joplin, which is plausible since the band owned the number one hit that summer. Heat still performs, but times have changed. Fito remains the sole member from the golden days.

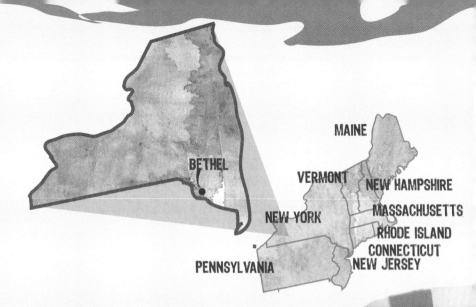

Only five British bands played at Woodstock: The Who, Ten Years After, Joe Cocker, the Incredible String Band, and the Keef Hartley Band. Ironically, the latter two bands didn't sign the necessary paperwork for inclusion in the documentary and are today mere footnotes.

Drummer Keef Hartley, who left John Mayall's Bluesbreakers the same time that Mick Taylor departed to take Brian's spot in the Stones, foolishly refused to sell out. When the Oscar-winning *Woodstock—Three Days of Peace & Music* premiered the following year, it helped launch Joe Cocker and Ten Years After to superstardom, while the Keef Hartley Band's performance was forgotten.

The clouds broke for the second day of the infamously wet event, and KHB hit the stage with full force, proficiently displaying their jazz-rock chops. The set consisted of a twenty-minute-long "Believe In You" (which was co-written by bassist Gary Thain and featured Mick Taylor's lead on *The Battle of North West Six*), followed by "Rock Me Baby," and closed with a forty-minute medley from their debut record *Halfbreed*. Miller Anderson on guitar, Henry Lowther on violin and trumpet, Lyn Dobson on tenor sax and flute (both of John Mayall's Bluesbreakers), and the late, great Gary Thain on bass completed the five-piece.

119

Next up was Santana, followed by the Incredible String Band, and Canned Heat. Darkness set in and Pigpen closed the Dead's performance with an energetic "Lovelight." Creedence Clearwater Revival riled up the crowd for the queen of the party's entrance.

The Kozmic Blues Band was on fire, and even though Janis Joplin had shot up in a porta-potty earlier that day, she delivered an electrifying performance. She encored with "Piece Of My Heart" and "Ball and Chain," both songs about being used by men. While clearly not a feminist, Janis was a liberated woman, which wasn't easy in the sixties—even for a star. Admission into the boys' club that rock & roll was (and to some degree still is) meant that she had to act like a thick-skinned broad and deny herself marriage and a calm, domesticated life.

Most people had already left by the time Hendrix closed the festival early Monday morning with Gypsy Sun and Rainbows, his temporary six-piece band. The two-hour set was plagued by technical snags, a poorly rehearsed band, and Jimi's out of tune guitar, but was elevated, of course, by his ferocious guitantics and "The Star Spangled Banner." At times his guitar sounded like falling bombs and stray bullets, but paradoxically Hendrix never said in public or private that it was an anti-war protest piece. He was proud of having served in the 101st Paratroopers and held deep respect for the military.

Consider what he told an English journalist in 1967 when he was confronted with America's involvement in the Vietnam War: "Did you send the Americans away when they landed in Normandy? The Americans are fighting in Vietnam for the complete free world. Of course war is terrible but at the present it's still the only guarantee to maintain peace."

"Machine Gun" was about the war and was often dedicated tongue-in-cheek to "all the soldiers fighting in Berkeley [or wherever he happened to play that night], you know what soldiers I'm talkin' about... and, oh yeah, the soldiers fighting in Vietnam too." At Woodstock he dedicated "Izabella" the same way. A few weeks later, when asked about the national anthem, Jimi explained, "We play it the way the air in America is today. The air is slightly static, see."

After Jimi Hendrix first tried psychedelics, in late '66, he started seeing notes as colors. In that context "The Star Spangled Banner" is a colorful canvas; a buzzed abstract piece filled with tracers and explosions. But with his performance etched onto film, and pundits pushing for its significance, it will forever stand as a defining anti-war moment of the psychedelic sixties. Actually, the one that deserves that distinction was released the previous summer and immediately banned.

"COMP'NEEEE! HALT! PREEEEZENT... ARMS!"

The Doors used "Unknown Soldier" as a vehicle for theater on stage. Jim stood stoically during a suspenseful drum roll while Robbie aimed his Gibson SG like a rifle. At just the right moment Densmore hit a piercing rim shot while Ray kicked a reverb unit, its springs creating an explosion, and Jim fell violently to the ground, hitting the stage with a boom. Then he'd lie completely still, finishing the song, singing, "It's all over, the war is over." The Doors' protest wasn't a fun sing-along like Country Joe's "I-Feel-Like-I'm-Fixin'-To-Die Rag"—"Unknown Soldier" was loud, powerful, and extremely visual.

Morrison

Trained in cinematics at UCLA's film school, Ray Manzarek and Jim Morrison directed and starred in a video for the song that turned into a groundbreaking achievement: it was graphic, theatric, political, and unlike anything produced before it. "Unknown Soldier" was the first music video to reach deeper than the self-indulgence and promotion seen in early efforts by Bob Dylan, the Beatles, and The Byrds. When MTV hit cable in 1981, it created a business built on an art form pioneered by the Doors.

In the video, Jim Morrison is tied to a pole on the beach and Robbie, Ray, and John pose as a mock firing squad. The execution commences, Jim crumbles, and blood spews out of his mouth. Grisly stock footage from the Vietnam War follows, showing distressed civilians screaming for mercy, burning napalm, and injured US soldiers. The video was of course banned upon its release. Nobody knows what Jim's father thought about it: George Stephen Morrison was the youngest admiral of the US Navy at the time. He never publicly said anything about his son, and why should he? Jim had already told journalists that his parents were dead. Several decades passed before the admiral opened up.

"The fact that he's dead is unfortunate, but looking back on his life it's a very pleasant thought," the senior Morrison admitted in *The Doors By The Doors*. "He knew I didn't think music was the best goal for him. Maybe he was trying to protect us."

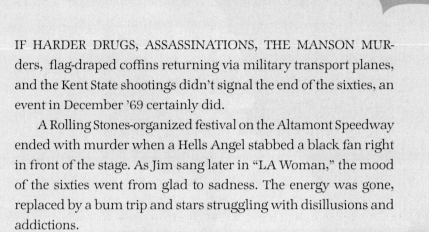

IF HARDER DRUGS, ASSASSINATIONS, THE MANSON MUR-
ders, flag-draped coffins returning via military transport planes,
and the Kent State shootings didn't signal the end of the sixties, an
event in December '69 certainly did.

A Rolling Stones-organized festival on the Altamont Speedway
ended with murder when a Hells Angel stabbed a black fan right
in front of the stage. As Jim sang later in "LA Woman," the mood
of the sixties went from glad to sadness. The energy was gone,
replaced by a bum trip and stars struggling with disillusions and
addictions.

One of the first albums of 1970 was The Doors' *Morrison
Hotel*, an uneven but gritty, blues-infected album with rockabilly
riffs, boogie-styled songs, R&B vocals, and lyrics for the man on
the highway and kid in the street, them versus us.

The subsequent tour began like a revved up R&B revue, but as winter turned to spring Jim's stage demeanor denigrated from animated to hugging the mike stand in an alcoholic stupor. Mundane lethargy hit others as well.

"Tomorrow never comes, man, it's all the same fucking day," Janis said in a moment of drunk epiphany on her live album *Joplin in Concert*.

She cultivated a new persona that she called Pearl, but Pearl was only a caricature of herself: a hard-drinking, loud and rude, feathery good-time girl with a penchant for binges and pansexual one-night stands. Whenever she wasn't on the needle she drank tequila, her new booze of choice.

By May the chaotic Kozmic Blues ensemble was history, replaced with a group of younger musicians that Janis was comfortably in charge of. "It's *my* band," she glowed. After rehearsing for a few weeks they went on tour, and Janis and the Full Tilt Boogie Band were well received by both fans and journalists.

A definite highlight of the summer of 1970 was the Trans Continental Pop Festival across Canada in a chartered train. If Woodstock was for the audience, *Festival Express* was a treat for the artists. For nearly two weeks Janis rode with Buddy Guy, The Band, the Dead, the Flying Burrito Brothers, and Delaney and Bonnie and Friends. They performed in cities along the way, but for the musicians it was the train ride that made it memorable. Impromptu jam sessions took place throughout the journey: blues in one cart, rock in another, country in a third.

"And all this time I've been thinking of you as a blues singer," Pigpen told Janis after listening to a drunk country recital with Rick Danko, Bob Weir, and Jerry Garcia. She retorted, "Hell, I'm from Texas, ain't I? Home of George Jones!"

Back from tour, Janis and the Full Tilt Boogie Band began recording for *Pearl* in Los Angeles. She raved to friends about a young man named Seth, but even his love and devotion were incapable of distilling the changes Janis so desperately craved in her life. Lonely nights at the hotel brought her back to the comfort of smack.

The Isle of Wight Festival took place in late August. Although the 600,000-attendance record surpassed Woodstock's, the performances by two of its biggest draws are best left forgotten.

Jim Morrison insisted on a near blacked-out stage during the set and sang on autopilot with his eyes tightly shut. London's underground paper *International Times* wrote, "the Doors copped out. The band was mechanical, bored & completely lifeless. Morrison sang well but it was the same old shit." *Friends* magazine concurred in its October issue: "The Doors were abysmal.

AFTON DOWN

ISLE OF WIGHT

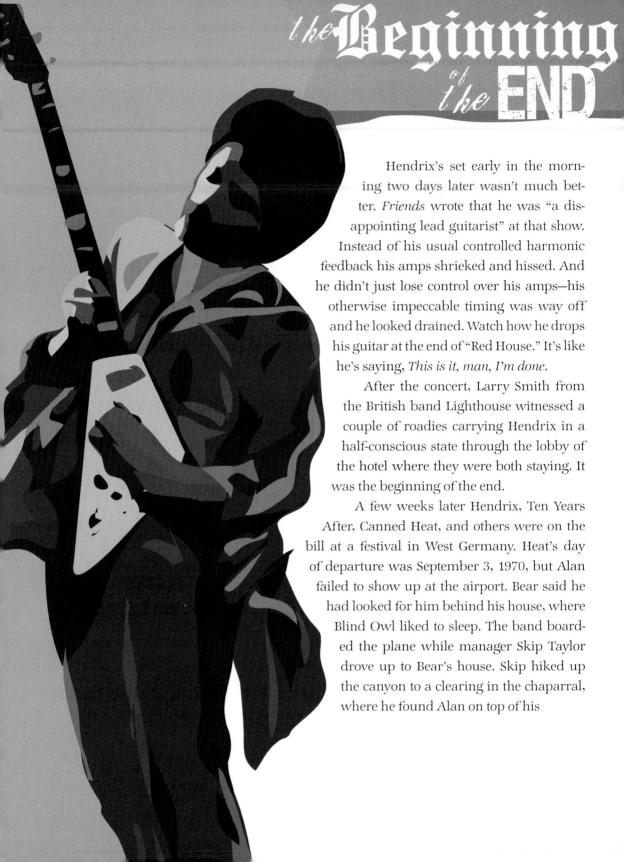

Hendrix's set early in the morning two days later wasn't much better. *Friends* wrote that he was "a disappointing lead guitarist" at that show. Instead of his usual controlled harmonic feedback his amps shrieked and hissed. And he didn't just lose control over his amps—his otherwise impeccable timing was way off and he looked drained. Watch how he drops his guitar at the end of "Red House." It's like he's saying, *This is it, man, I'm done.*

After the concert, Larry Smith from the British band Lighthouse witnessed a couple of roadies carrying Hendrix in a half-conscious state through the lobby of the hotel where they were both staying. It was the beginning of the end.

A few weeks later Hendrix, Ten Years After, Canned Heat, and others were on the bill at a festival in West Germany. Heat's day of departure was September 3, 1970, but Alan failed to show up at the airport. Bear said he had looked for him behind his house, where Blind Owl liked to sleep. The band boarded the plane while manager Skip Taylor drove up to Bear's house. Skip hiked up the canyon to a clearing in the chaparral, where he found Alan on top of his sleeping bag, calmly smiling, with his arms crossed over his chest. Next to him were two empty bottles—gin and Seconal. Alan Wilson was 27 years old.

"Bottom line is that he succeeded in committing suicide," Taylor says. "Alan believed in life after death, so he had to believe there was a better place that he should check out."

Taylor has something to say to those who claim Blind Owl's death was accidental: "Look, Alan Wilson was an intelligent man—he knew what the end result would be from a bottle of gin and a bottle of Seconal."

Canned Heat made it to Berlin and learned of their deceased bro by phone. They were devastated, but went on as planned. Bear opened with a slow blues number by Little Water, one of Owl's favorite harp players.

> "Last night I lost the best friend I ever had
> And now you are gone and left me
> You know I feel so sad."

Hendrix hit the stage shortly afterward and struggled through the last set of his life. The restless crowd booed and local Hells Angels did what they're known for: raising hell. "I don't give a fuck if you boo," Hendrix said from stage, egging them on with his large hands, "As long as you boo in key, motherfuckers." That was the Isle of Fehmarn's Love and Peace Festival for ya.

HOOKER ON ALAN

"I say that man was a genius," John Lee Hooker said about Al Wilson. "Inside him, that was beautiful. Beautiful." The two bluesmen recorded *Hooker 'N Heat* shortly before Alan died. It remained one of Hooker's favorite albums.

The last two weeks of Jimi's life were hectic. He complained of fatigue to friends, girlfriends, and journalists. Making matters worse, he consumed uppers to keep going and downers when he needed rest. In Århus, Denmark, he babbled incoherently all day and stopped "Message of Love" to say "I've been dead for a long time." After a very short set he told journalist Anne Bjørndal, "I'm not sure I will live to be twenty-eight years old. I mean, the moment I feel I have nothing more to give musically, I will not be around on this planet anymore."

Jimi Hendrix's life had been a tornado during the nearly four years that had passed since he arrived in London. He had changed the face of music but fumbled for a new direction. He recorded a backup track for proto-rap artist Jalaluddin Mansur Nuriddin (a.k.a. Lightnin' Rod), leader of the Last Poets. He told Mike Nesmith of the Monkees that he wanted to move towards R&B yet told a journalist that he wanted to play strictly acoustic. At the end of August, in an interview with *Melody Maker*'s Roy Hollingworth, he said, "I've given this era of music everything. I still sound the same, my music's the same, and I can't think of anything new to add to it in its present state. This era of music, sparked off by the Beatles, has come to an end. Something new has got to come and Jimi Hendrix will be there. ... I want a big band. I don't mean three harps and fourteen violins. I mean a big band full of competent musicians that I can conduct and write for. And with the music we will paint pictures of earth and space, so that the listener can be taken somewhere."

Two nights before his death, Jimi asked former Animals guitarist Eric Burdon if he could sit in with War, but the staggering guitar god was turned away. "For the first time I'd ever seen him, he didn't have his guitar," Burdon said later. "When I saw him without that guitar, I knew he was in trouble." It seemed Marbles finally had lived up to his nickname from the Chitlin' Circuit.

The next evening, Hendrix's recent girlfriend Monika Dannenmann, a German ice skater, picked him up from a party at three in the morning. Back in the hotel room, Monika took a sleeping pill and passed out, leaving Jimi awake. Wired from amphetamines, he decided, like so many late nights before, to pop a handful of downers so he could crash. Jimi probably didn't know that Monika's pills were significantly stronger than most prescriptions. The recommended dose was half of one pill: he took nine and left forty-one in the jar.

Jimi Hendrix puked sometime in the early morning of September 18, 1970, and asphyxiated in unconscious sleep. Before Jimi went out that last night of his life he had worked on a new lyric: "The story of life is quicker than the wink of an eye." Jimi's ended at 27.

GIVE A FUCK

DON'T

CLAPTON ON JIMI

"But the core of all his playing was the blues," Eric Clapton told *Guitar World* in 1994. Clapton, who was famous for his fat "woman tone," which came from playing Gibson guitars, revealed why he switched to the Fender Stratocaster. "Once he [Jimi Hendrix] wasn't there anymore I felt like there was room to pick it up."

Clapton's favorite axe from 1970 till its retirement in 1985 was a '56 Strat that he named Blackie.

Hendrix's death stirred Janis Joplin, who was still in Los Angeles recording. She wondered what people would say if she were to drop dead but told friends that the odds of two rock stars dying the same year were very small. Although Jimi triggered her comments, the death of another singer was still fresh in her mind.

The re-release of Bessie Smith's records in 1970 prompted a housewife to write the *Philadelphia Inquirer* and ask why the Empress's grave, which was near the city, remained unmarked. Sensing a great story, a journalist with the paper called Columbia Records, where an eager PR man decided to give Janis, who was also on their label, a call. Janis promised to fund a new headstone, but by the time the label got back to the journalist a successful local entrepreneur named Juanita Green had offered to do the same. As an adolescent Green was a hired housekeeper for Bessie, and the singer's suggestion that she should focus on education rather than entertainment had served her well. In the end, Joplin and Green agreed to split the cost of the stone. It was unveiled in August that same year. Janis stayed away from the ceremony, afraid her presence would district from the cause. Bessie's epitaph reads,

THE GREATEST BLUES SINGER IN THE WORLD WILL NEVER STOP SINGING
BESSIE SMITH
1895-1937

Eerily it was a matter of weeks before Janis was dead too. On October 4, 1970, her band recorded a new track, and Janis planned on adding her voice the following morning. But fate didn't grant her to record "Buried Alive in the Blues." Back at the hotel that evening, Janis Joplin shot up an accidental overdose from unusually pure heroin and died 27 years old.

139

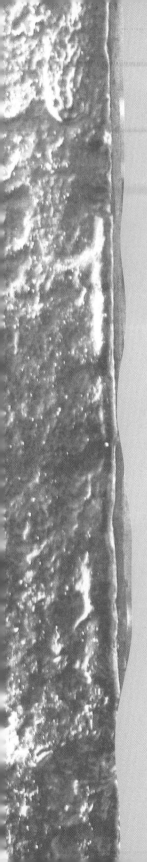

Jim Morrison held a debaucherous court at Barney's Beanery in LA the night following Joplin's death and told his entourage, "You're drinking with number three." He apparently forgot about Brian Jones. Pigpen told *Rolling Stone* that he planned a solo wake and would get righteously messed up on Southern Comfort, "just like she would've wanted."

Joplin's lethal dose came from French Count Jean de Breteuil, a young playboy and dealer to the stars, thanks to his suave mannerisms and steady supply of high quality horse brought in on his diplomatic passport. The count was in the country on an expired visa, and he knew he'd be put away for a long time if the cops found out where Janis scored the dope. His only option was to flee, so he called up his lover Pamela Courson and begged her to come to Paris with him. Morrison wasn't exactly psyched when he found out who she skipped the country with.

Morrison's life was becoming stressful, and it wasn't just because of Courson's heroin addiction and infidelity. He was unhappy that nobody took notice when Simon & Shuster published his collection of poems as *The Lords and The New Creatures*. In addition, he brooded over the outcome of his court case. The Florida prosecutor had no concrete evidence and offered conflicting stories from witnesses, yet the judge was convinced that Jim had exposed himself. When Jim returned to Miami for sentencing, he spent an evening belting out drunken blues numbers with Canned Heat, who were in town for a gig. The following day, Morrison received eight months of hard labor and a $500 fine for public exposure and profanity. Jim's lawyer filed an appeal that kept him out of jail—at least for the moment.

Morrison's contractual commitment to Elektra Records was over, and with the possibility of incarceration, it was time for him to move on. "He was through with this particular part of his career

1971	APR. 19, 1971	JULY 16, 1971
San Rafael High School kids in California start meeting at 4:20 p.m. to puff next to a statue of Louis Pasteur.	Judge Older sentences Charles Manson to death in his California Court.	The World's population is estimated to be 4 billion.

and his life," Jim's friend Frank Lisciandro said later. Paris was enticing, especially since France had no extradition agreement with the US for indecency charges. What Jim really wanted was space to reinvent himself.

Bill Siddons recalls Jim's remarks before his departure: **"He said, 'I don't know who I am, and I don't know what I'm doing at the moment. I even don't know what I really want, I just wanna go away'."**

Pamela was behind it all. It was her who pushed him to leave, and who told him to take his scrapbooks and write a theatre play."

Pamela Courson loved the idea of Jim Morrison the writer. It would keep him home, away from groupies and the drunken road. Jim wanted that too. It was his dream to write something of significance, something that would remain after he was gone, words that people could get lost in like he had been lost to Sigmund Freud, Friedrich Nietzsche, William Blake, and Arthur Rimbaud. He was sick of kids that screamed for "Light My Fire" and longed for a mature audience—people who would appreciate his intellect.

Moving to Paris made a lot of sense—it was where expatriates such as Ernest Hemingway, Getrude Stein, James Joyce, and Ezra Pound wrote their breakthroughs in the 1920s. The Atlantic Ocean would keep him isolated from the Doors hoopla and give him sufficient space to write.

Following Pam, Jim left for Paris in March '71. They stayed in a hotel at first but were soon offered a sublet in the old beautiful quarter of Marais. Jim set up a desk by the window. He worked on his essay "Observations On America While On Trial For Obscenity in Miami" and brought his notebook with him on long walks around town. Although their lack of French limited

JULY 27, 1971

The Allman Brothers plays closing night of Bill Graham's Fillmore East.

AUG. 1, 1971

40,000 people attend Harrison's Concert for Bangladesh in NYC.

the couple's social circle, Jim regularly visited moviemaker Agnes Varda, while Pam enjoyed attention from the high-flying crew that Count de Breteuil was part of. Pam and Jim still fought occasionally, but overall their last months were filled with bliss. They road tripped to Spain where they visited the Alhambra, boarded the ferry to Tangier, and drove south through the mountains to Fez and Marrakech.

Back in Paris Jim shaved off his beard and reached new levels of drunkenness in the tradition of the *Lost Generation*'s literati. Breaking away from work to walk around town frequently lapsed into disturbing multi-day benders. He puffed up from French food and drinks, chain-smoked No. 27 Marlboros, and spat blood after violent coughing fits.

Tere Tereba, a teenager who designed clothes for Pam's LA boutique *Themis*, hung out with Jim and Pamela June 27th. He died a week later, and Tereba wrote a short piece that same year, titled "Goodbyes," about their last time together. Jim showed her a hand-written book that was nearly finished and said it was soon ready for publication.

Tereba wrote, "Pam interjects that *'he wants to be immortalized'* and it does seem logical that a writer could achieve that state easier than a rock idol." Jim must've thought a lot about that. A few weeks earlier he told a journalist that 27 was too old to be a rock singer. Rock was still in its infancy, old rock stars didn't exist, and Jim had little idea that four quick years in the spotlight was enough to immortalize him as one of rock's de facto gods.Like Brian Jones's death, Morrison's has been subject to doubt and scrutiny. So far new books haven't brought us any closer to the truth. In a way we're farther from it than we were in 1971. Fact: Pam found him dead in the bathtub the morning of July 3. The coroner's verdict was heart failure from natural causes. No autopsy was performed because he didn't suspect drugs were involved. So what did he die from? Asthma medication coupled with excessive drink? Was cocaine involved? Did a sample of Pam's heroin kill him? As late as 1974, Ray Manzarek thought Jim Morrison faked his own death. "He could be just off wandering around somewhere," Manzarek suggested. The problem was that the two people who *saw* Morrison dead are dead themselves.

Count de Breteuil was in bed with Marianne Faithfull in Keith Richards's riverside mansion when Pamela Courson woke him up at 6:30 in the morning. De Breteuil rushed over to the apartment and instructed her to tell the coroner that Jim had a heart disease, then left hastily for a family mansion in Morocco. That makes me think *his* heroin was somehow involved with Jim's last night. Think about it: In less than nine months his dope had killed off two of rock's greatest stars. The Paris police were aware of his dirty trade, so fleeing was a necessary precaution.

De Breteuil OD'd a few years later; Pamela Courson followed in April '74, also aged 27.

Courson lived in an apartment in LA with her friend John Mandell, who found her on the couch with fresh needle tracks on her arm. Mandell told the cops that her *husband* had overdosed from heroin in Paris three years earlier. (Pam was buried in California, but Ray Manzarek has said that he hopes her urn will be united with Jim's remains in Paris: "It's a rock & roll love story. They should be together in one grave. Those two belong together.")

I think it's fairly certain that snorting heroin was at least partly the cause of Jim's death and that the dope came from de Breteuil. Parisian rock critic Herve Muller, who had befriended Morrison that spring, wrote a few days after Jim's death that the poet and singer had really OD'd in the toilet at the hip Rock'n'Roll Circus a day or two earlier than reported. Sam Bernett was the club's twenty-six year-old manager at the time, and in 2007 he published a French account of what he says transpired.

It's well documented that Jim was a semi-regular customer at the Circus and that he had been thrown out on a few occasions for drunkenly slandering patrons.

Bernett says Jim bought heroin that night from two dealers who frequented the club. Instead of heading home, he slipped into the bathroom, where he was found passed out in a stall half an hour later. An employee notified Bernett, who went to check on his famous customer.

"I raised his head gently, holding him by the shoulder to stop him [from] falling over. His face was grey, his eyes shut, there was blood under his nose, and whitish dribble-like froth around his slightly open mouth and in his beard," Bernett claims.

A doctor who was at the club pronounced Jim dead, but the two dealers asserted that he was merely out of it. They carried him through the vacant club next to the Circus and out the backdoor. From there they supposedly brought him back to Pam and dropped Jim in the tub hoping the water would revive him. To avoid a scandal, the owner of the Circus had everybody involved swear to keep the incident under wraps.

It's an interesting story, but it doesn't hold up to the light. First of all, how have the four or five witnesses managed to stay quiet about Jim Morrison's death for thirty-six long years? Who was the doctor? How did the dealers know where Jim lived? If they knew de Breteuil they could've asked him for directions I suppose, but that doesn't explain why the count was calmly in bed the following morning.

Sam Bernett offers vivid details about what he saw in that stall, yet errs when he describes Morrison's beard. Tereba writes that Jim was clean-shaven when she met him, and photos taken a couple of days before he died show the same.

Regardless of what the truth might be, news about Bernett's book *The End: Jim Morrison* hit the wire with a vengeance in June 2007 and predictably spilled over to countless blogs. Fact is that we can't get enough of our culture's most famous icons. We speculate, hypothesize, discuss & argue, adding bits & pieces until they become larger than life'

elevated to characters that harbor contradictions of Hellenic proportions.

Conflicting stories about the lives and deaths of gods were prevalent in Ancient Greece—two different accounts about Dionysus' birth exist— so why can't there be several versions of Jim, Brian, or Kurt's deaths? It's the stuff legends are made from. With the passage of time they'll appear to us as Hephaestus, Ares, Zeus, and Apollo did to the Greeks.

The press's coverage of rock's young corpses is a disguised warning peppered with irresistible words. Drugs. Excess. Sex. Dope. *That's what happens to those who choose an outrageous lifestyle and you better believe it!* Makes me think that puritan zealots must fume like pressure cookers whenever Keith Richards pops his raisin face on TV.

We expect rock stars to die before we do, but until 2007 there was no research to back up that suspicion. Dr. Mark Bellis and his team at the Centre for Public Health at Liverpool John Moores University released a report that summer titled "Elvis to Eminem: quantifying the price of fame through early mortality of European and North American rock and pop stars." Basically six researchers combed record sleeves from Virgin's *All-Time Top 1000 Albums* (which was put together after polling 200,000 fans, experts, and critics in 2000) and crosschecked all the personnel to see who was dead and who wasn't. They found that after two and twenty-five years of fame "pop stars tend to experience two to three times the risk of mortality expected in an average population."

OCT. 29, 1971	DEC. 18, 1971	MAY 3, 1972	JUNE 17, 1972
Guitarist Duane Allman (24) dies on his motorcycle. Bassist Berry Oakley (24) follows 13 months later.	*The US devalues the dollar.*	*Stone the Crows' Les Harvey (26) is electrocuted on stage.*	*Pigpen of the Grateful Dead plays his last show, but is too sick to sing.*

The report didn't mention the data pool's statistical mode so we queried Dr. Bellis. **Sure enough, out of all age groups the number of rockers who died at 27 stand out like bright poppies in a field of alfalfa.** Dr. Bellis tells us it's "difficult to attach any statistical significance level to this."

So there are more 27s than 28s (Shannon Hoon, Bradley Nowell et al) or 33s, but while statistics can't explain why, it's peculiar that Alan Wilson, Jimi Hendrix, Janis Joplin, and Jim Morrison died within ten months of each other. Incidentally, Jim Morrison was found in the bathtub two years to the day after Brian Jones was fished up from his pool. Water—the ancient symbol of death and rebirth, the element that can drown, nurture, wash away sins... or in fermented form numb our sorrows.

By 1971, Pigpen's liver had had enough. More than ten years of constant saucing had taxed it to the max and he was hospitalized for three months starting in August.

Shortly after the hospital released Pigpen, *Rolling Stone* magazine published its first profile of Jerry Garcia. In the interview he touched on Pig's situation: "It's sorta, like, stepping out of the blues story, cause, Pigpen is a sort of guy who's, like, been a victim of the whole blues trip—it's like Janis exactly—in which you must die. That's what the script says. So Pigpen went up to the line, and he's seen it now, so the question is how he's going to choose."

Pigpen tried to change his lifestyle, but he never fully recovered. It was too late. Pig was found dead on the floor of his tiny apartment in Corte Madera in March 1973. Ron "Pigpen" McKernan was 27 years old, and his cause of death was internal bleeding from a gastric hemorrhage. His epitaph reads "Pigpen was and is now forever one of the Grateful Dead."

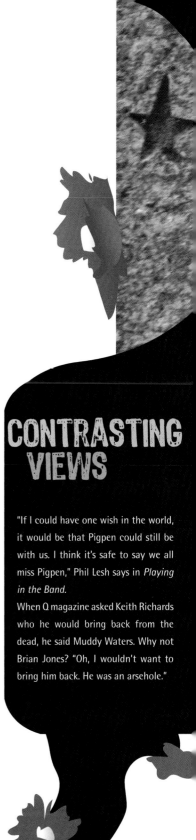

CONTRASTING VIEWS

"If I could have one wish in the world, it would be that Pigpen could still be with us. I think it's safe to say we all miss Pigpen," Phil Lesh says in *Playing in the Band*.

When Q magazine asked Keith Richards who he would bring back from the dead, he said Muddy Waters. Why not Brian Jones? "Oh, I wouldn't want to bring him back. He was an arsehole."

JULY 4, 1972	JULY 21, 1972	SEP. 17, 1972
The first Rainbow Gathering commences in Colorado.	Comedian George Carlin arrested for reciting "Seven Words You Can Never Say On Television."	The first episode of the M.A.S.H. sitcom airs.

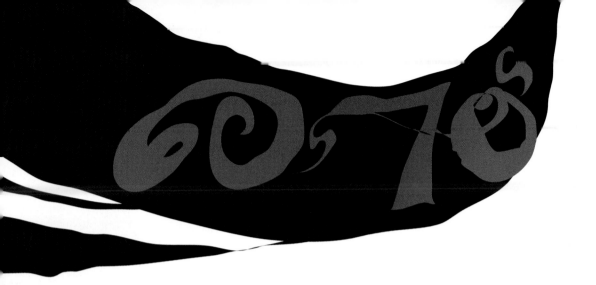

Few of the world's ideas are strictly original. They might seem new, but in reality their origin is drawn from other thoughts and inventions, repackaged with the unique stamp of personality and time.

Hendrix was a unique artist, but he didn't come out of nowhere. He drew on four decades of showmanship from the Chitlin' Circuit, the blues, soul, early rock, and the techniques of guitarists such as Steve Cropper and B.B. King. But Jimi packaged it differently than anybody else, hit London at the right time, and blew everybody away with his music, flair, and showmanship.

Art is creating original expressions, but other artists inevitably influence those expressions. Art is not rehashing what other artists have done before. The history of rock & roll is a case study in the explosion of movements—and in epigones. Hundreds of record-making bands molded on the Beatles are now forgotten, while there's only one Beatles.

The Beatles command the high chair of rock for obvious reasons: after years of honing their style in German bars and Liverpool's Cavern, the fab four broke barriers with their music, mop tops, music, and attitude. But the catchy pop songs

JAN. 13, 1973	FEB. 27, 1973	MAR. 17, 1973
Eric Clapton emerges from heroin seclusion and plays London's Rainbow Theatre.	*The American Indian Movement occupies Wounded Knee in South Dakota.*	*Harvest releases Pink Floyd's Dark Side of the Moon.*

pioneered by the Beatles were commercially out of vogue by the early seventies. **Cutesy pop stars were replaced by longhaired monsters that took Morrison's Dionysian sensualism to new levels in between ten-minute guitar solos that were pumped through seven-foot Marshall stacks.**

The first to complain, of course, was the Lizard King himself. Shortly after Led Zeppelin's debut album entered the charts, Morrison grumbled that "this riff-banging, power-mad English band represents the death of rock as I know it."

Led Zeppelin's image was already rough, but the old guard still commanded some respect. During the British band's first US tour the guys stopped by photographer Herb Greene's studio in San Francisco for some promo shots. Greene was an acclaimed photographer, and since he was as much of a hippie as his subjects, he enjoyed full access to the Haight-Ashbury milieu. The Grateful Dead happened to stop by on the same errand. First come, first serve, so while Herb was busy with Zep, Pigpen got bored with the wait. He had a .22 caliber gun on him, and like Pogo in the eponymous comic strip (that curiously ran in major dailies for 27 years), fired it off in the ceiling to punctuate his sentences. Rock's new bad boys bailed like sissy schoolgirls.

Morrison spent the last two years of his career moving away from the Lizard King persona, and even though he loathed it, many musicians picked up where he had left off. The new breed of rock stars embraced occult mysticism and subsisted on cynical hedonism, sex, drugs, and rock & roll for all it was worth.

Inspired by a Doors performance in Detroit, James Newell Osterberg left his real name behind and adopted a new identity and persona: Iggy Pop. It was 1967, and he was already jamming with the Asheton brothers and their buddy Dave Alexander, but seeing Jim Morrison perform changed everything.

Two years earlier Dave, or Zander as he was often called, won a bet by dropping out of high school forty-five minutes into his senior year. He and Ron Asheton left later that year for Liverpool in a wishful attempt to find the Beatles. It was 1965 and their dream of running into the pop stars on the street failed, but they caught an early gig with The Move and The Who at The Cavern. Having found their calling, they returned home, plugged in, and began playing music.

Their first band was The Dirty Shames and despite having never played out they earned a reputation in Detroit for being a killer band. Fact was they couldn't do much more than make noise along to records, but that didn't stop a local promoter from offering them an opening slot in Detroit for the Rolling Stones. Ron Asheton explained what happened next to author Joe Ambrose in *Gimme Danger: The Story of Iggy Pop*, "We were all excited until we realized, 'Wow we can't even play!' So we told the guy, 'I think we're going to be auditioning out in LA.' "

Their skills slowly improved. "I spent a year playing all the teen clubs, pretending I was Brian Jones," Ron Asheton told editor Jason Gross in an interview for the latter's outstanding *Perfect Sound Forever* online magazine in 2000.

With the Stooges they left the standard garage band fare behind and went for something new. Ron Asheton continued his conversation with Jason Gross: "My mother would come home and we'd just be blasting. She'd flick the switch to the basement light like a strobe light. She's had a stressful day at the office and she comes home to WRRRRANG, BEEEEEP, ZZZZZZZZ. I could

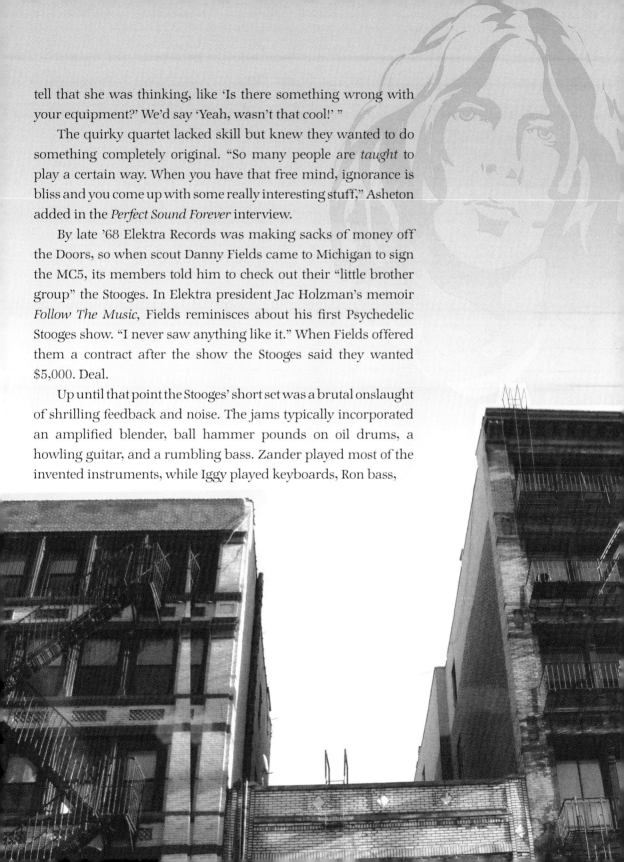

tell that she was thinking, like 'Is there something wrong with your equipment?' We'd say 'Yeah, wasn't that cool!' "

The quirky quartet lacked skill but knew they wanted to do something completely original. "So many people are *taught* to play a certain way. When you have that free mind, ignorance is bliss and you come up with some really interesting stuff," Asheton added in the *Perfect Sound Forever* interview.

By late '68 Elektra Records was making sacks of money off the Doors, so when scout Danny Fields came to Michigan to sign the MC5, its members told him to check out their "little brother group" the Stooges. In Elektra president Jac Holzman's memoir *Follow The Music*, Fields reminisces about his first Psychedelic Stooges show. "I never saw anything like it." When Fields offered them a contract after the show the Stooges said they wanted $5,000. Deal.

Up until that point the Stooges' short set was a brutal onslaught of shrilling feedback and noise. The jams typically incorporated an amplified blender, ball hammer pounds on oil drums, a howling guitar, and a rumbling bass. Zander played most of the invented instruments, while Iggy played keyboards, Ron bass, and Scott drums. For one gig Iggy played a vacuum cleaner (if you thought that Jon Fishman of Phish was this instrument's first virtuoso, think again).

The Stooges soon gained notoriety from Iggy's wild, raw, and sexual stage antics. He reengineered Jaggeresque strutting to become an act of androgynous burlesque, pretty much invented stage diving, and the, eh, art of smearing peanut butter all over his chest as well as cutting himself with shards of glass. "He was beyond Jim Morrison," Holzman writes in his book. "You had to be ready for something beyond stock outrageous."

"An influence on him was Dave Alexander, who was with a group of hoodlums [in high school]. I think he was fascinated by their attitude," Ron Asheton commented later.

With the record deal the Stooges abandoned their crude avant garage and sat down to mint actual songs from the rubble. The record came up a few songs short when Zander suggested they should try an Indian chant. "You'll get high, man," he insisted.

"I did and it was very relaxing. They actually had to stop us because we just wouldn't stop," Asheton says. "We had the candles going and the incense and everything. It was mesmerizing." The chant became the ten-minute "We Will Fall."

The Stooges eponymous debut album, produced by ex-Velvet Underground member John Cale, received mixed reviews upon its release. "This debut set is an exciting premiere from a new group whose inventive lead singer Iggy brings to every cut dimension, energy, and drama," *Cashbox* wrote, and speculated that it "could be a break-out" record. It didn't chart there, however. *Billboard Review*, where the record peaked at 106, opinioned that the Stooges "will benefit from a big push from the label to cop the same sales power of their best-selling Doors." A review of the band's first NYC gig, penned by Fred Kirby for the same publication, was published a month later: "The erotic performance of Elektra's Stooges was coolly received by most of the 2,000 in attendance. ... Iggy, clad only in cut-away blue jeans, swayed and gyrated, caressed and licked his mike stand, flung it into the audience, scratched his bare chest to the point of bleeding, rolled on the floor with lead guitarist Ron Asheton, among other things. ... The stage activity took precedence over the quartet's music, which may be good." The band toured non-stop for a year to support the album and progressed tremendously between their first and second record. Nearly six months later Kirby wrote another review: "Elektra Records has quite an act here!"

"The young kids don't look to orderly patterns of sound and meaning in them. Instead, their concept of music is much more free, less hung up," Dave Alexander told *Rolling Stone*. "We play sounds and create moods. Lots of people say play lots of blues, riffs and changes, but it's just our music, our way of putting sounds together. It's a group mood."

Unfortunately Zander's time with the Stooges was up. In August, the band played at the infamous Goose Lake International Musical Festival in Michigan. Residents had tried to quell the event in the weeks leading up to it, but to no avail. Ticket sales were reportedly at 70,000, but more than 200,000 people descended on tiny Jackson County. Twenty-two bands, including the MC5, Jethro Tull, Ten Years After, Mountain, Chicago, and The Flying Burrito Brothers performed, but it was an odd scene. The festival grounds were fenced with concertina wire and a police chopper patrolled overhead. The authorities feared the crowd would riot if they intervened, so they let the show go on as long as long as the freaks didn't escape with their drugs from the barbed corral.

Zonked on downers, Zander dropped like a pile of shit in front of his amp, unable to play. Iggy sacked him immediately after the show. *Funhouse* came out a few days later and it captured the original lineup's primal energy. Solid cuts like "Dirt," "Little Doll," "1970," and "Funhouse" originated as Zander-riffs, leaving us with the last licks of his short career.

JACKSON, MI.

JETHRO TULL
10 YEARS AFTER
SAVAGE GRACE
CHICAGO
MOUNTAIN
BOB SEGER
THE JAMES GANG
THE STOOGES
MC5
FLYING BURRITO
BROTHERS...

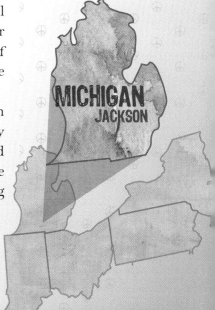

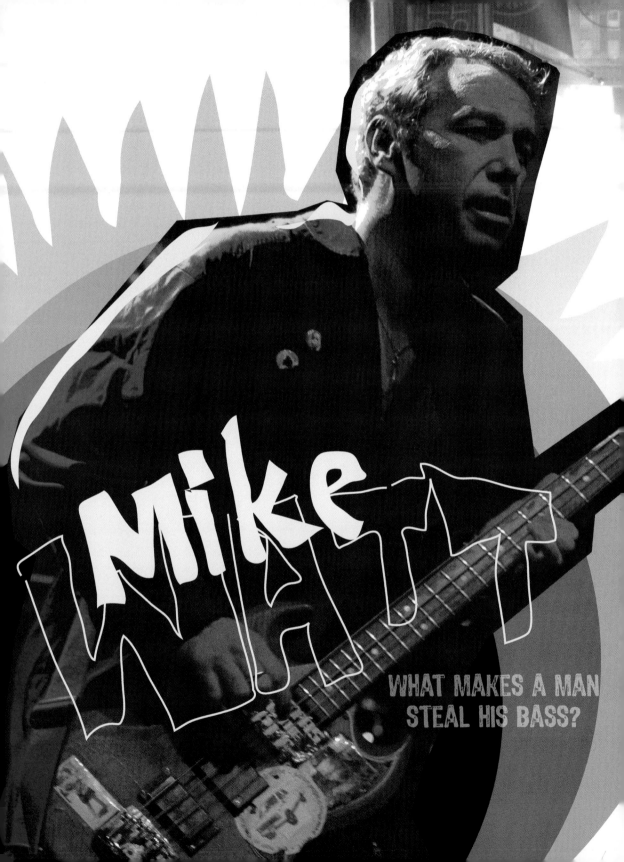

Mike WATT

WHAT MAKES A MAN
STEAL HIS BASS?

The Stooges quickly added Zeke Zettner on bass. Dave returned home, where he spent the next five years battling various addictions and health problems.

In 1972, David Bowie invited Iggy to record in England. The Stooges released *Raw Power* before the house crumbled from the lack of success and powder parties. Meanwhile, Dave Alexander's depressive drinking led to pancreatitis and subsequent hospitalization. Once there his lungs filled with fluid, and the Stooges' original bass player lapsed into pulmonary edema and died February 10, 1975, aged 27.

Iggy Pop continued his career in sporadic strides, but never stopped playing Stooges material. "We really don't communicate," Ron Asheton said of Iggy at the end of the nineties.

The Stooges reformed in 2003 and played occasional gigs with Minuteman Mike Watt filling in Dave's bass duties. In 2007 the band released *The Weirdness*. The reunion brought the band on the cover of more music publications than ever before. Curiously, Zander is never more than a footnote in any of those stories. "Dave hasn't been able to speak for himself, and maybe that's why people tend to forget him. I always try to acknowledge him with people," Watt says. "Dave was a lot about feel and groove and not so much bluster and to me that's a really essential thing—something I'm trying to work towards more and more."

In retrospect, the Stooges were an anomaly until 1975 when Danny Fields signed a new act. The Ramones picked up the former group's shambles from earlier in the decade and helped popularize them for a new audience.

"Maybe three people liked the Stooges in the whole area [Queens, New York]," Dee Dee Ramone says in *End Of The Century*, a Ramones documentary. "And everybody else was, like, violently against them. So if you liked the Stooges you had to be friends with each other."

The Ramones spurred a new movement and inspired the Sex Pistols and The Clash. Punk was ON and the Stooges was the genre's perverted father. *Rolling Stone* counts the group's first three records among its 500 Greatest Albums of All Time.

During the first half of the seventies, rock splintered into a myriad of subgenres. There was heavy rock, funk, blues-rock, **SOUL POP PROGRESSIVE ROCK** and **FUSION,** and each style suffered the loss of a 27. The one whose output rumbles the loudest is bassist Gary Thain, best known for his work with British heavy-cum-prog rockers Uriah Heep. The band never really conquered the American market like some of their behemoth British counterparts, but it they were successful in Europe, Japan, and Australia. Thain was part of Heep's most acclaimed line-up and played on four successive Top 40 studio albums and the double *Live*.

Critics are extremely genre conscious by profession, and they found Uriah Heep difficult to pin down. As a result the band was constantly ragged on. "We were never really taken seriously by the press, but the fans loved us and that kept us going," says Uriah Heep's keyboardist and principal songwriter Ken Hensley.

Uriah Heep sounded heavy and featured tightly arranged progressive rock passages yet managed to come off as popish. Listen to *Demons and Wizards* to hear what I mean. "Easy Livin'" is a seventies pop-rocker, while "The Spell" sounds like it would fit on a Yes or Pink Floyd album from the same era. *Demons and Wizards* went platinum and was one of the first to forge heavy rock and Tolkienesque lyrics—a link that's still alive and well. While we're on the subject of a seventies heavy band and magic motifs, the 1984 mockumentary *Spinal Tap* does undeniably bring aspects of Uriah Heep to mind.

Gary Thain was only seventeen when he left his native New Zealand, first to Australia, the following year by boat to England with his band Me And The Others. The nascent group played England, Scotland, and on military bases in Germany before they split up.

Excellent musicians are never unemployed for long, so Gary soon found himself in a promising trio called The New Nadir. They gigged Switzerland, Germany, and around London where Jimi Hendrix once jumped on stage for an impromptu jam at the Speakeasy. The New Nadir recorded an album produced by Joe Boyd, but with no release date in sight, Thain teamed up with the infant Keef Hartley Band.

KHB sounds like a cross between the Allman Brothers and Blood, Sweat & Tears thanks to its solid rhythm section and rotating cast of brass players and talented guitarists such as Miller Anderson and Junior Kerr (Kerr was later known as Junior Marvin, lead guitarist for Bob Marley's Wailers through *Exodus*,

NEW ZEALAND

NORTH ISLAND

SOUTH ISLAND

CHRISTCHURCH

FRIENDS & ANGELS

One of the most interesting side gigs Gary Thain did was to play on Martha Velez's debut record from 1970. For some reason *Fiends & Angels* has never been released on CD, which is strange considering that Britain's top blues musicians provided the backing: Eric Clapton, Jack Bruce, Keef Hartley, Mitch Mitchell, and members of Traffic, Free, and John Mayall's Bluesbreakers. Impressed by Velez's voice, Bob Marley helped write and produce her fourth record, *Escape From Babylon*, which is the only album that bears his production credit outside of the Wailers.

Kaya, Survival, Uprising, and *Babylon By Bus*). The Keef Hartley Band became a driving force in British blues, and Thain and Keef were the anchors throughout the group's six releases. The group ended when its namesake left for a solo career.

Musicians rarely live healthy lives, and Gary was no exception. He lived on a diet of soup, cigarettes, and an assortment of pills and illicit drugs. The result was visible to everybody around him: he was skinny, frail, and his body already prone to illness before Heep roped him in to replace Mark Clarke.

While Thain's constitution wasn't the strongest, his playing was. "Gary just had a style about him," Heep guitarist Mick Box says. "It was incredible because every bass player in the world that I've ever known has always loved his style with those melodic bass lines."

"Gary was a major part of the movement that brought bass players and the instrument itself more into the limelight," Ken Hensley adds. "His bass playing was so lyrical and yet forceful. People still talk about him! A musician's musician!"

Heep isn't typically listed at the top of '70s bands, but fans of rock bass echo Mick's observation. If Gary Thain played with any of the other big bands of that era, he would've been revered today like Zep and Who drummers John Bonham and Keith Moon. That's right, he was that good.

Gary Thain offered a syncopated, propulsive groove, which was a new thing in rock bass. It almost sounds like the brass on Motown's soul records. Spin Heep's *Live* 1973 album, where Thain is way up in the mix, and imagine his powerful bass as a horn section or a loud trumpet.

"Gary's musical contribution was more on the arranging side than anything else," says Ken Hensley, "but it can't be overlooked that his personality helped create the chemistry that carried the Heep into the rock & roll stratosphere."

Thain never used a pick; he plucked his heavy gauge strings using bare fingers. Crewmember Todd Fisher recalls a gig from Salem, Oregon, in early '72 when Gary winced in pain mid-set: "After the number he came to the side of the stage and asked in that raspy back-of-the-throat New Zealand accented voice *'Tawd! Do you have an adhesive bandage?'* As he held out this terribly bloody thumb, I saw that he had torn off the callous built up from many years of playing without a plectrum." The show and the tour went on, and Thain kept playing. Fischer adds, "Gary was able to get through at least one number, sometimes two, before he would come over to the me on the side of the stage to have me spray the open wound with ethyl chloride [an anesthetic]. Damn! The man wouldn't even let me tape it for him because he felt it would change his sound! Only he would know."

"It's total involvement," Gary once said about the band. "Something you must have, or you're wasting your time." And he walked the talk in all aspects of his life. This was a time before rockers employed personal dressers, and Gary, like Brian and Jimi before him, always looked like the rock star that he was. Tight pants, furry white plateau boots, flowing shirts, long hair, and the ubiquitous cigarette dangling from his mouth.

"Gary was hard to figure out," says Ken Hensley, "He always gave you the impression that he didn't care about too much of anything other than playing and living the hard rock life. He didn't seem to even consider the consequences of his addiction either to himself or those who depended on him. On reflection, we

161

were all like that to some extent. Even when we had to practically carry him on and off aeroplanes, he seemed to think it was just fun. But as a bandmate he was, at his best, a phenomenal musical resource, though he pretty much stayed out of anything non-musical, like meetings."

"Gary hardly socialized with the rest of the band," says Sonja Wagner (nee Sonja Gindl), Thain's friend and occasional lover. "He loved to be on stage and make music. Heep always had a great audience."

September 15, 1974, Heep played the Moody Coliseum in Dallas, Texas. The band was in the middle of "July Morning" when the bottom dropped out. "All I remember is going to the amplifiers to adjust the equalizers, the next thing that happened was I blacked out," Thain said later. A jolt lifted Gary's platform boots three feet from the stage in front of his Acoustic 370 bass amp, his mouth wide open, gasping for air. Blue smoke billowed from the amp and Gary fell face first on the bass while his legs bounced up behind him. Thain's body was still charged with god-knows how many volts from the faulty amp when the band stopped playing and roadies swarmed the stage. Thain was rushed to the emergency room where he was treated for electrocution.

Thain was on the hospital's critical list for several days, wavering between life and death, and the accident quickly escalated to become a fateful turning point in his life.

Heep manager Gerry Bron was hesitant to cancel the six remaining dates of the US tour so Thain could recover, which started a beef between Thain and Bron—and ultimately Thain and the rest of the band. "The music's been forgotten, and now it's become a financial thing," Thain complained to the press.

"He was very pissed off that Gerry Bron, our manager, did not seem to care about him and did not even place a call to see how he was," Mick Box says today. "This really hit a nerve with Gary and he felt very let down by the fact that he had given Bron and Heep everything and Bron as our manager never bothered to pick up the phone to see how he was."

"That last year wasn't too nice," says Sonja Wagner in her German accent. "They [Uriah Heep] didn't give him enough time to recover. They kept pushing him and he went back on stage far too soon."

Ken Hensley remembers Gary Thain's health issues differently. He says they stemmed from the bassist's drug use, not the electrocution. "Gary's health at this time was extremely poor and there were many moments during this tour where we were really struggling to keep him in shape."

Over the next few months, Gary's wife Carol took their baby Nathalie and left him, and the band gave him the boot. The press, reporting a statement issued by the band, first wrote that Thain had quit "following several months of indifferent health."

The next week, a band spokesman clarified that "Gary was asked to leave. Nevertheless, as we said in the first place, everyone associated with the band still wishes him the best of luck in his future projects."

Despite Thain's incredible talent, the truth was that the rest of the guys felt that they couldn't continue with his destructive abuse. "I remember he became personally and musically unpredictable and unreliable," Ken Hensley says.

Thain returned to London and began calling musicians, but nobody wanted to take on the sick and frail bass player. Gary Thain put down his last recorded tracks in his home studio with Pierre Roland (guitar), Bert Stockner (drums), Andy Bauz (saxophone), and Sonja Gindl (flute and vocals); the latter says the quintet sounded like a jazzier version of the Keef Hartley Band.

Gary Thain took his last breath December 15, 1975. After taking too many amphetamines, he decided to come down in his bathtub. Gary's girlfriend found him there, unconscious, and had him transferred to the nearby hospital where he was pronounced dead by "misadventure"—just 27 years old.

Rock lost one of its best deep-enders that day, but to the press it was just another dead rock star. A newspaper quoted his ex-wife Carol as saying, "Gary loved drugs of all sorts." Heep leader Ken Hensley was more diplomatic: "I always loved Gary as a person, he had a quality of irresponsibility that I always liked. I think he died because he misjudged what he was doing and it got the better of him."

SOUL POP

The pop-infused soul group Bloodstone started out in Kansas City as a high school doo-wop outfit named The Sinceres. The members eventually learned how to play instruments and blended pop, funk, and soul for a new sound. A few months after Bloodstone's debut, "Natural High," hit Billboard's Top 10, the group lost singer Roger Lee Durham following an equestrian accident July 27, 1973. Durham was 27 years old. His service as an airman for the US Airforce during the Vietnam War granted him interment at the Fort Leavenworth National Cemetery.

Bloodstone's sound proved perfect for many blaxploitation soundtracks, and in 1997 Director Quentin Tarantino used "Natural High" in *Jackie Brown*, an homage to the genre. Listen for the song in the scene where Jackie (Pam Grier) walks out of jail with confident strides and bail bondsman Max Cherry (Robert Forster), who's there to give her a ride, is struck by her graceful beauty.

PROG ROCK

Another talented bass player, composer, and vocalist was Helmut Köllen of the German group Triumvirat. He replaced his cousin after the band's debut release and participated on two of the greatest concept albums of the era, *Illusions on a Double Dimple* and *Spartacus*.

The trio promoted *Illusions* as a support act for Fleetwood Mac on a forty-date US tour and holed up in the studio to record the follow-up. Geoff Emerick, who's known for engineering *Sgt. Pepper's*, did the same for *Spartacus*, and the record blew up on both sides of the Atlantic. The album chronicles Spartacus' slave rebellion against the Roman masters. Yup, a grand—some would say pretentious—prog rock epos. The record stood on its own but lacked a hit single, so Triumvirat remained a supporting act, touring with Grand Funk Railroad in Europe and Supertramp in the US.

Köllen left the band at the end of the tour in LA and began working on a solo album. He wanted to explore a new direction but found himself back with the band a year later.

After a long recording session in May '77, he parked the car in his garage and listened to a tape of his unreleased solo tracks. Although it's unclear whether it was an accident or suicide, the 27-year-old Helmut Köllen was trounced by monoxide. Köllen's solo album *You Won't See Me*, named after his favorite Beatles song, was released posthumously later that year by EMI's Harvest label.

FUSION

In the seventies, mixing jazz and rock morphed to a style of its own known as fusion. One of the great, albeit hardly remembered bands of this genre was Chase.

"We played with Sly and the Family Stone, the Spinners, and Herbie Hancock during my 17 months with Bill [Chase] and my own collection of live bootlegs proves that Chase kicked ass almost every time we took the stage," bassist Dartanyan Brown writes on his website. He was twenty-three when Chase folded, but his memories linger more than thirty years after the terrible accident that killed four of the band members.

Led by trumpeter Bill Chase, his eponymous nine-piece band (that included four trumpet players) recorded its first album in 1971, which was nominated for a Grammy. The follow-up *Ennea* didn't do nearly as well, and Chase suffered a slew of personnel changes and lack of innovation until Wally Yohn joined. The ferocious interplay between Bill and Wally became part of the trademark sound; Bill's trumpet chasing the whirls of Wally's oscillating keyboard. Like all of Bill's bands, this last incarnation of Chase was tight as a pickle jar.

"I still have tapes of one day in April '74 at the Half-Note in NYC where Herbie had his press party and performance in the afternoon with the HeadHunters and we played our NYC coming-out party on the same stage that evening," Brown reminisces.

Pure Music entered the Billboard charts on April 27 where it climbed to number 155. The disc placed third on jazz mag *Down Beat's* chart.

At the end of the summer, the band was scheduled to play at a fair in Jackson, Minnesota, but a roaring rainstorm barred the group from ever playing again. An airplane carrying bandleader Bill Chase, drummer Walter Clark, guitarist John Emma, and keyboardist Wally Yohn crashed close to the airstrip and killed them and the pilot.

Wally Yohn was 27 years young.

August 1, 1971, George Harrison walked out on Madison Square Garden's huge stage, cleared his throat and said, "We're gonna try one with just these acoustic guitars." Pete Ham from Badfinger was standing next to him. It was Harrison's *Concert For Bangladesh*, and out of more than two dozen musicians (including Bob Dylan and Eric Clapton), Pete was the man he wanted for a duet. Their stripped-down version of "Here Comes the Sun" is one of the best cuts on Harrison's double album.

The show was a rare moment in the bright stage lights because the story of Pete Ham and Badfinger reads like a Greek tragedy, where the hero's trajectory goes from good to bad and there's no resolution other than death. This reversal of fortune occurs because of a *hamartia*, or mistake, made by the hero. Badfinger's mistake was trusting managers and labels that were paid to take care of them.

Three years before Harrison's charity concert, the Beatles founded Apple Records as an artist's label. Badfinger, then known as The Iveys, was one of its first signings.

The four Iveys boys had spent the last few years communing with and under the guidance of the patriarchal Bill Collins, a manager who promised success if they followed his plan. Collins encouraged all of them to work on songwriting, and with a single released, Pete often worked entire nights in the studio at their London digs. The boys were still heavily influenced by the Beatles and hadn't yet found their true sound—or name for that matter. "Maybe Tomorrow" sounded dated, especially when compared to, say, Jimi Hendrix.

In early '69 The Iveys had the misfortune of promoting their debut disc on *The Lulu Show* the same night that Jimi Hendrix guested. Britain's super group Cream had recently broken up and Jimi cut "Hey Joe" short live on the air to announce, "we're gonna stop playing this rubbish and dedicate a song to The Cream regardless of what kinda group they might be in."

Drummer Mike Gibbins later summed up the evening to Iveys/Badfinger biographer Dan Mantovina: "Here we were in suits as The Iveys, and Hendrix is doing Cream songs—on fucking heroin!" The group was still in its incubation stage, and it took a full-length LP and a name change for the metamorphosis to reach completion.

The Beatles tracked *Abbey Road* at the time, and Paul McCartney was commissioned to make the soundtrack for a movie titled *The Magic Christian* (starring Ringo Starr, Peter Sellers, Raquel Welch, and a pre-Monty Python cameo by John Cleese). He made a demo recording of "Come And Get It" for the flick and decided to give The Iveys a stab at it. The group completed the mission to Paul's satisfaction, so he continued the recording sessions, allowing the group to work on original material. One of the songs was bassist Tom Evans and Pete Ham's "Carry On Till Tomorrow," which ended up being used for the opening scene. Paul taught the lads about recording and arranging, and as his neophytes progressed he granted them more creative freedom.

It was time for a name change. The Iveys bore associations to the older Merseybeat scene, which was very passé. They started a list. Paul McCartney suggested Home, John Lennon suggested Prix (pronounced pricks), but it was eventually Apple chief Neil Aspinall who came up with the winner: Badfinger. The name came from a nascent Lennon-riff titled "Bad Finger Boogie" (as the riff evolved it became "With a Little Help From My Friends.")

Badfinger's first single "Come and Get It" reached top five on the British charts, while their debut album, titled *Magic Christian Music* to capitalize on the expected hoopla surrounding the movie release, received mediocre reviews upon its release in 1970.

Rolling Stone's John Mendelsohn wrote, "Even when they're so unbearably cute that you want to take them off for a minute to clear the air with Led Zeppelin or something, you can't help but be cheered by their presence."

Badfinger entered the seventies with strong songs, not long jams. Instead of a wall of Hi-Watt stacks, they played through small Vox or Fender Silverface amps. Instead of double bass drums and a forest of cymbals, Mike Gibbins sat behind a small, standard five-piece drum kit. They didn't have a glitzy stage act either; they were just four guys singing incredible songs. "We're just ordinary," Mike Gibbins told *Rolling Stone* in '71. "We write our own songs and we like simplicity and rock and roll, and we're basically a three guitars/drums lineup," Ham added. The writer noted Ham's "John Lennonish sad-eyed stares into the audience."

Pete was a typical Welsh male: introspective and quiet. He never talked about his feelings, but his lyrics are often autobiographical and incredibly expressive.

Badfinger's sophomore release *No Dice* received far better reviews than their first—*Rolling Stone* even lauded it "one of the best records of the year." The problem was that most reviewers compared Badfinger to the Beatles, pitted their songs against Lennon-McCartney compositions, and pointed out Ham's "McCartney-esque voice." Although the comparisons were usually favorable, the omnipresent Beatles affiliations started to strain the band.

"Sure, we were influenced by the Beatles," they lamented to *Melody Maker*, "like ten million other groups."

The Beatles connection cast a cursed shadow over the band throughout their career, as journalists habitually pointed out that a) Tom Evans looked like Paul's brother; b) Paul wrote their first single; c) Tom or Pete sounded like Paul; d) they were an Apple band; and e) because of Badfinger's session work on "Imagine"/"Come And Get It"/*All Things Must Pass*/"It Don't Come Easy" they were really John/Paul/George/Ringo's backup band.

"I've never come across any remotely serious substantive interview with any of the band members on their *music* [my emphasis] from the period Pete was alive," Matovina told Ken Sharp in an interview for *Beatlefan* magazine in 1998.

An American named Stan Polley was keen on managing the band, and he set up the group's first American tour in 1970. "We were dashing around like zombies gigging all over America," Pete said in an interview the following year. Badfinger played forty-six dates in less than two and a half months, often with grueling drives in between gigs. After playing Lincoln, Nebraska, they drove 1,500 miles to make it to Pullman, Washington the following day. A month into the tour, over three consecutive nights they performed in Fort Worth, Texas; drove 1,100 miles to the next gig in Fargo, North Dakota; then traveled more than 1,600 miles southwest to Las Vegas.

At the end of the tour, the band made a grave *hamartia*—they signed a management contract with Stan Polley. Polley already managed notable musicians such as Lou Christie and Al Kooper, and he made a lofty promise that he could make them all rich if the band invested all their proceeds into Badfinger Enterprises Inc., a corporation co-owned by the four members,

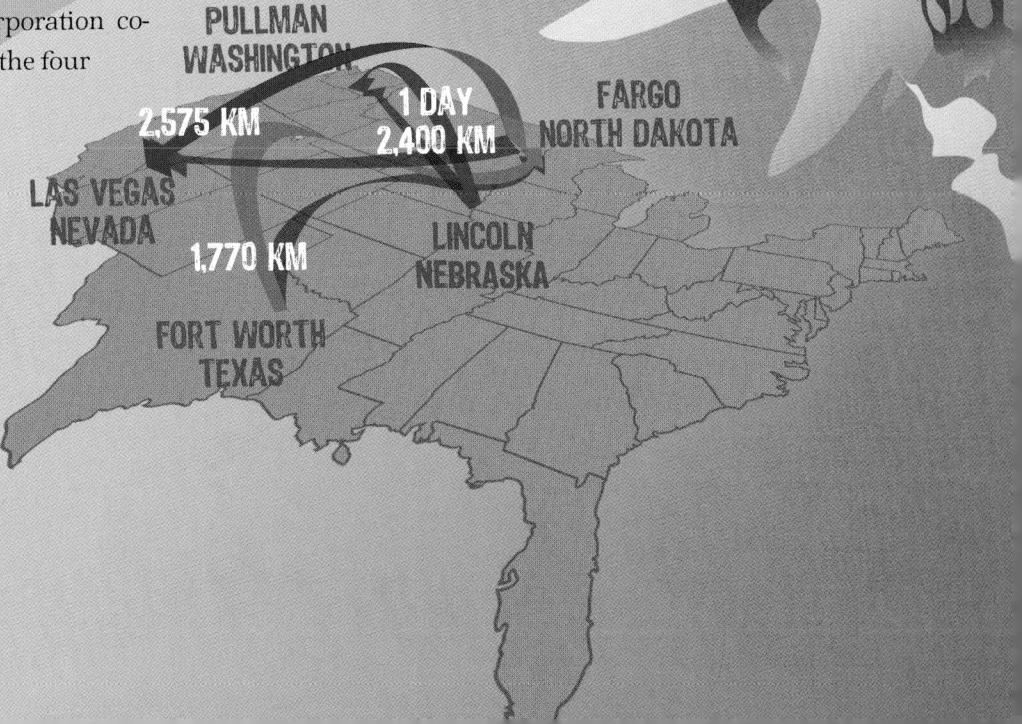

PULLMAN
WASHINGTON

2,575 KM

1 DAY
2,400 KM

FARGO
NORTH DAKOTA

LAS VEGAS
NEVADA

1,770 KM

LINCOLN
NEBRASKA

FORT WORTH
TEXAS

Bill Collins, and himself.

The lads continued to churn out hits—four top ten over three years—but instead of reaping rewards from their successes, the members were paid a modest salary. They had made it, yet lived like starving musicians, drove used cars, and ate on the cheap. In 1970 the soles of Pete's only pair of shoes were falling off. Most bands with a few hit records would plow money back into the band, buy new equipment, stage lights, whatever. But Polley had a different plan.

Apple Records was disintegrating, and an unfortunate legal battle over publishing copyrights halted the British release of the group's third album, *Ass*. **The cover illustrated where they were: a donkey gazing across an expanse of desert towards a giant hand in the sky holding the promised golden carrot. Put together, the three album titles read No Dice, Straight Up Ass.**

Since Apple was dismantling operations, Polley negotiated a new deal with Warner Brothers Records. He was an unscrupulous businessman, and he set up the WB contract so he could plunder advances while the band was forced to comply with a Sisyphean schedule: tour, record, tour, record, tour, record, with no time allotted for rest, rehearsals, or writing songs. The contract called for six LPs over three years with $225,000 advanced per album and an additional $100,000 advanced for the copyrights.

"There never seems enough time to do things. We'd like to spend more time rehearsing and we'd like longer in the studio, but there's only 24 hours in the day," Pete Ham complained to a journalist.

BADFINGER'S CHART TOPPERS

"No Matter What" from *No Dice* reached number five in England and number eight in the US, while the George Harrison-produced "Day After Day" from *Straight Up* went gold in America—one million in single sales. "Baby Blue" from the same album reached number fourteen on the Billboard charts, but was never released in the UK.

In March '73 American singer-songwriter Harry Nilsson received a Grammy for his version of "Without You."

When Stan Poses, the vice president of Badfinger Enterprises, realized that the contracts between the band and Stan Polley were set up so Polley had a lock on all the assets, he decided to leave. "He has control of everything," Poses warned Pete and Tom. The WB deal still wasn't signed, but somehow Polley convinced the guys to ink it.

The band was nudged back into the studio. In the past they'd used producers such as Paul McCartney, Geoff Emerick (famous for his work with the Beatles on *Revolver, Sgt. Pepper, The White Album,* and *Abbey Road*), George Harrison, Todd Rundgren, and Chris Thomas (whose latest gigs were Procol Harum's *Grand Hotel* and Pink Floyd's *Dark Side of the Moon* which he worked on simultaneously), but this time they started without one, and it turned into a collective mess. Pete wrote song after song, but the other members, and increasingly guitarist Joey Molland's girl Kathy, vetoed them. Kathy was a loud American who demanded a say in band affairs and pushed for Joey's songs. Pete, the quiet Welsh, felt overrun, but it wasn't in his nature to pick a fight.

I CANT LIVE........   I CANT FORGET....

Starting in '73, Pete's songs delved into spirituality, mortality, frustrations, and writer's block. He didn't understand their creative direction and was upset with the touring schedule—they toured with no album to promote, then were told not to tour when *Ass* finally came out. He defended Polley whenever someone questioned the manager's integrity or the way that Badfinger's business was run. **Stan had promised he'd take care of them and Pete trusted him. Pete's flaw, if you can call it that, was that he believed in good vibes and that people would stay true to their words.**

As the mid-seventies approached, living a creative life was becoming harder for Pete and the rest of the band. Legal wrangling enriched a herd of lawyers and distracted business managers working for Warner Brothers, Apple, and Badfinger Enterprises. Copyright issues with Apple dragged on and WB requested audits for where money placed in escrow accounts had gone. Contracts and forms presented in court by Stan Polley were backdated, doctored, and rife with false signatures. Some of his actions were careless, yet the tangle made him somehow invincible.

Another blow came in early '74 with the release of their first album for WB. The group's intended title, *For Love Or Money*, was left off, and they had no creative input on the cover. Back on tour they played through house systems or local rentals, and although they often filled the small venues, the group was plagued by terrible sound. As soon as the tour concluded they were forced straight back to the studio. Morale was running close to mutiny. Both Tom and Joey frequently cussed Stan Polley for his lock on their dough; Pete, of course, wouldn't believe it.

After the recording sessions the band had a meeting with an agent in the UK, presumably to discuss the upcoming British tour,

SEP. 9, 1973
Country-rock founder Gram Parsons (26) dies after mixing too many drugs in a motel room near Joshua Tree National Park.

SEP. 20, 1973
Singer-songwriter Jim Croce (30) dies in a plane crash.

but the meeting took an ugly twist when they discussed rumors about WB canceling their contract because of money missing from escrow. During the meeting Joey's girlfriend Kathy called in. She said she had talked to people at WB who assured her everything was okay. Pete's built-up frustrations uncharacteristically erupted. He stood up and yelled, "I don't want Kathy managing the band! I'm leaving."

Pete Ham was done with the band and finished with touring. He found a cottage in Wales, where he wanted to build a studio so he could keep writing songs. Polley was shopping for a solo deal when somebody at Warner Brothers called Pete and said they were interested in *him*, not Badfinger without Pete Ham. Pete might've felt that he owed it to the band to continue, so he showed up a few weeks later in time for the tour. Badfinger was now a five-piece: Tom Evans, Mike Gibbins, and Joey Molland had added keyboardist Bob Jackson in Pete Ham's absence.

Ham was quieter than usual and hardly allowed himself to joke around like he used to. At least the rest of the band had a good time on the road. For Joey Molland it was a fun last blow. He quit at the end of the tour and left Tom, Mike, and Bob in the street saying, "Well, look, it's my wife. I cannot go against my wife."

The loss of Joey Molland's songwriting added to Ham's pressures back in the studio. With Badfinger's career submerged in an abyss, Pete started to fear he had written his last hit. He still tried to work, but his demos became increasingly introspective, paranoid, and manic.

FEB. 8, 1974	JULY 27-30, 1974	JULY 29, 1974	OCT. 30, 1974	JUNE 29, 1975
KISS releases its eponymous debut album.	The House of Representatives Judiciary Committee impeaches President Nixon on three counts.	Cass Elliot (32) of The Mamas & the Papas dies from a heart attack.	The Rumble In The Jungle: Muhammad Ali knocks out George Foreman in the 8th round in Zaire.	Musician Tim Buckley (28) snorts his final line of heroin and ODs.

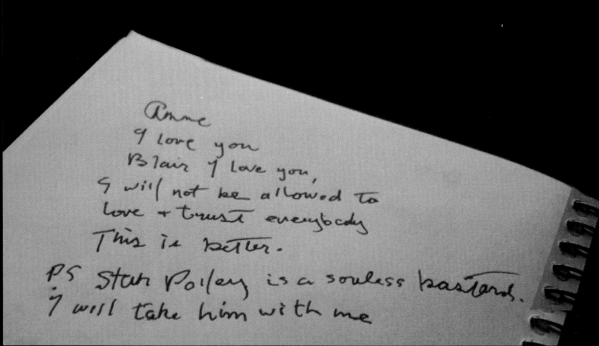

To make matters worse, Warner Brothers asked a California court to cancel the company's contract with Badfinger in December '74. It argued that the money missing from escrow was a breach of contract. Their latest disc, *Wish You Were Here*, and their back catalogue were pulled from the shelves, effectively choking the band's business.

Pete Ham purchased a new house, but soon thereafter Badfinger's salary checks from Polley stopped clearing. Ham felt the squeeze and was overcome with hopelessness. His checking account was in the red, the band no longer felt like family, and he couldn't write songs. How could he support his girlfriend Anne Herriot, her son Blair, and their baby that was only weeks away from being born? He frantically called Polley, but his manager's secretaries and assistants wouldn't connect him.

Ham finally admitted to Evans that Stan Polley had screwed them over and that it was time do something about it. Pete said he "knew a way out." He downed several triple scotches at the bar and said goodbye.

Anne Herriot found Pete Ham the next morning at the end of a rope in his garage studio. It was April 23, 1975—three days before Pete's 28th birthday—and his presumable last words were scribbled in one of his songbooks. It read:

Anne
I love you
Blair I love you,
I will not be allowed to
love + trust everybody
This is better.

PS Stan Polley is a souless bastard.
I will take him with me

Pete Ham crafted "Without You," a powerful ballad with dramatic verses and a brilliantly sad melody line, by fusing what he already had with a chorus from a scrapped Tom Evans song; "I can't live if living is without you." The song took a prophetic twist in 1983 when Tom Evans (36) hung himself in the garden after eight more years of failed records and dead-end tours. He never got over Pete's suicide mentally or professionally.

"Without You" is Badfinger's most famous song, yet few people know or acknowledge that Pete and Tom wrote it. Harry Nilsson was awarded a Grammy for his version in the early seventies, and Heart, Air Supply, Clay Aiken, Kelly Clarkson, Natalia Druyts, and many others have rerecorded it since then. **Mariah Carey went gold with "Without You" in 1993; it helped make her album Heartbox a diamond record—that's ten times platinum—with 7.9 million albums sold in the US alone. Why don't some of these pop artists turn on fans and journalists to Badfinger?**

In the history of rock Badfinger's lawyer fees are second only to the Beatles'. Their copyright issues and releases are still a complete mess, leaving Joey Molland and the estates of Pete, Tom, Mike, and original manager Bill Collins with petty change for their amazing artistic legacy.

"Songwriting is one of the greatest pleasures in my life," Pete Ham once said. He breathed music and wrote songs that are now considered pop standards, but he was ruined financially, robbed creatively and ultimately raped emotionally to a point where he felt he could no longer be allowed to love and trust anybody.

The press instilled Badfinger with insecurities about their own material to such a degree that the band rounded out its shows with standard rock & roll covers instead of featuring their own songs.

178

MAR. 19, 1976	APR. 1, 1976	JAN. 27, 1977	MAR. 27, 1977
Paul Kossoff (25) of Free dies from drug-related heart problems.	*Steve Jobs and Steve Wozniak founds the Apple Computer Company.*	*EMI kicks the Sex Pistols off its roster.*	*The worst aviation disaster of all time kills 583 people on the island of Tenerife.*

When Harry Nilsson won the Grammy for his version of "Without You," he demonstrated the worth of Ham and Evans' songwriting.

"Music doesn't have to be bad to be commercial," Pete Ham asserted, something his back catalog strongly demonstrates. All of Ham songs inherit superb melodic and lyrical qualities, and his guitar playing was good enough for Duane Allman to ask if he could join the band at their hotel and jam after a Badfinger show in Georgia.

One of Ham's finest recorded moments is found in the song "Timeless," as heard on *Ass*. The song builds slowly to a climactic chorus and a long, tormented guitar solo that runs to keep up with an increasingly thick blanket of swelling white noise.

Bud Scoppa wrote in his review for *Rolling Stone* that the song "might easily be mistaken for an inspired Clapton-Harrison collaboration."

The lyrics and the arrangement's harrowing quality would be the perfect title track for a biopic on The 27s.

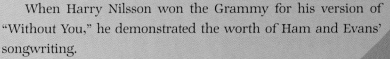

PUNK POWER

Critics frequently categorized Badfinger's music as out-of-sync with the times. Ironically, the still-unknown punk band the Sex Pistols took over Badfinger's rehearsal space in London's Denmark Street soon after Pete's death.

Rubber and leather fashion maven Malcolm McLaren figured his style had a better shot at becoming vogue if it had music to go with it. McLaren molded the Sex Pistols from the Ramones' carefree attitude, but the band soon took on a life of its own. The Pistols only released four singles and one studio album during its turbulent three-year career but left a lasting legacy.

In January 1978, the group encored a San Francisco show with The Stooges' "No Fun." At the end of the song vocalist Johnny Rotten rhetorically asked the audience, "Ever get the feeling you've been cheated?" The original incarnation of the Sex Pistols ended with a pop when Rotten threw the mike on the stage and walked off.

PULLING A POLLEY

Dan Matovina's *Without You: The Tragic Story of Badfinger* and Al Kooper's *Backstage Passes & Backstabbing Bastards: Memoirs of a Rock 'N' Roll Survivor* tell wretched stories about Stan Polley's management style. When ex-client Charlie Calello and his young son stopped by Polley's office to claim his money, Polley told him to leave at gunpoint.

During a 1971 Senate Investigation Committee hearing Stan Polley's name came up as a liaison between a corrupt judge and organized crime, but nothing came of it. Polley eventually phased out of the entertainment business, but he kept swindling and embezzling money.

In 1991 a California court ordered Polley to return $250,000 that he had defrauded an aeronautics entrepreneur. He finagled a way to stay out of jail and was put on probation. Polley didn't make a single payment to the guy he swindled and continues to live out his old days as a free man in Southern California.

Badfinger's sound—euphonic harmonies, tight guitar riffs, and short and melodic solos—was later dubbed power pop. Pete Townshend coined the term to describe The Who's music in an interview in the heat of Swingin' London, but it never stuck.

The term doesn't show up in *Rolling Stone* mag's pages until 1978 when it was casually sprinkled in record reviews. In the last issue of the decade, writer Tom Carson took a stab at an explanation: "Power pop is a definite step backward—an artistic retreat—from the daring of punk." The article's header defined it: "Power pop: good old rock & roll."

Power pop is rooted in British invasion bands such as The Beatles, The Kinks, and The Hollies, the riffs and energetic drumming of The Who, and the vocal harmonies of The Everly Brothers.

Badfinger, along with American groups The Raspberries and Big Star, created the recipe for what is now considered true power pop. The genre's three progenitors had dissolved by 1975 with little more to show than a few hit singles, under-appreciated albums, death, and depression.

Most music journalists were in the fog about those bands (with Bud Scoppa as a clear deviant), but somehow Townshend's term was reintroduced at the end of the '70s to describe the music of Cheap Trick, The Knack, 20/20, The dB's, The Cars, and so on. The style influenced R.E.M., the Gigolo Aunts, and the Replacements in the '80s, while the '90s saw the Posies, the Flaming Lips, Matthew Sweet, the New Pornographers, Teenage Fanclub, Ben Folds Five, and perhaps the biggest success of them all, Weezer. Power pop tendencies are audible in the music of Ryan Adams, The Postal Service, the late, great Elliot Smith, and on Wilco's *Being There* and *Summerteeth*.

SEP. 16, 1977	OCT. 20, 1977	JAN. 23, 1978
Mark Bolan (29) of T.Rex dies in a car crash.	Lynard Skynard members Ronnie Van Zant (29), Steve Gaines (28) and Cassie Gaines (29) die in a plane crash.	Guitarist Terry Kath of Chicago dies after saying, "Don't worry, it's not loaded."

While Badfinger looms large in power pop, near-mythical status has been reserved for a low-key quartet from Memphis, Tennessee.

Big Star released two incredible studio albums and toured modestly before it dissolved in 1975. Big Star isn't a household name, yet the group's music has been played through the TV in most living rooms.

In 1998, the producers of *That '70s Show*, a Fox sitcom about teenagers growing up in a Wisconsin suburb in the 1970s, chose Big Star's "In the Street" as the theme song (after the first season, the song's producers asked Cheap Trick to rerecord it) and featured other originals by the same group throughout the show's eight-year run.

FEB. 18, 1978

Nigerian Afro-beat founder Fela Kuti marries his 27 singers and dancers in a traditional Yoruba ceremony.

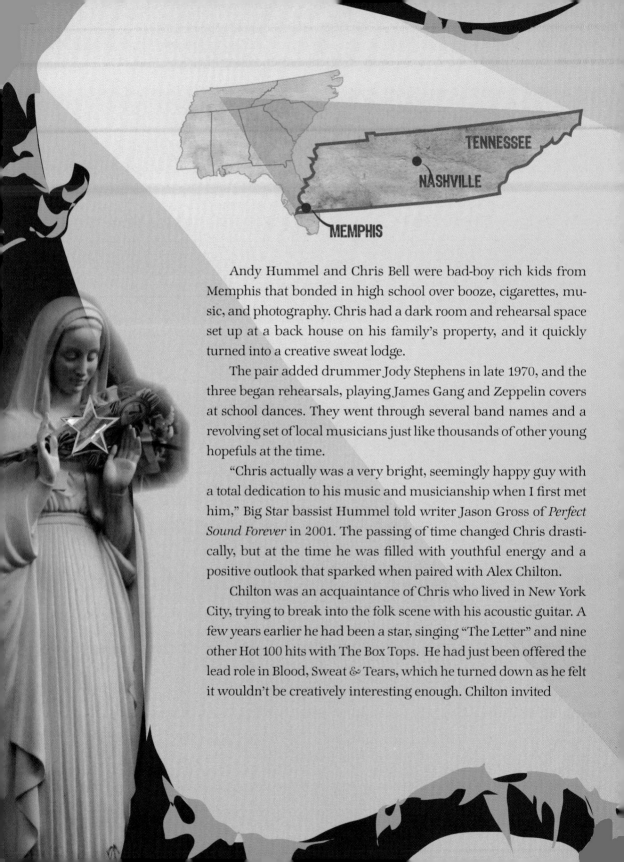

TENNESSEE

NASHVILLE

MEMPHIS

Andy Hummel and Chris Bell were bad-boy rich kids from Memphis that bonded in high school over booze, cigarettes, music, and photography. Chris had a dark room and rehearsal space set up at a back house on his family's property, and it quickly turned into a creative sweat lodge.

The pair added drummer Jody Stephens in late 1970, and the three began rehearsals, playing James Gang and Zeppelin covers at school dances. They went through several band names and a revolving set of local musicians just like thousands of other young hopefuls at the time.

"Chris actually was a very bright, seemingly happy guy with a total dedication to his music and musicianship when I first met him," Big Star bassist Hummel told writer Jason Gross of *Perfect Sound Forever* in 2001. The passing of time changed Chris drastically, but at the time he was filled with youthful energy and a positive outlook that sparked when paired with Alex Chilton.

Chilton was an acquaintance of Chris who lived in New York City, trying to break into the folk scene with his acoustic guitar. A few years earlier he had been a star, singing "The Letter" and nine other Hot 100 hits with The Box Tops. He had just been offered the lead role in Blood, Sweat & Tears, which he turned down as he felt it wouldn't be creatively interesting enough. Chilton invited

Chris to come out and form a folk duo, but Chris declined, opting to stay in Tennessee and focus on electric music, college, and his new job as an engineer-in-training at John Fry's nascent Ardent Studio. Alex returned home a few months later and found himself at Ardent, tracking late night songs with Chris. With Chilton on board, the group abandoned cover songs in favor of originals. Alex brought "Watch the Sunrise," "When My Baby's Beside Me," "The Ballad of El Goodoo," and the riff for "In the Street." Chris had a few too: "Feel," "Try Again," and "My Life Is Right."

Each member brought something to the table, but would invariably add to the other's tunes, thus creating a new and unified sound. Chris was a British Invasion fan, and aspiring to be like the great Lennon/McCartney songwriting team, the compositions became Bell/Chilton. Chris smoothed out Alex's rough and edgy folk songs while adding something melodic, such as the beautiful thirty-second intro to "Watch the Sunrise" and the change from the subdued verse to the crashing chorus on "The Ballad of El Goodoo."

"I would suggest a few things, changes etc., to Alex's numbers and he would similarly add to mine, but really it was a separate thing," Chris said later. True to his studio's name, owner and producer John Fry let the group experiment for free after hours, and over the next year the still-unnamed group tracked their debut album.

"Well, Chris *was* in charge. I would pretty well credit him with recording and producing that LP. Of course, he had a lot of artistic help from Alex, but Chris was the technical brains behind it," Hummel said in the *Perfect Sound Forever* interview.

Ardent moved across town, and with the tracking done, Chris went into overdrive. "His producing was agonizing, very meticulous, and quite frankly a bit overdone in my opinion. He spent

ARDENT STUDIOS

Ardent Studios lives up to its name. Since 1966, when John Fry built his first equipment in his parent's garage, Ardent has been associated with quality recordings in all sorts of genres. *Led Zeppelin III* was mixed there, and Ardent has done work on albums by Isaac Hayes, Soundgarden, The Replacements, ZZ Top, The Staple Singers, Bob Dylan, Stevie Ray Vaughan, Cat Power, Waylon Jennings, Lynyrd Skynyrd, Leon Russell, The White Stripes & The Raconteurs, North Mississippi Allstars, The Allman Brothers, and many, many more.

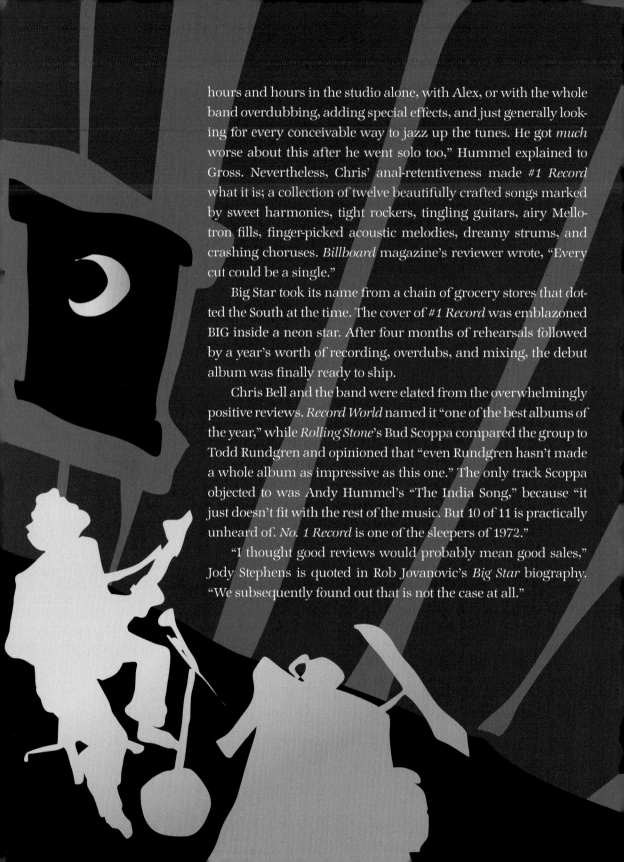

hours and hours in the studio alone, with Alex, or with the whole band overdubbing, adding special effects, and just generally looking for every conceivable way to jazz up the tunes. He got *much* worse about this after he went solo too," Hummel explained to Gross. Nevertheless, Chris' anal-retentiveness made *#1 Record* what it is; a collection of twelve beautifully crafted songs marked by sweet harmonies, tight rockers, tingling guitars, airy Mellotron fills, finger-picked acoustic melodies, dreamy strums, and crashing choruses. *Billboard* magazine's reviewer wrote, "Every cut could be a single."

Big Star took its name from a chain of grocery stores that dotted the South at the time. The cover of *#1 Record* was emblazoned BIG inside a neon star. After four months of rehearsals followed by a year's worth of recording, overdubs, and mixing, the debut album was finally ready to ship.

Chris Bell and the band were elated from the overwhelmingly positive reviews. *Record World* named it "one of the best albums of the year," while *Rolling Stone*'s Bud Scoppa compared the group to Todd Rundgren and opinioned that "even Rundgren hasn't made a whole album as impressive as this one." The only track Scoppa objected to was Andy Hummel's "The India Song," because "it just doesn't fit with the rest of the music. But 10 of 11 is practically unheard of. *No. 1 Record* is one of the sleepers of 1972."

"I thought good reviews would probably mean good sales," Jody Stephens is quoted in Rob Jovanovic's *Big Star* biography. "We subsequently found out that is not the case at all."

At the time Ardent Studios acted as an independent extension of Stax Records, and Fry and his crew of young engineers tracked the likes of Isaac Hayes, Albert King, Leon Russell, and Booker T. and the MGs for the label. With Big Star on the infant Ardent Records, Stax's machinery could come to good use. On the other side of town, Stax was eager to branch out from its usual R&B and soul records to the profitable rock & roll segment, so the two Memphis studios signed a distribution agreement. Consequently *#1 Record* was pushed through Stax's network of regional independent distributors. The problem was that those guys were used to black Memphis soul, not anglophile pop, so a lot of them were nonplussed with Big Star. Should they take in copies of this strange music or let it be? That ambivalence soon became a problem. Rave reviews and promising radio play didn't translate to fat sales since few potential buyers were able to find the disc at their local record store. Ardent countered the struggle with hard footwork, calling and shipping directly to individual stores, but it amounted to little more than a band-aid to a leg in a bear trap.

Scoppa was right on target describing *#1 Record* as a sleeper, one of those great albums that didn't generate initial buzz, but would go on to outlive most of its contemporaries.

Big Star hit the road that fall and showcased its album on at least seven dates through Tennessee, Arkansas, Georgia, Louisiana, and Mississippi. After the last gig at the University of Mississippi the band and its modest crew left Oxford. Chris's Chevy Camaro was pulled over for no apparent reason other than transporting a group of longhairs. The cops searched the vehicle, and when they found a modest amount of pot, they threw Chris and passengers Alex, Andy and friend Vera Ellis in jail. The foursome stayed there until their parents bailed them out the following day.

Bad news followed them back to Memphis. Stax had signed a new distribution deal with Columbia Records, and the latter pulled all Stax releases from the independent distributors in an effort to streamline its operations. **The move meant that the few Big Star records available for sale across the country were pulled from the shelves. The band was devastated, but Chris took it the hardest. He had put his heart and soul into the record and had seen it favorably received by the critics, only to have it thwarted by corporate machinery.**

With Chris flopping on the bottom of the barrel, his older brother David intervened by taking him out of the country on a trip to Europe. Conditions didn't improve, and David noted later that his brother "drank an alarming amount of bourbon and was generally inconsolable." Chris returned to Memphis later that fall, quit Big Star in November, returned to the band for a few sessions, and quit again. He spiraled downward in a bout of drugs and depression, and Big Star's productive environment was replaced with impulsive acts of retaliatory destruction. Acoustic guitars, vintage basses, cars, and rehearsal tapes were jabbed with screwdrivers, smashed against the wall, kicked in the parking lot, or simply disappeared.

"Then of course he was so intense about it, the failure of Ardent and Stax Records to get the first record, which we felt was good and saleable, into the stores and its resulting failure totally freaked him out. That along with the emotional turmoil going on

SEP. 7, 1978

The Who's Keith Moon (32) dies from prescribed medication intended to wean him off of alcohol.

DEC. 27, 1978

Following 40 years of dictatorship, a Spanish referendum approves a new constitution.

in his love life at the time just broke him down, and he became what we would now call clinically depressed," Hummel said in the 2001 interview. But it wasn't just that. Critics focused on Alex Chilton, which isn't surprising considering he was the only familiar name in the group. Sadly, Chris's contributions were largely ignored. More than a third of Bud Scoppa's review in February '73 was about Chilton:

"When he came to realize that picking and starving in New York wasn't necessarily on a higher karmic level than cutting slick singles in Memphis, Alex headed back home to reconcile his two musical stages and to see what he could get together. What he got together was Big Star, and Big Star is really something," Scoppa noted. Never mind that it was Chris who invited Alex into the fold. "When Alex joined up there was no fuzz on who was the band. It was the three of us with Alex joining to make it four," Andy Hummel told writer Kent Benjamin for a 2004 *Pop Culture Press* piece on Big Star.

Sonic evidence includes Chris Bell's tracks "Try Again" and "My Life Is Right" on the Rock City recordings (tracked late '69 and early '70; the rest of the band included Tom Eubanks, Jody Stephens, and Terry Manning), which were done prior to Alex Chilton's return to Memphis: they already carry the jangly Big Star sound.

From 1972–74, Chris Bell went in to rustication at his family's home, and he was bitter and confused about his sexuality. Some of Chris's friends suspected he was homosexual, and Chris may have struggled to come to terms with it. David says Chris attempted to do himself in (*"It's suicide / I know I tried it twice,"* Chris sings in "Look Up"). Even though he carried an enormous load of emotional baggage, Bell found strength to work on his music. He cut demos for new songs and continued to grow lyrically. Although he was no longer in the band, he occasionally saw the other members, and fragments of his songs ended up on Big Star's *Radio City* in the form of "O My Soul" and "Back of a Car."

David Bell worked in Europe but kept in touch with his brother through letters and the occasional visit to Memphis. He was home on summer vacation in '74 when he walked in on Chris "pulling with his teeth on a rubber tourniquet, a syringe in his hand." Chris had been terrified of syringes, but not so anymore. David saw no other option than to take him away from Memphis and the drugs. They booked studio time at a French château where Elton John had just recorded, and David said he'd bankroll an album as long as Chris stayed clean. In addition to the Bells, Ardent engineer and drummer Richard Rosebrough tagged along to help with the recording.

The Memphis trio were treated like stars by the château staff, and the studio's British engineer had a fortuitous connection. Claude Harper had worked at Apple with Beatles knob-wiz Geoff Emerick, and he was able to set up a few days with Emerick at George Martin's AIR Studios in London.

Over the course of three days at AIR, Chris laid down vocal and guitar tracks for "I Am the Cosmos," and Emerick made a new mix of the song. An acetate of Paul McCartney's "Junior's Farm" arrived on the third day, and they chuckled when they heard it was recorded in Tennessee. McCartney was due in the studio the following day, and with Emerick's help they met Paul and Linda in Studio 2's control room—the room where all the pre-Apple Beatles recordings had been put to tape. It was only a ten minute meet 'n' greet, but Chris cherished every second of it. "It was the singularly most heavy moment of my life," he said later.

Back in Memphis he reconnected with John Fry, Ardent, and even his old bandmates, who were busy finishing a third album (*Third* remained unreleased until 1978). Chilton added vocals to Chris's fragile acoustic love song called "You and Your Sister," and another friend wrote and conducted a string session for the same tune.

Around this time Chris became a reborn Christian and was so devoted he'd walk up to strangers to tell them about the gospel. His newfound religion made its way into songs like "Better Save Yourself," "There Was a Light," and "Look Up." The Lord kept him drug free and helped him stay focused and meet life with a positive outlook. Now all he needed was a record deal.

He went back to London and combed the scene with David for producers, A&R men, and journalists. At night Chris played whatever club gigs he could round up. A trip to Berlin yielded a few memorable solo spots. "When Chris was treated like a professional, he rose to the occasion brilliantly. It confirmed my belief that given the proper circumstances, his talent would truly soar," David Bell wrote in the liner notes to Chris's posthumous solo album.

Chris Bell soon drifted back to Memphis and spent the next couple of years playing locally. Jody Stephens played drums in one of these groups, The Baker Street Regulars, and their sets featured Chris's songs, tunes from the Big Star record, and a random assortment of covers. The band folded soon after Jody quit, and Chris found himself with Keith Sykes's band. He was still religious, but Sykes remembers that Chris was paradoxically fascinated with the rumors that Led Zeppelin worshipped the devil.

Bell was a ripping lead guitarist who could also pick emotional passages on his Gibson sunburst. This duality also applied to his voice: he sounded like Robert Plant yet was capable of supporting another lead with a beautiful harmony. After six years of dedication, he gave up his dream of a career in music. Instead he played tennis, attended a cultish church in Florida, and managed a Danvers, a restaurant chain owned by his father.

In the fall of '78 Chris Stamey, who ran a small label, tracked Chris down. He had heard about "I Am the Cosmos" through the

STAIRWAY TO HEAVEN

"Stairway to Heaven," Led Zeppelin's apocalyptic song from *Led Zeppelin IV*, was filled with metaphorical references to a songbird flanked by a soothing brook, two roads, the Lady who shines a white light, and pagan references to Pan as the real savior masked as the piper who will lead us to reason if we join him.

After listening to Jimmy Page tinker with the riff in front of a huge Victorian fireplace, Robert Plant grabbed a pen and spilled the lyrics onto the page. "All of a sudden my hand was writing the words. I just sat there and looked at them and almost leaped out of my seat," Plant explained later.

Hammer of the Gods—The Led Zeppelin Saga author Stephen Davis writes, "It expressed an ineffable yearning for spiritual transformation deep in the hearts of the generation for which it was intended. In time, it became their anthem." The song is still the most requested song on classic rock stations in the US.

grapevine and funded the issue of 1,000 singles with "You and Your Sister" as the B-side. "I Am the Cosmos" is Chris's masterpiece, an existential, angst-filled cry for help. It's difficult to give it a listen without being moved by Chris's flair, sincerity, and desperation. It's all there, an emotional genius cut into the vinyl grooves.

In the early morning of December 27, 1978, Chris Bell drove home in his white two-door Triumph TR-6. Chris had rehearsed with his new band earlier that evening, but he was in a weird state. He had popped a fist of Mandrax and complained about what it took to make it in the music business.

Shortly after 1 a.m. Chris wrapped the Triumph around a lamppost and died on the scene. A blood sample showed he wasn't drunk, but the hospital never checked for traces of drugs or medications. It's unlikely that he committed suicide, so friends and family have always considered it a tragic accident. Chris Bell was 27 years old, and the born-again died on John the Apostle's feast day.

Since his death more than thirty years ago, Chris Bell's legacy as a songwriter has grown steadily, especially among musicians. In 2005, psychedelic poppers the Flaming Lips compiled and released *LateNightTales*, an officially sanctioned mix tape of what they listen to at home. The collection includes "Speed of Sound," Chris's melancholic letter to a departed lover. It sums up his talents as a songwriter, vocalist, instrumentalist, and lyricist with his keen sense of harmony, the jangle of an acoustic 12-string guitar, a less-is-more guitar solo using volume swells that echo his loneliness and desperation, and finally the flawless studio production that sounds full of zest and color.

BIG STAR TODAY

Thirty-five years after Big Star's debut, the band's popularity is at an all-time high. Alex Chilton and Jody Stephens are touring as Big Star with Posies members Jon Auer and Ken Stringfellow completing the lineup. The quartet recorded *In Space* at Ardent Studios, which was released September 27, 2005, and a film crew is working on a feature-length documentary about the history of the band. No word on *Big Star Story*'s release date yet.

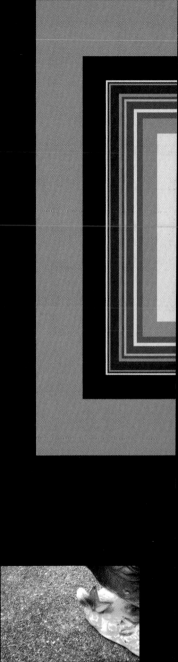

ECHO & BUNNYMEN

WITH THE EIGHTIES APPROACHING, ROCK HAD BECOME stale and idiosyncratic. Instead of looking for creative ingenuity in their artist roster, corporate labels too often relied on changing technology to cover-up artistic mediocrity. **Drums sounded like they were played on the far end of a hangar, drenched in the reverb from digital studio processors, a new technology that had just entered the market. Guitars were glossy thanks to chorus pedals, and the musicians appeared in the same sheen: hair-sprayed plastic people proudly wearing neon colored clothes, hoop earrings, and faux leather. On the surface it was the worst decade in the annals of rock.**

That said, there were a few highlights. Behind the sheen, new wave bands not only stripped the lead guitarist's badge and banished him or her (yeah, punk and new wave were rife with talented women) to focus on rhythm, texture, and melody. The movement also offered refreshing lyrical depth. The best American example is the Talking Heads, but many came from the UK. I'm referring to the Cure, pre-stadium U2, Simple Minds, Siouxsie and the Banshees, the Smiths, and Echo & the Bunnymen.

FEB. 2, 1979

Sid Vicious (21) ODs from heroin shortly after he's bailed out for the murder of his girlfriend Nancy Spungen (20).

JUNE 29, 1979

Little Feat leader Lowell George (34) dies from a heart attack.

JULY 1, 1979

The Sony Walkman goes on sale in Japan.

EDINBURGH

LIVERPOOL

LONDON

Liverpoodlians Ian McCulloch, Will Sergeant, and Les Pattinson formed the Bunnymen in 1978 as a trio and released their first single the following year on a minor label. They replaced Roland the drum machine (often assumed to be "Echo") with seventeen year-old Pete de Freitas in time for *Crocodiles*, the group's debut album.

Listen to pretty much any track from the eighties, and you can date it by the sound of the wimpy drums. Not Pete de Freitas's: his drumming was something else. He trimmed down the forest of cymbals favored by so many heavy hitters and didn't favor the studio processor's *more* knob. Instead he focused on playing clean and energetic, and utilized tams to their fullest potential.

Like his electronic predecessor, de Freitas was a machine, a human metronome, and he hit those skins with the same ferocity later made fashionable by Nirvana's Dave Grohl.

Not quite as subtle is the Bunnymen's influence on Coldplay— compare *Siberia*'s "In the Margins" to the general feel of Coldplay's *Parachutes* to hear what I mean. The influence is hardly a big secret: during Coldplay's 2002 tour Chris Martin frequently played "Lips Like Sugar" as a solo piano piece. Ian McCulloch took notice

AUG. 27, 1979

Lord Mountbatten assassinated by the IRA.

SEP. 27, 1979

Guitarist Ian McCulloch (26) of Stone the Crows and Paul McCartney's Wings ODs.

NOV. 17, 1979

Jethro Tull bassist John Glascock (28) dies from a heart defect.

and hung out during some of the recording sessions for *A Rush Of Blood To the Head.*

Ten years before Kurt Cobain and Courtney Love name-checked the Bunnymen, Courtney spent a few months latching on to the then-vibrant Liverpool scene. She was eighteen and financed the excursion with a trust fund granted by her foster parents. Love and a friend met Julian Cope of Teardrop Explodes at an after-show party at a hotel in Ireland and befriended him.

"A young girl with a dark feather cut sat in the biggest armchair, dispensing pills to everyone. She said she was 16 and her father was a road manager for The Grateful Dead (bassist Phil Lesh writes that Love's dad, Hank Harrison, was a college buddy who occasionally booked gigs for them in the early days). She said there was a picture of her on the back on the *AOXOMOXOA* album at nine years old," Cope writes in *Head-On*. "She was completely off her head, the first person I'd met who was almost intolerably crazy."

Love caught up with Teardrop Explodes in London and paid her way with LSD sent from her father in California. But after a while Cope had had enough: "She was everywhere. ... every minute of every day the Adolescent would be screaming long and into the night. I rang de Freitas and told him that I was sending the Adolescent up to Liverpool to stay with him at my old place." Cope had invited Pete to stay at his crib after Cope's ex-wife moved out. "Even at my most paranoid, I trusted Pete pretty much completely. But he wasn't the tidiest dude in the world."

The American duo quickly became a fixture at Liverpool's revitalized club scene, but Pete, who had attended a privileged public school (that's British for private) wasn't too pleased with the arrangement. "Even de Freitas, a man normally known for his capacity to chill out in the most extreme situation, was

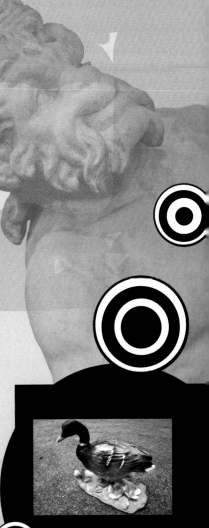

DEC. 27, 1979

Three days after invading Afghanistan, the Soviet Union installs a puppet ruler.

JAN, 1980

The Rubik's Cube goes on sale.

FEB. 19, 1980

AC/DC vocalist Bon Scott (33) dies from alcohol poisoning.

worried," Cope writes. Courtney's dad kept shipping packages laden with acid and MDA to the apartment in Cope's name. Pete finally took matters into his own hands. He threw their belongings down the stairwell and wrote a note instructing the American girls to get the hell out.

With or without adolescent visitors, the Bunnymen kept their momentum. Pete's drumming, coupled with Les's deep end support, Will's minimalist guitar playing, and Ian's ethereal voice that sang gloomy, socio-introspective lyrics pushed the band to the forefront of British music—at least in terms of critical acclaim. *Heaven Up Here* peaked at a very respectable number ten in the charts, but for most of their career, the Bunnymen chose going on a limb over the track to safe and profitable stadiums. They toured the Outer Hebrides, Iceland, and the Scottish countryside without a PA or an entourage, filled their sets with covers by the Talking Heads, the Doors, the Rolling Stones, and Wilson Pickett in Scandinavian clubs, yet the Bunnymen could sell out successive dates at London's prestigious Royal Albert Hall.

Never afraid of reinventing themselves, the band moved from post-psychedelia influenced by Velvet Underground and the Doors to a moody powerhouse, and dared to release *Ocean Rain*, a string-fuelled acoustic masterpiece from 1984. The latter showcased what de Freitas could do with a pair of soft brushes.

McColloch's hair withstanding, the Bunnymen frequently changed their appearance as well. **They pioneered Indie garb, first with camos, then with those long, black raincoats that Indie fans and bands wore through the nineties. Now you know who to hail or blame.**

Ian McCulloch became notoriously known as Mac the Mouth for his acidic outspokenness. He frequently hyperbolized the

MOBY

"When I was growing up I was obsessed with Echo & The Bunnymen," Moby mentioned in an interview. "I still love that aesthetic, that hybrid of electronic elements with rock elements and dance music that has a sort of pained, emotional quality to it."

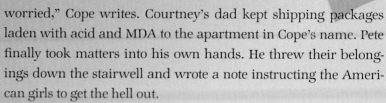

SEP. 25, 1980
Led Zeppelin drummer John Bonham (32) dies from asphyxiation after a grotesque drinking binge.

OCT. 27, 1980
T.Rex' Steve Took (31) asphyxiates on a cocktail cherry.

MAY 11, 1981
Bob Marley succumbs to cancer at 36.

Bunnymen while bringing everybody else down—especially Bono and Bruce Springsteen. "No Cuban heels and no flags, those were two of the golden rules," he said in a stab at both. Few journalists could resist printing the quote monster, but as a profession, music journalists generally agreed with Mac the Mouth. "The Bunnymen are as superior to your U2s and whatever as a peacock is to its turds," the *New Musical Express* wrote in 1984.

Later that year the band announced a year-long sabbatical from writing, touring, and recording. Pete cruised through France and Spain on his Ducati crotch rocket. After only six months the band came back with a single. Mac the Mouth's verbal onslaughts and the fact that the band still hadn't "sold out" gave them cred to keep it up. Unfortunately the Bunnymen's inter-band relations were strained. They lacked direction after *Ocean Rain*, the self-proclaimed "greatest record ever made." Pete was the only one to talk and act on his frustration. "I rather be riding me bike," he said.

In 1985, Echo & the Bunnymen headlined the prestigious Glastonbury Festival, and they were confident enough to hit the stage without a setlist. In the midst of a dark, rainy evening, they threw down a wide selection of covers (including the Rolling Stones' "Paint It Black," James Brown's "Sex Machine," Bob Dylan's "It's All Over Now Baby Blue," and the Doors' "Soul Kitchen"), dug deep into their catalog, and premiered a couple of new tracks. Both the crowd and music critics left ecstatic from the sheer raw power of the set.

A few months later a slick single titled "Bring On the Dancing Horses" was released to great reviews. "Without resorting to any kind of crass commercial strategy, 'Bring On the Dancing Horses' sounds like its been aimed straight at the top," *New Musical Express* opinioned and added that it was "monumentally moving."

MAR. 20, 1982	MAY 8, 1982	NOV. 30, 1982	1983
Ozzy Osbourne guitarist Randy Rhoads (25) dies in a plane crash.	Legendary Canadian racecar driver Gilles Villeneuve dies in his No. 27 Ferrari.	Michael Jackson's Thriller released; it goes platinum 27 times over.	The Compact Disc, the original 8-bit Nintendo, and the McNugget all hit the market.

Sounds Magazine dubbed it "a slick electro-kaleidoscope," while *Melody Maker*'s reviewer praised it "Single of the year." Unmoved by the reviews, de Freitas simply wasn't psyched on it: "I think it sounds a bit flat ... it's absolutely polished. I prefer the demo. That's got an edge to it."

Any band that's been around for more than a few years ultimately releases some sort of *Best Of* collection. Bunnymen's was released later that year with the title *Songs To Learn and Sing*. Always the cynic, Pete commented, "The company want us to reach a broader audience, and it's their idea of a way to do it. They think it'll help." It did. *Songs To Learn and Sing* quickly became a dorm room favorite, but behind the scenes the Bunnymen were bickering among themselves. They'd released some fantastic albums and succeeded as the indie cool big-name alternative to mainstream, but they had no idea what to play from there. "I still feel like I want to get out every other minute," Pete said. "If you're working closely with the same people all the time, it's obvious that you're going to get fed up."

Les Pattinson asked de Freitas to be his baby's godfather, but New Year's Eve—the day before her christening—Pete called from the airport and said he wouldn't make it. He craved a radical change and had dreamed up a philosophy based on artist and percussionist Tim Whittaker's "Duck" paintings and Bokononism, an invented religion in Kurt Vonnegut's *Cat's Cradle*. Nah, he wasn't looking for TV-style salvation; it was something temptingly unholy, a quest far more important than the Bunnymen and a christening. At least he had the decency to announce his departure. *As Bokonon tells us, "It is never a mistake to say goodbye."*

De Freitas flew to New Orleans with Tim Whittaker, Andy Eastwood, Johnno, and Send No Flowers's Tim O'Shea. The

MAR. 1, 1983

Swatch introduces its iconic watches.

JULY 25, 1983

Metallica releases its debut album Kill 'Em All.

OCT. 25, 1983

Microsoft releases its first version of Word.

fearless five set up shop in the finest hotel Pete could find and became The Sex Gods. Pete decided he'd sing and play guitar, and Bunnymen-extra Mike Mooney and Psychedelic Furs' sax player Mars Williams joined the ad hoc crew. The Sex Gods soon became synonymous with one of rock's worst debaucheries, orchestrated and funded by Mad Louis, Pete's new alter ego.

There was an improvised looseness surrounding the crew in NOLA—part Bokononism, part the Duck. Whittaker explained the theory of The Duck as sort of a middle road. There's good, there's bad, and somewhere in between is the Duck. Pete took it one step further. The Duck represented the ultimate good. At one time it had been Indo-Europe's most important sacrificial animal, and Pete infused it with all sorts of mythological power, some real, some invented. In Julian Cope's words, "By the time Pete was finished, the Duck had, in his own mind, become a shaman spirit which would descend upon The Sex Gods and fill them with an awe-inspiring Michigas, or Creative Spirit."

De Freitas shut out the Bunnymen's Liverpool, but he kept Julian Cope updated on the group's outrageous outings and frantic fragments of his metamorphosing philosophy: "From my end of the telephone ... it just sounded as though they were all taking large amounts of drugs," Cope wrote later. Instead of being infused with the Duck's savory creative power, Pete's trip mached straight toward the wall of self-destruction.

De Freitas nearly stopped eating and substituted old-fashioned nutrients with acid, molly, booze, and cocaine. He stayed awake for eighteen days straight, keeping a barrier between himself and everybody else with a pair of mirrored sunglasses. To avoid falling asleep Pete abstained from sitting down, opting instead to circumambulate the room while manically scribbling his thoughts in a notebook. Andy, by the way, was the appointed

1984

The Sony CD Walkman (known as the Discman) enters the market, offering portability and 16-bit sound for those on the go.

NOV. 25, 1984

Nearly fifty musicians record "Do They Know It's Christmas?" under the moniker Band Aid.

JUNE 27, 1985

The legendary Route 66, which began construction in 1927, is decommissioned.

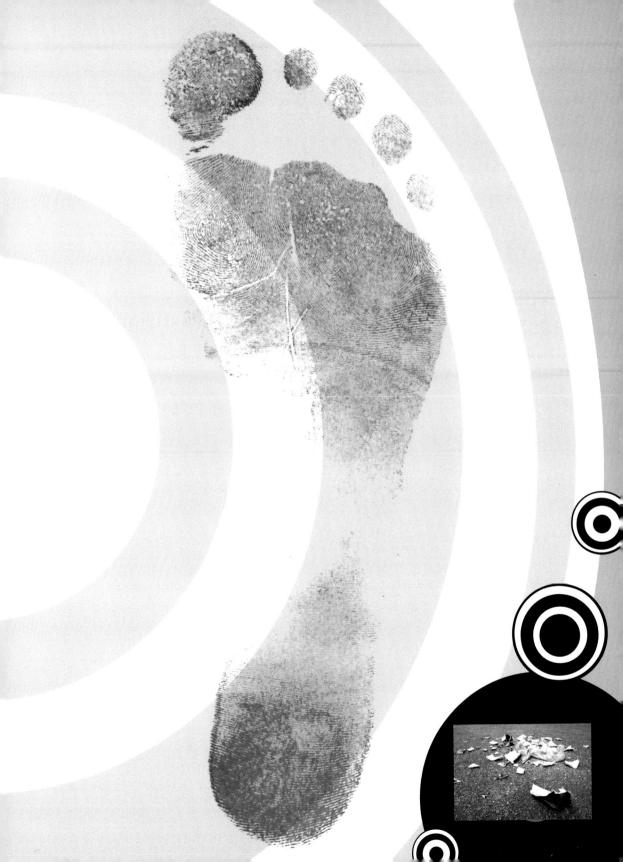

biographer and documented the debacle for posterity using a film camera, tape recorder, and a large book that was known as *The God Logs*. *"Write it all down," Bokonon tells us.*

"I was philosophizing with a sledgehammer," Pete admitted later. "I was very much involved with what I was thinking, which I guess was bordering on insanity. I just thought I'd take it to its limit." And nobody argues that he didn't. He showered at least three times a day to wash away the tingling sensation stemming from the combination of sleeplessness and too many drugs.

During a two-week stretch, the fine print about operating heavy machinery was clearly illegible to de Freitas, who managed to total an old Dodge Meadowbrook, a '72 Vista Cruiser, and two motorcycles. The Bunnymen had a tour planned, but Pete called Mac, resigned, and asked for £15,000 as restitution for all the smokes Mac had bummed off of him over the years. The singer never sent the money, but shipped a few cartons in the mail along with a note asking the AWOL drummer to return home.

The request went unheeded, so manager Bill Drummond flew over to talk some sense into the deserting drummer. Unexpectedly, he found the bizarre scene inspirational.

"He was literally king of the world out there, calling himself Mad Louis, living this extraordinary dissolute lifestyle straight out of a Jack Kerouac novel in which anything was possible. And it really was until the money ran out and he had to come home to reality," Drummond noted three years later. He added that Pete's mentality inspired him quit his management gig back in Liverpool and start recording his own album (which includes a thank-you song titled "Ballad For a Sex God.")

With the coffers depleted, debts piled high all over town, and

JAN. 4, 1986

Thin Lizzy frontman Phil Lynott (36) dies from heart failure and pneumonia.

SEP. 27, 1986

Metallica bassist Cliff Burton (24) dies after the tour bus crashes in Sweden.

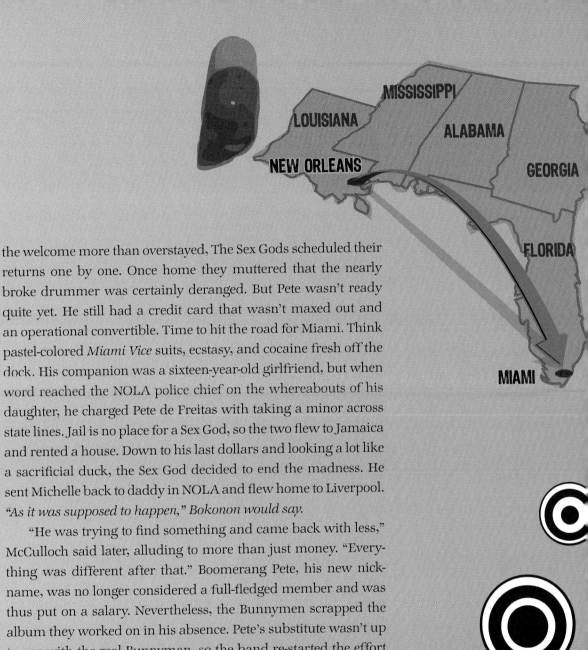

the welcome more than overstayed, The Sex Gods scheduled their returns one by one. Once home they muttered that the nearly broke drummer was certainly deranged. But Pete wasn't ready quite yet. He still had a credit card that wasn't maxed out and an operational convertible. Time to hit the road for Miami. Think pastel-colored *Miami Vice* suits, ecstasy, and cocaine fresh off the dock. His companion was a sixteen-year-old girlfriend, but when word reached the NOLA police chief on the whereabouts of his daughter, he charged Pete de Freitas with taking a minor across state lines. Jail is no place for a Sex God, so the two flew to Jamaica and rented a house. Down to his last dollars and looking a lot like a sacrificial duck, the Sex God decided to end the madness. He sent Michelle back to daddy in NOLA and flew home to Liverpool. *"As it was supposed to happen,"* Bokonon would say.

"He was trying to find something and came back with less," McCulloch said later, alluding to more than just money. "Everything was different after that." Boomerang Pete, his new nickname, was no longer considered a full-fledged member and was thus put on a salary. Nevertheless, the Bunnymen scrapped the album they worked on in his absence. Pete's substitute wasn't up to par with the real Bunnyman, so the band re-started the effort with blank reels. Former Doors keyboard player Ray Manzarek joined the quartet in the studio and added his signature organ

APR. 27, 1987

Time magazine sports U2 on the cover as "Rock's Hottest Ticket."

licks to a remake of "Bedbugs and Ballyhoo" as well as a cover of "People Are Strange" that found its way onto *The Lost Boys* soundtrack. "They're one of my favorite bands," Manzarek told *Rolling Stone*. The Doors connection that had long lurked in the shadows was out in the open.

In a rare candid moment with Bunnymen biographer Chris Adams, McCulloch admitted that the odd "Zimbo" chant heard in 1981's "All My Colours" originated at a rehearsal session where he started singing "Jimbo, Jimbo, Jimbo" as a nod to Jim Morrison. The song, which is about holding on to something that's already lost, has since featured the cryptic chant, which is repeated like a mantra: "*Zimbo, Zimbo, Zimbo, Zimbo, Zimbo... Zimbo, Zimbo, Zimbo, Zimbo, Zimbo.*"

In hindsight the recordings with Manzarek ended an era—the Bunnymen couldn't take each other any longer. McCulloch decided it was time to leave, while the remaining trio surprisingly decided to push on with a new singer. Pete might've kept it up so he would still have a paycheck to bankroll his latest band. No longer The Sex Gods, Andy Eastwood, Tim Whittaker, and de Freitas formed The Divine Thunderbolt Corps with two other guys and de Freitas's new girlfriend singing lead. DTC's sets consisted of old spirituals and obscure country songs on which Pete played either drums, banjo, or guitar.

In 1989, Julian Cope invited Pete and Andy to help him plan a video for a new song titled "China Doll." The video's plot was developing attraction between a young girl and a good-looking, mysterious motorcycle man—a role Pete knew how to play extremely well. The vid came together nicely, and after it was produced Pete excitedly saddled up on his motorcycle hugging two huge plastic bags filled with videotapes meant for the Liverpool crowd. Cope suggested that shuttling two hundred or so miles from London

with that kind of cargo wasn't the safest strategy, but Pete just shrugged and rode off with an unconcerned smile worthy of the WWII kamikazes DTC was named after.

Two months later, on June 14, 1989, Pete left London once again for Liverpool. An old lady named Hannah Cantrell entered freeway A51 without looking for oncoming traffic, and Pete slammed into her car going 60 miles per hour. He died instantly. Pete de Freitas was only 27 years old and the proud father of a baby named Lucy.

Eulogies followed quickly by Cope, the Bunnymen, and manager Bill Drummond. The latter said Pete "was the one who could talk to each of them when they weren't talking to each other" and added that "he always loved being in a rock & roll band, living in hotels and all that, while the others loathed touring and only wanted to get back to Liverpool."

Pete embodied rock & roll like no drummer since Keith Moon—both were inventive musicians and notorious partiers. Moon dug through hotel room walls, while The Sex God transcended Hunter S. Thompson's druggie exaggerations and lived to tell about it.

De Freitas was fuelled by an existential drive to race off the highway, opting to explore the narrow back roads. Cope succinctly jotted in his journal that de Freitas was "more interested in the journey than the destination." Pete's been dead for nearly two decades, but the spirit of The Duck still darts somewhere across the skies on an Italian-made motorcycle.

LOVE'S PETE

In December '97 Courtney Love stuck a photo of Pete de Freitas in her journal and wrote, "Looking at pictures from Liverpool. How sad it makes me seeing this old Bunnymen book. Pete de Freitas RIP."

Courtney and the rest of Hole included the Bunnymen's "Do It Clean" in many live sets, but they weren't the only ones to cover their songs. The Flaming Lips played "All That Jazz" for a while and Pavement closed out shows with "Killing Moon."

The Bunnymen's atmospheric music lends itself to soundtracks. Listen for "Killing Moon" in *Donnie Darko* (2001) and *Grosse Pointe Blank* (1997) and "Bring On the Dancing Horses" in *Pretty In Pink* (1986).

CONTRARY TO WHAT MOST RECORD EXECS AND MAIN-stream America thought, Nirvana's "Smells Like Teen Spirit," didn't emerge without warning from the damp woods of the Pacific Northwest. The band's pre-MTV growth and buzz was the product of more than a decade of laborious efforts by the underground music movement.

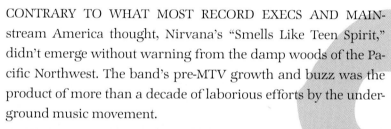

At the tail end of the seventies, stadium rock and glitzy disco dominated the charts. Although it was enough to satisfy listeners at large, small fractions of dissatisfied urban youth revolted. Using pawnshop instruments and often fuelled by emotion more than technical skill, first generation punk screamed like stepping on a rusty nail.

Punk's gloomy outlook sprung from a different seed than flower power's, but the two species had a lot in common. Both renounced the status quo, and musical chops didn't preclude anybody from writing songs and starting a band.

210

The landscape had changed significantly in the ten or so years that had passed since the Summer of Love. Clubs either booked soulless cover bands or had been converted into discos. Punk changed that. The money wasn't yet in it, but dimmed lights and cans of second-hand paint converted run-down basements across the country into a network of happening venues for the burgeoning underground. "Punk brought the club scene back and there were a lot of artist-people making expressions. It was very empowering," Minutemen-alum Mike Watt says today.

Lurking in the shadows of the American eighties was a creative clique of young groups that kept punk's Do It Yourself spirit alive, furthering the art of rock without support from the industry. Bands and die-hard fans created underground labels, fanzines, and mixed tapes as tools to spread their music to the people.

LA-based Black Flag created its own label called SST, and its first signing was a nascent trio named the Minutemen from San Pedro, California. Contrary to popular belief, the name was not a reflection on the length of their songs, but a reference to the colonial elite militia—and a kick in the nuts to a group of right

wing reactionaries that had been active in the sixties.

Singer and guitarist Dennes Boon was into history and was a proactive observant of the messy geo-politics of the day. Frightened by the Cold War's nuclear standoff and Reaganism's financial and military support of brutal Latin American regimes, D. knew instinctively that the past can teach us a lot about the present and the future. The colonial minutemen fought from tree to tree in civilian clothes against an outnumbered force fighting in a perfect column or a line. They were elite vigilantes that stood up for the common man against the uniform—a fitting analogy to the trio's philosophy.

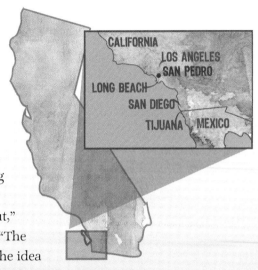

"When the 1970s ended, punk rockers burned out," Minutemen bassist Mike Watt told me in Denver. "The Minutemen were caught in a weird space. We liked the idea of self-reliance, but didn't think punk was a specific kind of music. To us it was more a state of mind. Ten years later they called it alternative music."

The Minutemen wrote songs, dozens of them, but they were almost anti-songs. Traditional song structure was abandoned, often lacking choruses and cut short, hardly clocking in at over a minute, yet the listener could always extract a piece of wisdom, a thought or an epiphany from the harmonious whirlwind.

Many of Boon's songs were about self-inquiry and often spawned from heated discussions with Watt on long drives in the Ford Econo van between gigs. "We'd discuss everything," Watt says. "I'd ask him, '*What's on your mind D?*' and we'd discuss what was going on and what needed to get done." On more than one occasion they pulled over to settle heated arguments fist to fist.

D. Boon was a working-class hero, the kind that shows up every other generation or so to prove once again that mad chops and good looks aren't prerequisites for stardom—personality, a message, and a talent for musical hooks will do.

He bounced, he shook, his guitar rasped and shrieked, and he screamed about politics, injustice, and pedestrian life. His guitar sound—always sinewy clean, never distorted—contrasted Watt's deep bass, and the two formed a musical yin and yang of sorts, while drummer George Hurley completed the circle.

To cut costs and keep it, to use Minutemen lingo, econo, the band booked studio time at night, recorded on used tape, were well-rehearsed, and recorded tracks in the order intended for the album so the master didn't have to be sequenced. Unlike most bands, the Minutemen used albums to promote their shows, not the other way around.

"We divided our world into gigs and fliers," Watt says. "A mix tape, radio interview, record, and poster were all fliers, just means to get people to come to the gig, which was all that mattered." SST couldn't accommodate their voluminous output, so the band often gave away songs to tape fanzines and radio stations, which brought attention to the band and upcoming gigs in the area.

CALEXICO

Indie rockers Calexico covered "Corona" with a mariachi horn arrangement on their 2004 EP *Convict Pool*, and Yonder Mountain String Band included a live version of the same song on *Mountain Tracks, Vol. 4.*, released in 2006.

By the early eighties the web of underground clubs in urban centers around the country served punk and hardcore bands like the Minutemen, Black Flag, Hüsker Dü, the Dead Kennedys, Sonic Youth, the Replacements, X (which was produced by Ray Manzarek), and many, many more.

Just like *That '70s Show* introduced Big Star to a national audience, Minutemen's *mersh* contribution is the song "Corona," which was adopted as the theme song for MTV's *Jackass* in 1999.

The lyrics are typical Minutemen: an epigram complete with musings on how scarcity leads to greed leads to emptiness, then

> *I could see it in my eyes there on the beach*
> *I only had a Corona*
> *five cent deposit.*

Not bad for a fifty-one word song.

"Corona" came off of Minutemen's post-punk opus: *Double Nickels On the Dime*, a cataclysmic double that spanned spoken word, jazzy punk, longhaired country, chicken funk, "Three Car Jam," and beyond. Boon's angular guittacks, rhythmic stutter, and frantic solos had veteran reviewer David Fricke write, "*Double Nickels*' best moments go far too quickly." It's difficult to linger Grateful Dead-style when forty-five tracks are pressed into four sides of vinyl. *Rolling Stone* included *Double Nickels* on its 500 Greatest Albums of All Time in 2003. Not bad for a record that was mixed in one night and cost $1,500 to record.

Hardcore fans responded favorably to Fricke's back-to-back review of the Minutemen with SST labelmate Hüsker Dü's double *Zen Arcade*. Reader Danny Catalano of Florida commended *RS* for having "once again shown a knowledge of the new and progressive music scene that so many other publications lack. Although punk may be dead, the American hardcore scene is still alive and trashing and, for those brave enough to look below the surface,

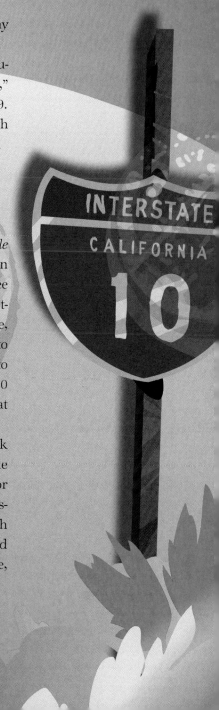

HISTORY LESSON

still putting out some of the most exciting, intelligent and politically active music since the Sixties." *Rolling Stone* largely ignored the hardcore scene in favor of corporate rock, but by 1985 it was at least trying. Sure, Fricke mixed up Mike Watt and George Hurley in his review, but the publication continued its fascination a few months later with a feature titled "Punk Lives."

The following year R.E.M.'s Michael Stipe listed Minutemen EP *Project: Mersh* in his top ten picks of year. For the Minutemen it was a brave departure. *Project: Mersh* was expensive ($2,400), especially when you consider it had only six songs (some even had choruses!). The extra cost paid for fade-outs, a couple of trumpet solos, and first class production.

The title was a pun on the music biz, audiences who buy into it, and themselves (maybe *this* will help us reach listeners on college radio?). The record sold miserably in comparison to *Double Nickels*, but it was a cleverly titled experiment instigated by SST.

Nevertheless, Stipe was a big fan, and R.E.M. invited the Minutemen to support them on a tour at the end of 1985. R.E.M. was an extremely happening band at the time, but Hurley, Watt, and Boon hadn't heard of them. They were in a different scene, and since the Minutemen read fanzines, not national music rags, they had never heard of R.E.M.

The Minutemen still rolled econo, while R.E.M.'s growth from the coolest band in Athens, Georgia, to a national act that played for 2,000 to 5,000 people, meant that there was a certain culture clash. R.E.M.'s crew, record company, and production manager made life miserable for the Minutemen. "The only four guys who liked us was the band," Watt lamented in Michael Azerrad's *Our Band Could Be Your Life*.

R.E.M. invited San Pedro's finest up on stage for the final encore of the tour. "It was the last time I played with D. and I played guitar—I was his bass player!" Watt says. The Minutemen joined

R.E.M. on "See No Evil," a song by Television, a mutual inspiration.

A few days later Boon left for Phoenix to spend Christmas with his girlfriend Linda Kite's family. He was ill with fever and slept in the back of the van, while Linda drove and her sister Janine rode shotgun. They had driven through the night from San Pedro, and it was about four o'clock when Linda zoned out at the wheel. She woke up in the median, but overcorrected and flipped the van. The two sisters suffered minor injuries, while D. launched through the backdoor, broke his neck, and died on impact with the Dime. "I had just turned 28 and he was 27," Watt remembers. "I still haven't seen his grave, you know." More than twenty years after that tragic accident he still chokes up every time he talks about his best friend's death: "I know where it is, but I just can't make myself go up there." Instead he opts to celebrate Boon's birthday every year by writing him a poem.

"You can bet that in ten years there'll be groups who sound like the Minutemen—maybe they'll even cover their songs," wrote Mark Coleman in a review of the posthumous *3-Way Tie (for Last)*. No band that followed sounded like the Minutemen, but their influence is heard in bands such as the Red Hot Chili Peppers (who dedicated 1991's *BloodSugarSexMagik* to Mike Watt) and Sublime. Bradley Nowell, who only made it to twenty-eight, sampled Boon declaring *"Punk rock changed our lives"* for the intro to "Waiting For My Ruca," the first track on Sublime's debut album *40 Oz. To Freedom*.

the year is 1985

HÜSKER DÜ

As soon as Hüsker Dü signed with Warner Bros. Records in 1986 the group became one of the first hardcores accused of selling out (another early "sell-out" were The Replacements who signed with Sire and released *Tim* in late '85. Most fans feel that 1984's *Zen Arcade* (a double album timed by SST to be co-released with Minutemen's *Double Nickels On the Dime*) is far superior to WB-released *Candy Apple Grey* and *Warehouse: Songs and Stories*. But the latter were products of the band's internal turbulence, not the influence of their label. Hüsker Dü took pride in that they retained complete artistic control in the WB deal and that the label would reach places where SST's limited distribution network wouldn't. Sonic Youth and other alternative bands that followed used Hüsker Dü's deal as a blueprint for their own move to the majors.

On the eve of Hüsker Dü's *Warehouse* tour in '87 manager David Savoy committed suicide. "I take full responsibility for [David's] suicide," Grant Hart told Q magazine in 2006. "It was a direct result of the pressure of working for Bob [Mould] and me, because he was being forced into a two-faced situation."

The two songwriters struggled with addictions and creative and personal differences, and Savoy was thrown in the middle. He was only 24 years old when he jumped off a bridge to his death. Mould characterizes Savoy's suicide as "the beginning of the end" of the band, which folded a few months later.

BY THE MID-EIGHTIES BLACK FLAG'S SST LABEL HAD ESTABlished itself as a lightning rod, and its prodigious releases bore a distinct quality that wasn't found on any other label, big or small. In 1985, *Los Angeles Times* noted, "The company has matured into a showcase for some of the best alternative rock bands in the country." Of course the money wasn't there to support more than the basic activity of any label—releasing records. "You have to be prepared to sleep on the floor," SST's Jordan Schwartz said in a feature where Michael Goldberg gauged the temperature of the hardcore scene for *Rolling Stone*.

SST was like Motown Records had been back in its heyday: It represented a *sound*. The label's roster included Bad Brains, Dinosaur Jr, Hüsker Dü, the Meat Puppets, Negativland, Saccharine Trust, Screaming Trees, and Sonic Youth. All those groups were rooted in punk and hardcore, but would add their own unique twist to the mix that set them apart from the rest, be it heavy guitars, pop sensibilities, drone tunings, speed or slur. Even with their inherent differences, the SST label unified them in some sort of underground/hardcore/alternative way, and the kids bought into it. "By the time I was 17, it was probably getting

a bit ridiculous: if it wasn't on SST, I didn't want to know about it," Dave Lang wrote in a retrospective article about SST Records for *Perfect Sound Forever*, an online mag that stocks an impressive cache of original music essays and interviews. "There was something just so mythical about the label; the selection of bands was so eclectic, yet so keeping in line with [the] individualist aesthetic it so firmly believed in."

SUB POP RECORDS

Sub Pop Records, although no longer a true indie label (Warner Music Group owns 49 percent) is still successful with bands like The Go! Team, Fleet Foxes, Iron and Wine, Postal Service, Flight Of The Conchords, Band of Horses, and The Shins.

Bruce Pavitt was a Seattleite who watched intently from the trenches of DIYism. He spent the early eighties publishing a fanzine named Sub Pop that focused on bands from the Pacific Northwest and the Midwest. He deliberately chose those two regions because they were largely ignored by the New York & Calicentric record industry. For a while he alternated print issues with compilation tapes of underground bands, and he was quite successful, at least with his acute sense of who was making it happen.

By the mid-eighties Pavitt penned a regular column for Seattle's alternative weekly, *The Rocket*, but he was anxious to start a label. He studied the rise and fall of specialized and alternative labels and learned from their trajectories. Sub Pop Records was born after he enlisted KCMU DJ and promoter Jonathan Poneman as his partner and investor.

The label's first releases were Soundgarden's *Dry As A Bone* and an EP by Green River, a Seattle-area band that included future members of both Mudhoney and Pearl Jam.

"I remember Bruce [Pavitt] putting his arms around us and telling us that Seattle was just going to be the hugest thing—before anybody had ever suggested it. Both those guys were visionaries,"

JUNE 25, 1988	AUG. 12, 1988	MAR. 24, 1989	AUG. 1989
Red Hot Chili Pepper's Hillel Slovak (26) dies from a heroin overdose.	Grafitti artist Jean-Michel Basquiat (27) succumbs to a speedball.	Exxon Valdez hits Prince William Sound's Bligh Reef, spilling 11 million gallons of Alaskan crude.	Nintendo's Game Boy debuts in the US.

Soundgarden's Chris Cornell said in an interview in 1994.

Soundgarden, Mudhoney, and TAD quickly became the label's most promising bands, integral to Pavitt and Poneman's strategy. They painted a picture of Seattle that only existed in their heads, but they figured shrewd promotion, marketing, and hype would help create it. Even though Seattle lacked a decent club for up and coming bands, Sub Pop marketed it as the new rock city. Charles Peterson's stark and gritty black and whites captured its image, and Jack Endino's bare-bones production epitomized its sound.

In 1988, the financially strapped label splurged on airfare for a select group of British music writers to attend Lamefest, their annual artist showcase. Cobain biographer Charles Cross writes that the name was "a stroke of genius: It immediately disarmed any possible criticism, while appealing to the disaffected music fans who wore T-shirts that read 'Loser' (the label sold as many of these as they did records)."

Sup Pop's strategy paid off—"Grunge City" was favorably covered on the other side of the Atlantic with Mudhoney as its flagship. Mudhoney's Mark Arm, Seattle's premier opinion-maker, had coined grunge in the mid-eighties to describe the local strain of metal-infused punk, but it was already starting to become a catch-all term for bands from the Northwest. "It was just overkill—sheer overkill and maximum hype," Pavitt admitted in 1992.

A little farther down on Lamefest's bill was a band called Nirvana. The show marked the official release of the group's first album, Bleach.

Since the band's inception in 1986 Kurt Cobain and Krist Novoselic had gone through several names and four drummers. They'd played a few dozen gigs in the Puget Sound area and had

NOV. 9, 1989	FEB. 11, 1990	MAR. 19, 1990
The 27-mile wall that divided East and West Berlin finally falls.	*The South African apartheid regime releases Nelson Mandela; he was cumulatively incarcerated for 27 years.*	*Mother Love Bone's lead singer Andrew Wood (24) ODs.*

JOHN PEEL
(1939-2004)

was a legendary English DJ who worked for BBC Radio 1 from '67 until his death thirty-seven years later. Peel wasn't bound by a specific musical style, he just played music he liked. Peel was one of the first to spin reggae and punk on British airwaves and was also an early champion of electronica. Over the course of his long career, more than two thousand artists recorded four thousand live-in-studio sessions for his program known as *Peel Sessions*.

cut a demo that Kurt carpet-bombed to labels across the industry, but Nirvana was only one of innumerable hopefuls. More than anything Cobain wanted to be on Touch and Go or SST. Black Flag/SST's Greg Ginn remembers listening to the tape but felt that "they were not that original. It wasn't bad, but it wasn't great either."

Pavitt and Poneman heard it differently and offered to release Nirvana's first single. "I was definitely grabbed by Kurt's voice. It was so emotionally versatile. There were some great songs there as well. But it was different. There was a confident quality that most other demos lacked," Poneman told the *Seattle Times* in 2008. There was no contract involved and the band never made a dime from "Love Buzz," but at least the 1,000 singles run established them as recording artists. Nirvana scraped together a tour up and down the West Coast, playing for audiences that were scarcely larger than the number of people who worked the venue.

With Sub Pop in dire straits, Nirvana paid $600 to record *Bleach* (actually guitarist Jason Everman loaned them the money and was never repaid), but it still bore Sub Pop's logo and was distributed through their channels. The songs covered a range of styles, so the album sounded a little schizoid, but it was a promising first effort. The upside was that college radio DJs could play several cuts from *Bleach* without sounding redundant.

Everman made the trio a quartet, and they hit the road for Nirvana's first national tour, which was scheduled to last two months. The crowds were a little bigger than they had been on their previous tour, but it was still a struggle. They crashed on people's floors or pulled off the road to sleep and didn't eat much to save money for gas. The tour kept on rolling thanks to proceeds from peddling T-shirts that read, "Nirvana: Fudge Packin', Crack Smokin', Satan Worshipin' Motherfuckers." They'd also acquired

JAN. 8, 1991

Def Leppard's Steve Clark (30) dies from a mix of uppers, downers, and alcohol.

MAR. 1, 1991

Oliver Stone's The Doors biopic recruits a new generation of fans.

the habit of smashing their instruments at the end of most sets, and although they were pawnshop finds, the routine took a toll on the band's depleted coffer.

Kurt's health started to deteriorate during the tour. Even though it was summer, he carried a constant cold and his stomach flared up in agonizing pain. The band blamed his diet. He absconded from drinking and smoking, but refused to eat vegetables and dined exclusively on fried, fatty foods.

The tour ended when Kurt decided it was time to go home. They skipped two weeks of dates and drove from New York to Seattle in fifty hours. Jason was out of the band, but in true Kurt style, Nirvana's leader avoided the confrontation and never told Jason to his face, he just stopped calling.

Back in Seattle, the band fixed their tattered equipment and recorded tracks for the *Blew* EP. "About A Girl" summed up the direction Kurt's songwriting was headed. It was largely autobiographical (about how his father had wanted Kurt's sister to be a boy) and featured a heavy sound, vocal harmonies, and a catchy hook.

In the fall of '89 Nirvana packed up with TAD for a European tour that coincided with a date in Berlin the day after the Wall came down. The posse numbered eleven, and it didn't take long before the van felt like a small cage with too many monkeys. But at least Nirvana played in rooms filled with captivated audiences. The hype write-ups jammed *Bleach* firmly in the British indie chart's top ten, and legendary DJ John Peel eagerly invited the trio to cut tracks for his show. With the exception of a few concert reviews, the British press had nothing but praise for Nirvana. To the band's cancerous dismay, the pretense for most of the articles was that the three logger dudes from Nirvana were backwoods, rednecked, trailer trash from wood pulp Aberdeen, USA.

Potential fans were easily fascinated by the image, but Kurt wavered over whether to love or loathe Sub Pop's deliberate stigmatization—at least in the beginning. The marketing ploy worked to their advantage and Nirvana became the new voice: an angry, fiercely energetic, talented, and lyrically intriguing group.

By mid-1990, Sub Pop churned out new discs weekly, but cash wasn't coming in nearly as fast as the label's burn rate. The company's distribution channels were still in a quagmire, and co-funding dozens of bands on the road at any given time proved expensive, all while trying to match major label offers who were by now extremely interested in the alternative music scene. Sonic Youth, Dinosaur Jr, Teenage Fanclub, and fIREHOSE—Mike Watt and George Hurley's new trio—had all left indie for the big league, so Nirvana thought it might be the way to go for them, too.

If external turbulence wasn't enough, Kurt and Krist decided it was time to can Chad. This time the duo manned up and told the drummer to his face that it was time to split ways. Danny Peters replaced Chad on drums, but not for long. Nirvana had their eyes on Dave Grohl, the drummer for a DC hardcore band named Scream, and when Scream folded they invited Dave to come up to Seattle. "We knew in two minutes that he was the right drummer," Krist told Michael Azerrad in *Come As You Are*. Grohl shared a similar musical background with the duo and really got Kurt's songs. But most of all he was a loud hitter in the tradition of Zep's John Bonham and Bunnymen's Pete de Freitas.

With Dave on board, Nirvana finally gelled as well as it ever would, both artistically and socially. Dave moved in with Kurt, and the two delinquents shared an extremely gross apartment in Olympia. Cleaning wasn't on their agenda—not much was. They spent most of their downtime either sleeping or mute, but at least the evenings were filled with rehearsals. Kurt did, however, develop a new hobby of sorts: he nursed a once-a-week heroin habit.

After an intense courting period by all the major labels, Nirvana went for a strong deal with Geffen, Sonic Youth's new home. Pavitt and Poneman felt betrayed, but they weren't capable of breaking Nirvana to the world-at-large in the way that Geffen could. On the upside, the buyout kept Sub Pop away from declaring bankruptcy.

Nirvana recorded *Smells Like Teen Spirit* in LA, and Dave introduced them to a certain Courtney Love, whom he knew through his ex-girlfriend. Kurt and Courtney had met two years earlier after a show in Portland.

Love was a notorious chick on the indie circuit and her band, Hole, had just released its debut album. Pretty On the Inside burned up the charts, especially in the UK where the music press fed on her persona with similar anthropological candor as it had with Kurt.

Courtney Love's apartment in LA was conveniently down the street from Nirvana's recording studio, a geographical advantage conducive to flirting. By their own accounts, the two lovers bonded over drugs and mutual respect for the other's music. For those around that witnessed the odd mating ritual, Kurt and Courtney were a perfect match.

1991

JAN. 12, 1992

*Sony introduces the
MiniDisc recorder.*

AUG. 18, 1992

*Wanderer Chris
McCandless (24) starves
to death in the Alaskan
wilderness.*

1992

*The US Constitution's
27th Amendment ratified.*

The Next NIRVANA

SMELLS LIKE TEEN SPIRIT CONQUERED THE WORLD IN 1991, and Nirvana became the first power trio to make it BIG since the Jimi Hendrix Experience. Grunge meant fuzzy punk, but that didn't matter to the press who were quick to lump Pearl Jam (straight-up rock), Soundgarden (dark rock with odd time meters), and Nirvana (poppy punk) kings of the Seattle grunge movement. It was like the "Summer of Love" all over again for mainstream media, descending on Seattle this time instead of San Francisco.

MSM's incessant quench for everything grunge led to the infamous "Lexicon on Grunge" hoax. A *New York Times* reporter named Rick Marin hounded Sub Pop sales rep Megan Jasper for grunge slang until she finally caved in and fed him what he asked for. The *NYT* published a sidebar with the terms Jasper craftily invented for the article. Grungers, whoever they were, never used *lamestain* to describe the uncool, nor was *wack slacks* a term for ratty jeans. Frank Thomas exposed the hoax in his journal *The Baffler*, and *NYT* demanded an apology, believing Thomas was a prankster. His response was piercing: "when The Newspaper of Record goes searching for the Next Big Thing and the Next Big Thing piddles on its leg, we think that's funny."

Kurt Cobain probably thought it was funny too. He hated the term "grunge," but given the amount of press it received, the "King of Grunge" was hard-pressed to fight what had granted him fame. It was a contradiction that would feed his internal struggle for the rest of his life.

Nirvana sounded new compared to their musical peers on MTV, but Kurt mined the past for influences. He had the punker's DIY ethic, wore flannel shirts like the beats and Neil Young, wrote poppy songs influenced by the Beatles, and cranked the amp for distortion. Cobain found his voice with songs about his dysfunctional family, abandonment, teenage rebellion, loneliness and frustration. He wrote what he knew, as the old credo goes, and Kurt struck a chord with adolescent minds across the world.

The autobiographical snippets that ended up in his songs were basically updated blues lyrics that contained clever, yet always elusive, storytelling from the rough side of the tracks.

There's little doubt Kurt lived a blues-filled existence and had done so since his parents divorced when he was eight years old. He had stints living with his mother, in his father's trailer, with various family members, and even with a friend's family who adopted him until they lost patience with Kurt's negativity and disobedience. Whenever conflicts arose he retreated or was banished, forced to fend for himself until someone else took him in.

Kurt famously claimed to have lived under a bridge, but that was a clever fabrication on his part, intended to make him even grittier. He did, however, spend nights in his beater car and a cardboard box.

Growing up, this lack of permanence made him realize that he never fit in, and art became a placebo for his self-esteem. He played guitar and drums but was also increasingly fond of creating collages using pen, paint, and magazine clippings pasted on dolls or random flea-market treasures. The works were always sexually deviant, bizarre, and grotesque. A woman with penises in place of her breasts. Flipper babies. Diseased vaginas. Etcetera.

DURING THE YEARS BEFORE HE REACHED WORLDWIDE fame, Kurt Cobain desperately reached out for attention from anybody remotely related to the industry. There's no other way to make it of course, but "paying one's dues" is an emotionally taxing process. **Becoming an artist is like boarding a crowded subway with two heavy duffels and your internal organs strapped on the outside.**

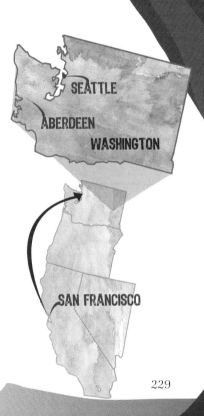

The goal is to make it through those narrow doors with both bags and the organs not too badly bruised before the train leaves. Kurt's tactic was to downplay success, and that protected him from the inevitable downers that come with failure. Expect the worst and you won't be disappointed.

Once he was famous, Cobain's disdain for the promotional treadmill became infamous among music writers. This behavior was deeply rooted in the punk code: sell out and loose cred. No self-respecting scenester would ever want to appear like a sell out. Kurt, of course, was a mastermind. His elusive persona garnered

229

him more press while retaining cred with a generation of record-buying kids.

You might recall that Love excerpted and published Kurt's notebooks as *Journals* in 2002. The notes provide a glimpse into his strange mind but also demonstrate his artistic and promotional acumen. The margins are filled with t-shirt designs, concert poster sketches, ads for Nirvana's records, their bios, and so on. He was so prematurely engaged that he composed in-depth interviews with himself long before he even had a stable band. There's no doubt that Kurt wanted to rise to the top, but once he reached that goal a new predicament transpired: he realized that not everything bundled with fame and glory was enjoyable.

Journals reveal that despise, hate, and death are three words he liked to use. "I hope I die before I become Pete Townshend," blurts one entry in the middle of a diatribe directed at the rock press. Fittingly *The Observer* had The Who's frontman, who has battled with his own demon squad and lives to talk about it, review *Journals* in 2002. Townshend was honest; he praised Kurt's talents, but called him out when he smelled manure: "What follows appear to be the scribblings of a crazed and depressed drug-addict in the midst of what those of us who have been through drug rehab describe as 'stinking thinking.' That is, the resentful, childish, petulant and selfish desire to accuse, blame and berate the world for all its wrongs, to wish to escape, or overcome and, finally, to take no responsibility for any part of the ultimate downfall. Me? An Expert? Of course. Been there, done that." No doubt Pete, no doubt.

AT LEAST COBAIN WAS HIGH-IN-THE-SKY HAPPY IN EARLY '92. He nodded off during the pre-*Saturday Night Live* photo shoot and injected too much after the show. A few days later, Courtney found out she was pregnant and Kurt proposed. The couple married February 24, 1992, on Hawaii's Waikiki Beach. The following year, while working on a Nirvana biography, Azerrad recorded Kurt describing his wedding day: "I just did a little teeny bit so I didn't get sick."

That summer, *Vanity Fair* published an interview with Lynn Hirschberg a few weeks before Courtney Love was due. According to the article, the soon-to-be mother admitted to using heroin before she found out she was pregnant. As a retort, the most rocking couple since Sid and Nancy vehemently claimed the quote was taken out of context. Courtney, of course, is all about image, and although far from everything that comes out of her mouth is true, the article caused a backlash of negative criticisms from around the world. People who had never heard about Courtney Love now cussed her name, and papers everywhere flaunted headlines in thick type along the lines of "Cobain Baby Born a Junkie." Love's response to the writer was to release a Hole bootleg that left no doubt. The song was called "Bring Me the Head of Lynn Hirschberg."

Here's the postscript: Nearly three years later Courtney spotted Lynn Hirschberg at an Academy Award après party. Love snatched the closest blunt object she could find—Quentin Tarantino's statuette for *Pulp Fiction*—and stormed over wielding the Best Director award like a medieval club. The Oscar was later returned in mint condition.

While Seattle bands lumped as grunge became stars, the vibrant Seattle punk scene kept churning out more talent. The Gits formed in 1986 at Antioch College, Ohio, and relocated three years later to the Emerald City. Fronted by the talented and dynamic Mia Zapata, the group released a slew of successful singles and gained notoriety for putting on energetic shows.

Mia Zapata was born and raised in Louisville, Kentucky, where she sang, played guitar, and painted. Like Janis Joplin, she was influenced by blues singer Bessie Smith and turned into a helluva performer. Listen to the live version of Smith's "Graveyard Dream Blues" on the quartet's unofficial debut *Private Lubs* (reissued as *Kings & Queens* in 1996) for an example of both.

The official debut album followed in 1992 and was called *Frenching the Bully*. The reviews in the local and punk press were ecstatic. Word of mouth allowed them to tour Europe, where fans dug their raw "Seattle sound;" a tight, fast, and almost jazzy punk variety.

In '93 the band began to record *Enter: The Conquering Chicken*, a record the band, fans, and many in the record industry expected would be their breakout album. Unfortunately the band's career was unexpectedly thwarted when Mia was raped, mercilessly beaten, and murdered on her way home from a party late at night on July 7. Mia Zapata was 27 years old.

Her gruesome death touched Seattle's music community in a profound way. Her friends organized a self-defense group called Home Alive and organized fund raising concerts and CDs that were supported by Pearl Jam, The Presidents of the United States of America, Heart, and others, including Nirvana, who played a benefit show the month following her murder. After the Seattle Police Department's investigation dead-ended, the remaining members of the Gits hired a private investigator to look for fresh leads. Three years passed, and without signs to break the case, it was featured on a string of true crime TV shows including *Unsolved Mysteries, American Justice, Cold Case Files,* and *America's Most Wanted.*

Nine years passed before the murderer was caught. After a Cuban immigrant was arrested in a Florida burglary, his DNA was entered into the national databank. The sample matched a profile found on Mia's body, and in 2004—eleven years after her brutal death—Jesus Mezquia was sentenced to 36 years in prison for the heinous crime.

Kurt Cobain and Courtney Love's daughter Frances Bean was born August 18, 1992, but it didn't take more than five days before things took an ugly turn. This time it was undeniably *in* context. Somebody
at the hospital had faxed Courtney's medical records to The *Los Angeles Times*, which confirmed that the mother "received daily doses of methadone, a heroin substitute used to treat narcotics addiction." The authorities for LA's child welfare threatened to have Kurt and Courtney's custody taken away. For a month Frances was forced to stay with Courtney's sister while her parents fought the case in court. They weren't even allowed to spend time alone with her and were forced to submit to humiliating pee tests. It was March '93 when the court finally dismissed the case and Kurt and Courtney regained their parental rights and responsibilities.

Biographer Charles Cross's tireless research paints a convincing picture that it was Kurt, not Courtney, who was on the sharper end of the needle. Love's appetite for heroin wasn't nearly as insatiable as Kurt's. She had problems, no doubt, but her main addiction was pills.

The last year of his life, Cobain's heroin addiction was so excessive that even cold-hearted dealers refused to sell him more. Kurt's solution was to ask other users to score him junk for a cut of the bag.

As early as 8th grade, Kurt romanticized the drug in his journals by spelling it "heroine," which was actually a good approximation of the drug's etymology. German scientist Felix Hoffman synthesized the substance from opium poppies in 1897 and named it "heroin" because most of his test subjects behaved *heroisch* under its spell. Not only that, pharmaceutical giant Pfizer thought it was a great substance to beat morphine addiction and to use in children's cough syrup. Sleep well kiddo.

Heroin derives from a semi-synthetic process, but the power locked within the picturesque bulbs in its natural state has been known at least since Mesopotamian times. Hypnos and Thanatos, the Greek gods of sleep and death, are often adorned with poppies, which helps explain why the Greeks and Romans paid respect to their dead by offering poppies at their gravesites. Look at any number of paintings depicting the Passion of Christ and you'll discover these magical flowers displayed for the same reason. While many drugs are arguably not as dangerous as society makes them out to be, heroin is no joke. Virtually every major city center in the western world is a testament to its high human cost, and it's no coincidence that heroin has killed more rock stars than any other drug.

Nirvana's last tour was a downer for everybody involved. It was early March '94, and Kurt was moodier than usual, sick of everything and everybody. Daily phone calls to Courtney, who was in London, ended with screaming matches. Two days before a break in the European tour, Kurt said enough was enough. He split for Rome and waited for Frances and Courtney to appear. When they arrived, Courtney was too zonked from painkillers to have sex and passed out, leaving him hanging. The following morning, she found her husband unconscious on the floor with a bloody nose, his hand clutching a three-page suicide note. It took twenty hours at the hospital for Kurt to come back to life from his self-medicating cocktail of sixty Rohypnols. Courtney didn't mention the note to anybody, so his bandmates, Nirvana's management, record company, and the rest of the world believed it was an accidental overdose.

The most revealing sentence in Kurt's suicide note was published in Cross's riveting biography. During an attempt to

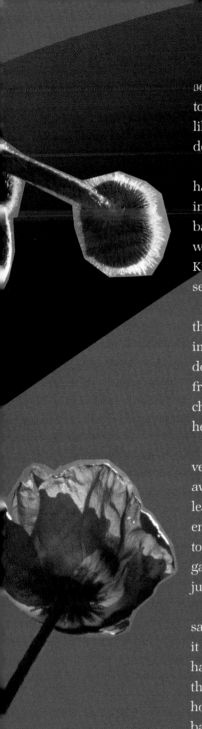

sober up a few months earlier at a rehab center, the doctor had told Cobain it was now or never. Kurt wrote, "Dr. Baker says that, like Hamlet, I have to choose between life and death. I'm choosing death."

Even after Kurt came to, he still felt the deep existential pain that had made him attempt the unspeakable. He had a dealer visit him in the hospital, shot up, and continued the binge as soon as he was back in Seattle. The police visited the Cobain residence twice that week after they received 911 calls from Courtney. The cops left with Kurt's guns on their first visit and brought Kurt downtown after the second.

In a desperate attempt to curb Cobain's heroin habit, Love ruled their mansion a drug-free zone. Kurt took note and began to nod off in sleazy motel rooms and at his dealer's whenever he could. His doses were reportedly too big for a single syringe, and when a junkie friend chastised him for being so incredibly reckless she received a chilling answer: "He told me he was going to shoot himself in the head. He said, half jokingly, '*That's* how I'm going to die.' "

Krist Novoselic tipped off Kurt Cobain about an upcoming intervention, so Courtney Love felt compelled to host another, but to no avail: Kurt wouldn't listen. She left for LA to clean up her own act, leaving Kurt to his own vices and devices. After a dangerous weekend binge, he finally saw the writing on the wall and booked a flight to LA on the same errand. He shot up real good and bought a twenty-gauge shotgun before he left town. After three days at the clinic he jumped the fence and flew back to Seattle.

Before the sun rose over Lake Washington on April 5, 1994, Kurt sat in his bedroom and composed another suicide note. This time it was for real. The shotgun would end what the dangerous drugs hadn't. Carrying the gun, a box with the potent works, cigarettes, the note, and a can of soda, he headed outside and entered the green house in the back. He sat on the floor, fixed himself up, placed the barrel in his mouth, and pulled the trigger. Kurt Cobain was 27 years old.

"It's a very dangerous business," Iggy Pop commented without specifying whether he was referring to the music industry or heroin. "It's very dangerous for the practitioners." Indeed.

DURING THE NINETIES, SEATTLE WAS KNOWN FOR ITS STAR-bucks lattes and stars on heroin. "Kurt broke my heart," Kristin Pfaff told the *Minnesota Nightly*. Kristin was Hole's bass player, and she and Kurt had developed some sort of a friendship. "She's a fucking talented musician, she's also a beautiful soul. I think she's so beautiful, but if I ever told her that, and Courtney found out, it would be hell," Kurt told his friend Dylan Carlson. Seven weeks after Kristen's interview, the *Minnesota Nightly* ran a story titled "Kristin Pfaff broke our hearts."

Pfaff's first brush with music was when she recorded her own lyrics to girl scout songs using a portable tape recorder. She played classical piano and cello in her teens and picked up the bass while studying at Boston College. She took a year off from school and transferred to the University of Minnesota where she majored in Women's Studies and attended writing classes at the English department.

Kristin Pfaff was an honors student and a driven activist, more so than any of the other 27s. In Minnesota, she co-founded a community radio, fought for better campus security, and was part of a sit-in at the dean's office to raise awareness about sexual violence on campus.

She found a great musical outlet in Janitor Joe, a hard-driving punk trio. Her playing was more dynamic there than it would ever sound in Hole. She wrote several tracks on the '93 release *Big Metal Birds*, including "Boys In Blue" and "Limited Edition." The Minneapolis trio toured clubs to promote *Big Metal Birds*. The alternative music press enthusiastically received the record, and the thumbs up pushed Janitor Joe along in the cutthroat music biz. The band even attracted a small following.

Courtney Love and guitarist Eric Erlandson were scouting for a new bass player when they spotted Kristin Pfaff laying down the low end for Janitor Joe at a gig in LA. Erlandson and Love thought Pfaff would be perfect for Hole and invited her to join.

Hole's first disc, *Pretty On the Inside*, released in 1991, was an indie blockbuster that had even outsold Nirvana's *Bleach*. By 1993 Hole's prospects appeared even brighter: they had just signed with DGC Records, a subsidiary of Geffen Records, and Courtney was married to the biggest rock star in the world. Hole's next disc was poised to be a mainstream breakout.

Nevertheless, Pfaff wasn't convinced, so she initially declined and continued on with the Janitor tour. Once back in Minnesota, she decided to join Hole as a temporary bassist and moved to Seattle so she could attend rehearsals and get to know her new band.

Pfaff joined the band permanently after the quartet successfully recorded *Live Through This*. "That's when we took off. All of a sudden we became a real band," Erlandson admitted later. Erlandson and Pfaff became a couple of sorts, but it didn't take Kristin long to learn something about Hole's fierce leader. "Courtney's scary," she confided in a friend. "If I take a hike, she'll make me look bad or do something to make my life miserable." She decided to split while the rest of Hole waited for their record's release. Kristin left for Minneapolis in February '94 and reunited with Janitor Joe for a European tour. The break from the Seattle

APR. 27, 1994

Nelson Mandela sworn in as the President of South Africa.

seattle

IOWA

MINNESOTA

MINNEAPOLIS

WISCONSIN

ILLINOIS

INDIANA

MICHIGAN

PARTNERS FOR A DRUG FREE AMERICA

After Kristin Pfaff's death her mother, Janet Pfaff, began volunteering for Partnership for a Drug Free America (PDFA), the organization behind the infamous "This Is Your Brain on Drugs" campaign. Although several PDFA campaigns have been misleading, holding up the platinum record for *Live Through This* that Kristin never had a chance to see demonstrates hard drugs' consequences in a very real way.

Live Through This was released just four days after Cobain died, but Kristin waited until June before she ventured back to Seattle. Once there she packed up her things in a rented U-Haul and was ready to jet out of town the following morning. Nobody knows exactly what happened her last night, but a friend who stayed over said she took a bath. The next morning was June 16, 1994; her friend busted the locked door and found Kristin Pfaff dead in the tub with a needle nearby. She was 27 years old, packed up and ready for a new start.

Many believed Courtney was somehow responsible, that Kristin's death was a carefully orchestrated murder set into play since she was set to leave Hole for good. The authorities didn't suspect foul play and ruled it an accidental overdose.

Conspiracy theorists take Max Wallace and Ian Halperin's books *Who Killed Kurt Cobain* and *Love & Death: The Murder of Kurt Cobain* to heart.

scene with all its star junkies and dealers did her good, and after Kurt died she decided to make it permanent.

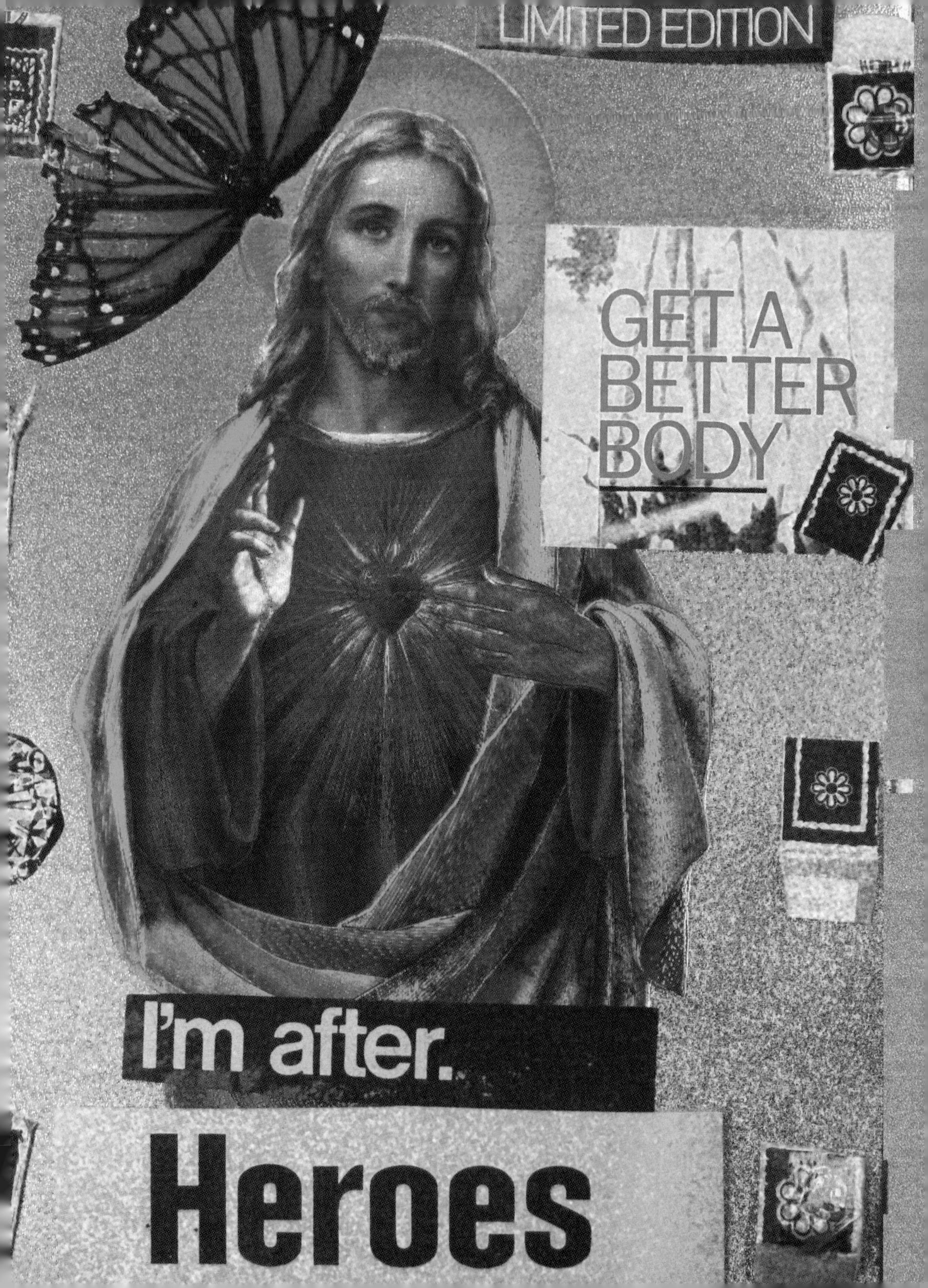
LIMITED EDITION
GET A BETTER BODY
I'm after.
Heroes

"YOU KNOW WHAT LIFE'S LIKE AFTER THIRTY - I DON'T want that," Kurt once said. That he was obsessed with his own death should be clear to anybody who listened to Azerrad's taped interviews (as heard in *About A Son*, a documentary from 2007). Richey James Edwards of the Welsh Manic Street Preachers was a huge fan of Cobain and thought of him as a kindred soul who was also suffering from existential depression. After a post-gig interview in 1991 with *New Musical Express*'s Steve Lamacq—who inferred that the band's image was an artistic mask and that the music alone should say enough—Richey took him aside and said, "Believe me, we are for real." Then he carved "4real" into his left forearm using a razor blade. "I was really fucked off," Richey explained later. **"I didn't know what I could possibly say to him to make understand." Afterwards NME photographer Ed Sirrs snapped one of rock's most iconic images: Richey displaying his bloody arm before he was driven to the emergency room for treatment.**

Edwards suffered from vicious bouts of depression, anorexia, alcoholism, and self-mutilation. The latter started when a fan handed Richey a cutlery set before a gig in Thailand with a note that urged him to cut himself on stage that night. He did.

"I'm on my own, I'm very selfish," Richey said in an interview. "*Self disgust is self-obsession*—that's the truest line on there, probably." Richey referred to "Faster," a song he wrote for Manic's monumental *The Holy Bible* from '94. The lyricist (and second guitarist) cut his wrists on the eve of the record's release, but he convinced his bandmates that it wasn't a suicide attempt. "In terms of the S word, that does not enter my mind. And it never has," Richey insisted in an interview, but few outside of his closest circle believed him.

OTHER POSSIBILITIES:

The Holy Bible is one of the top three records of the 1990s. 4real.

It's a creative collaboration, a defining masterpiece with a fat sound, hard flanging hooks, and sinewy leads accentuated by drummer Sean Moore. The stark lyrics about religion, eating disorders ("4st 7lb"), and iconoclasms were emancipated from Richey's troubled head, while bassist Nicky Wire filled in the last quarter. Guitarist James Dean Bradfield says he struggled to set music to the dire stanzas, but the result is astonishing.

The Manics grew up together in working class Wales, surroundings Kurt Cobain could've related to. Richey was the driver and art director in early incarnations of the band. He photographed and designed their self-released "Suicide Alley" single in '89. Three years later he contributed lyrics and modeled his chest and tattooed left arm on *Generation Terrorists*, their album debut. His skills on the guitar improved enough to play on *Gold Against the Soul*, which was released a year later. The track "Life Becoming a Landslide," also found on the eponymous EP, portended *The Holy Bible*'s grim lyrics.

Even though the record climbed to number six on the UK album charts, it took a few years for critics and listeners to wrap their heads around it. The Manics are virtually unknown in the US (partly because their US distributor insisted on censoring songs and album designs in the name of morals and decency), but the Brits revered them as the hippest in Brit pop. In a way the Manics filled the same role on Britain's musical landscape as the Bunnymen had before them. Not coincidentally, the quartet sported military fatigues and draped their amps with camouflage nettings a la Echo & the Bunnymen anno 1980.

OCT. 21, 1995

Shannon Hoon (28) of Blind Melon dies after a cocaine bender.

SPEAK SO MUCH OF THE ABYSS

The controversy surrounding Richey and death continued with the *Bible* track "Die In the Summertime," but Richey spun that one too, claiming it was written before he experienced self-destructive tendencies: "Die In the Summertime was basically an old man looking back over his life, over his favorite period of youth, his childhood, basically. Everybody's got a perfect mental time of their life and that's what that song is about. And it was written last summer."

Sure, that's one interpretation. Although mentally ill, Richey commanded an incredible intellect. He was drawn to very heavy stuff such as the Holocaust, Albert Camus, Fyodor Dostoevsky, Van Gogh, Sylvia Plath, and Joy Division's Ian Curtis. His artistic, literary, and musical heroes lived short, depressed, yet productive lives.

For a while he wore a T-shirt that read "Kill Yourself" and in an early interview he had the audacity to tell readers of *Smash Hits* to die before they reached the age of thirteen. The idea was that life past childhood was filled with constant suffering.

"He's just a mess. Fucking nutter, the boy is," Nicky Wire said after Richey was interred at the Priory, the same mental institution that Brian Jones had stayed at in '67.

The Manic's final gig as a four-piece took place at the London Astoria in December 1994. They'd completed a successful European tour, which included stops in Scandinavia, and the group played loud and incredibly tight. After Christmas break they reconvened up at a demo studio in Surrey. Richey was in great spirits. "It's nice that the last time we were together was just unbelievably pleasant and nice. Just like it used to be. It was just lovely. Perhaps because he knew he was going," Sean Moore told the BBC ten years later. The day before a promotional visit to the US, Richey disappeared from the hotel where he was staying. A note addressed to his sometime girlfriend read, "I love you." His passport and wallet were found at his apartment in Cardiff Bay, which proved he had stopped by there after he left the hotel. But no more

REGRETS NO

"I have no regrets. Regrets are meaningless. You can't change yesterday or tomorrow. You can change only this present moment."

—Richey James Edwards

clues were discovered until two weeks later when Richey's abandoned car was found near the Severn Bridge. The battery was flat, and it looked like someone had spent several nights in the vehicle. Could he have jumped from the bridge, his body dragged from the Severn into the Bristol Channel and from there to the Atlantic Ocean? "That's the only time that I genuinely ever thought that, you know, he's dead," Moore said.

Despite no confirmed sightings since February '95, the remaining band members still deposit Richey's royalty shares into an escrow account in case he resurfaces.

"Personally I still think he's alive, although I've got no physical evidence or reason to think that he is. But I do... how can you accept that he's dead when there's no body, no evidence whatsoever? It's irrational," Nicky Wire says today.

Melody Maker's Taylor Parkes wrote, "Nirvana were all about certainty. The Manics, on the other hand, are all about doubt on every level, even down to Richey's sexual ambiguity. Which is why it's so appropriate that Kurt shot himself and Richey just went missing."

Richey's heroes fall into two categories: they either staged their own disappearance or they committed suicide. More than a decade has passed since he vanished, but The Manics, Richey's family, and innumerable fans still believe he's alive. Is he peaced out in a monastery somewhere, or was that Richey James Edwards someone spotted on the beach in the Canary Islands or Goa, in Mexico or Iceland?

"He was a very intelligent guy," says Simon Price, who wrote *Everything (A Book About The Manic Street Preachers)*. "If he wanted to disappear, he could've done it."

DYKE'S RAP

Dyke's influence on rappers is evident. Before Tupac Shakur (a.k.a. 2pac) died from a drive-by shooting at 25, he sampled "Let a Woman Be A Woman, Let A Man Be A Man" on "If My Homie Calls;" Public Enemy snatched "We Got More Soul" for its "Anti-Nigger Machine;" and Big Daddy Kane used "Broadway Combination" for "Chocolate City."

WITH THE EXCEPTION OF ARLESTER "DYKE" CHRISTIAN and Roger Lee Durham, the seventies were largely devoid of African-American 27s. Rock was a mostly white endeavor, but black musicians contributed immensely to other genres of course. Think Miles Davis's droning, psychedelic, jazz-funk; Sly and the Family Stone's funk/rock/soul mix; soul-pop a la Marvin Gaye, Al Green, and Bloodstone; the disco of Jackson 5, or the rhythm & bruise of Ike & Tina Turner.

By the early eighties, a confident art form emerged from America's dense and dangerous inner cities. Born on urban streets in the seventies, young kids excluded from disco's coke glam threw block parties where DJs Kool Herc, Afrika Bambaataa, Eddie Cheeba and others spun beats from soul and funk records while toasting and rapping on top. Just like James Brown popularized tight drumbeats in the early sixties, these pioneering artists resurrected rapping, another form of expression suppressed by yesteryear's slave masters.

The gift of gab, known in parts of West Africa as *nommo*, was—and still is—extremely important. Healing potions, rituals, necromancy, and even war, are powerless without words. Spin the time dial to the mid-seventies, and these quickwittedfasttalkin' deejays elevated street speak to a new and competitive art form.

"It is my opinion that the colored people of this country have done four things which refute the oft advanced theory that they are an absolutely inferior race, which demonstrate that they have originality and artistic conception; and, what is more, the power of creating that which can influence and appeal universally." These words come from *The Autobiography of an Ex-Colored Man*, a fictional novel published anonymously in 1912. James Weldon Johnson, a noted African-American artist and intellectual, admitted he was the author in time for the 1927 reprint.

Weldon's character referred to ragtime, the most popular craze in America at the turn of the nineteenth century. If you've seen the caper film *The Sting* starring Robert Redford and Paul Newman, you've heard Scott Joplin's rag "The Entertainer," which is featured throughout the Oscar-winning movie (never mind that the plot takes place in 1936, thirty-four years after Joplin wrote the rag). Ragtime was the first truly American musical style to gain widespread popularity, and jazz derived from a mix of that and the blues.

Today, ragtime's best-remembered musician is Scott Joplin, but at the time his friend Louis Chauvin was equally famous within the tightly knit rag scene.

Chauvin was born in St. Louis, Missouri, and although he died without leaving recordings, we know that his ivory chops were legendary in vaudeville circles all over the Midwest.

"Chauvin emerged from the urban subculture of St. Louis," says Ed Berlin, a ragtime scholar and author of three books on the genre. "Chauvin's reputation is astonishing when one considers it is based on his contribution to "Heliotrope Bouquet," a mere 32 measures of music, less than three minutes including repeats. However, its ethereal beauty is unlike anything else coming from the ragtime years, and he certainly impressed Scott Joplin who was the era's standout composer. This piece of music is unlike anything else ever composed."

Louis Chauvin couldn't read music, but his friend Scott Joplin notated "Heliotrope Bouquet" and added the latter half. We're only left with two other compositions that bear Louis Chauvin's name, but at least these glimpses provide context to his legend.

Chauvin frequently warmed up by hammering double-time octaves in opposing directions using the entire keyboard. In 1904 he won player Tom Turpin's piano contest at the Rose Bud Club, and since Joplin was known as the "King of Rag Time Writers," Chauvin was soon taglined "King of Rag Time Players."

"The list of contestants demonstrates that as the winner, Chauvin's talent must have been formidable," Berlin says. If someone hummed him a composition Chauvin could sit down and play the piece note-for-note, adding harmonies and changing the arrangement to make it his own.

Even though Louis's best known talent lay in fast runs on the keys and incredibly technical impromptu compositions, he was also known as a fantastic singer and a fluid dancer. One account claims Chauvin "had an insatiable thirst for women, opium, and alcohol."

Louis Chauvin died in Chicago March 26, 1908. He was 27 years old, and the cause of death was complications from syphilis.

To paraphrase Weldon Johnson, African-American art forms' universal influence and appeal continued to grow over the course of the twentieth century.

There's jazz.

Then rock was minted from the blues, and styles such as doo-wop, soul, and funk all proved to be popular supplements as well.

Hip-hop is in its own league, however. In the past white players mimicked black musicians, often creating a slightly new style, but hip-hop has turned the entire world on to not only the music, but also its fashion, attitude, and style.

Like the blues, hip-hop's ethos is to create something from nothing, *makin' a way outta no way*, and it's not surprising that a lot of hip-hop's brightest came from the front lines of urban decay.

Take New York City's E Line to the end and get off at Jamaica in the South Queens borough. In the early nineties rappers threw down hip-hop jams in Baisley Pond Park there. One of the young men who made a name for himself was Raymond Rogers who called himself Freaky Tah.

Tah's high school buddies DJ Spigg Nice, Pretty Lou, and Mr. Cheeks were there too, and the crew began to jam as a unit. The Lost Boyz appropriated its name from *The Lost Boys* (a teenage vampire movie that featured Echo & the Bunnymen's version of the Doors' "People Are Strange" on the soundtrack).

The Boyz slung drugs to get by but quit after another dealer they knew was shot. The Lost Boyz soon debuted the single "Lifestyles Of the Rich & Shameless," and it climbed up Billboard's Hot 100 thanks to its hypnotic creed *"some died wit the name, some*

MAY 25, 1996	MAY 29, 1997	JUNE 10, 1997
Bradley Nowell (28), Sublime's lead singer and guitarist, dies from a heroin overdose.	*Singer-songwriter Jeff Buckley (30) drowns on an evening swim.*	*Black Panther member Geronimo Pratt exonerated after 27 years in jail for the murder of a 27-year-old teacher.*

die nameless, it's all the same game, all the same pain." Based on the single and the promise of more party jams, Uptown Records added the Lost Boyz to its roster. "Renee" followed and was included in the spoof movie *Don't Be A Menace To South Central While Drinking Your Juice In the Hood.*

"Cheeks and Freaky were the star players on the team," Pretty Lou says. Freaky Tah's throaty voice was the response to Mr. Cheek's call, the story's chorus, the adlibbing backup—the hype man. "He was that big spark that started the engine," says his brother Tito. "He loved his fans and loved being on stage." Like Public Enemy's Flavor Flav, Tah's role in the group was irreplaceable. Tahleek's deep rasp is found all over their '96 debut *Legal Drug Money*; he even rocked the mike on "1,2,3." The record is part contemplation and part celebration of the Queens they emerged from. Even the song titles speak collectively of a greater story with "Get Up," "Music Makes Me High," "Jeeps, Lex Coups, Bimaz & Benz," "All Right," "Straight From Da Ghetto," "Da Game," and so on.

NOV. 22, 1997

INXS singer Michael Hutchence (37) hangs himself.

MAR. 27, 1998

The FDA approves Viagra for treating male impotence.

SEP. 27, 1998

Google launches its search engine.

NOV. 30 - DEC. 9, 1999

The WTO riots in Seattle marks the first major anti-globalization rally.

The album commanded the top spot on the rap/hip-hop charts and climbed to number six on the Billboard 200, going gold in the process. Several cuts from *Legal Drug Money* charged up the singles charts, such as "Music Makes Me High," which outsold LL Cool J, Outkast, Jay-Z, and Mary J. Blige in November '96.

The Lost Boyz managed to stay out of the East Coast/West Coast beef that claimed the lives of Tupac Shakur, Biggie Smalls, and many others. In an otherwise bling-filled scene, the Lost Boyz pioneered plain white tees as part of the hip-hop uniform.

Tah never forgot about who he was and where he came from and invested time in prepping kids from his hood in the rap game. His crew was known as the 134 Allstars and included 50 Cent, Lloyd Banks, Bang 'Em Smurf, Sha Monteloc (now Money XL), Mutt-Lo, Na Tha Natural, Ava Denero, Huey P., and Tony Yayo. The group soon went on to form G-Unit. "Tah inspired me man, Tah came from the same struggle I came from so he showed me that I could really do it," Tah's cousin Domination said in a 2005 interview with *Riotsound*. "I used to freestyle on the block and Tah used to have me battling grown cats."

When Tah wasn't hanging with his crew, he might ride the bus so he could sign autographs or pass out CDs and t-shirts. He was in the street all the time, and on his birthday he'd throw a BBQ for the south side of Queens. "That's why 95 percent of everyone knew who Tah was," Tito says.

In 1997, the Lost Boyz followed up with *Love Peace & Nappiness*. Tah stepped up on two of that album's essential tracks "Why?" and "Get Your Hustle On," while "My Crew" paid homage to their hood. The album went gold, and the single "Me & My Crazy World" placed in the middle of Billboard's Hot 100 chart.

March 28, 1999, the Lost Boyz entourage celebrated Mr. Cheeks's birthday at the Sheraton Hotel in Queens. Well after

SCREWED UP AND DEAD

Thanks to DJ Screw and his Screwed Up Click, Houston's rap scene rose to the top among late nineties Southern rap. An early member and collaborator was Mr. Fat Pat (or P.A.T), nee Patrick Lamont Hawkins, who went to Sterling High with Screw. The two were buds through thick and thin and slowly raised the Screwed Up Click to underground prominence.

Fat Pat released *Ghetto Dreams* in 1998, and its single "Tops Drop" scored at number five in the US rap charts. Riding the wave, he quickly put out *Throwed In Da Game*.

An Austin promoter and notorious drug dealer known on the streets as Weasel (his real name is Kenneth Eric Watson) failed to pay the Screwed Up Click for a show, but taped, filmed, and hustled it without permission.

Shortly thereafter Weasel's safe house was robbed, and he suspected Fat Pat had something to do with it—a payback of sorts. Fat Pat denied the accusation and said that he was no longer in the game—strictly music for him now.

A little later Weasel invited Fat Pat to an apartment under the pretense to pay him for the show. "I'm like, don't mess with that cat," Screw said later in an interview. Fat Pat went to the meeting anyway, and Weasel killed him with a shot in the head. DJ Screw: "Basically, because he thought Fat Pat had something to do with him getting robbed."

Fat Pat was 27 years old when he was murdered by Weasel.

EURODANCE

If you've lived or visited Europe in the last fifteen years you've heard the cheesy bubblegum sound of Eurodance. The beats, lyrics, and choruses are designed like a clever virus to rule dance floors and airwaves from Ibiza to Tromsø for a month or so—just long enough to record and release something new.

Passion Fruit was one of these pop groups and in '99 it released "The Rigga-Ding-Dong-Song," which charted Top 10 in fourteen countries. Internal tension split the group, but management decided to continue with a fresh crop. In 2000 and 2001 Passion Fruit released a trio of high charting singles (all big in Germany of course) and the album *Spanglish Love Affairs*, but the Eurodance fairytale ended grimly on November 24, 2001. After a performance in Berlin they boarded Crossair flight 3597 to Zurich. On its way to landing the pilot descended below minimum altitude and crashed into a hill, killing twenty-four of the thirty-three on board. Passion Fruit members Nathalie van het Ende and 27-year-old Maria Serrano-Serrano were among the victims, while Debby St. Marteen survived. Proceeds from Passion Fruit's posthumous single, "I'm Dreaming of... A Winter Wonderland" went to the crash victims' families.

midnight Tah said goodbye and left the party. As he walked through the main doors of the hotel, a man on the street shot him in the head and escaped in a car that sped off.

Freaky Tah was pronounced dead at 4:20 a.m.; the incredible hype man was only 27 years old.

In 2001, Kelvin Jones pleaded guilty to murdering Raymond Rogers and received fifteen years to life, while driver Raheem Fletcher was sentenced to seven years for chauffeuring the getaway car.

Shortly after Freaky Tah's death, his father Linford Rogers told reporters that his son "kept ties with the kids in the neighborhood. He checked their report cards. He bought them sneakers and jackets. He always told them, 'You do the right thing and I'll do the right thing.' "

The socially conscious Talib Kweli pays his respects in "Good Mourning" off Reflection Eternal's 2000 album *Train of Thought*. He raps "Freaky Tah, rock rock on."

Eight years later, *XXL Mag* asked Mr. Cheeks about Freaky Tah's murder. "I couldn't believe somebody shot my nigga. I never thought something could happen to a nigga, 'cause we just represented the hood and everything we stood for was Queens. I never thought that something would even go wrong, so it bugged me out. It just fucked us up."

INK & DAGGER

Philadelphia's Ink & Dagger was an unusual hardcore band. Over the course of its career, the band played a hypnotic fusion of aggro punk riffs and noisy techno. Ink & Dagger dented the indie circuit with this sonic stew coupled with, at least in the beginning, a dramatic vampire theme that Vampire Weekend picked up on brought fame a few years later.

"It was very discouraging to have people only see us as 'that emo-goth-core band that wears makeup' when there was much, much more to the puzzle," singer Sean Patrick McCabe said in an interview with *Ink19*, a fanzine. "I can understand that some people never really took this band seriously," he added.

Ink & Dagger had a reputation for putting on fierce shows with symbolic dress-ups and unusual stage props—at one show the members puked on Christmas trees, an act perhaps interpreted as a statement against consumerism.

The group might seem odd to the uninitiated, but behind the noise and makeup they were a reflective punk unit fuelled by McCabe's fiery but intelligent lyrics and a propensity to shock. "Think of a vampire as a metaphor for the world," says Robby Redcheeks, Ink & Dagger's former roommate and road manager. "Blood is a person's energy and vampires feed off of it. It had nothing to do with vampires per se, but was more a metaphor for punk rock and the society."

"My brother Sean was totally into whatever he was doing and so psyched you'd think he was nuts," Brian McCabe says. Bassist Joshua Brown still laughs every time he tells the story about when Sean threw yogurt at the vegan band Earth Crisis. "It went everywhere on stage and Earth Crisis, who are these stormtrooper kinda guys, went crazy, but Sean was out of there before they could do anything. They still knew it was him who did it though."

"Sean McCabe was an unexplainable force," Robby says, " One of the most intelligent people I've ever known and also one of the craziest."

McCabe orchestrated an Internet prank in 1996 to prove the power of the new medium. The hoax took place on an early message board. He made up a story about a deadly accident, including details about the upcoming funeral service. People started calling from all over, and when he was finally called out on fabricating the story, he posted that George in their band Forthought had made him do it. The aggression soon shifted to innocent George. Sean let that run for a little while and posted, "Don't believe everything you read on the Internet."

Sean McCabe was always up on technology; he made posters and fliers using the latest software and worked at a Kinko's copy center for a while. "He robbed a shoebox worth of $100 copy cards that he sold to other punk rock kids for $20 a pop," Brian McCabe says.

Both Robby Redcheeks and Brian McCabe feel that the next band Sean was in really killed. "Sean's best band was Crud Is A Cult. They were a straightedge hardcore band, and kept it straight at least for a little while... until they all fell on the wayside," McCabe says and laughs. Brown, who played with Sean in both Crud and Ink & Dagger, agrees: "We went from being against drugs and alcohol to a druggie-hippie-hardcore band."

They were extremely influential in the Philly hardcore scene, but it was only later, touring as Ink & Dagger, that they reached a wider audience—perhaps even more so a few years after they disbanded when the creators of *Amped*, a the snowboarding video game for Microsoft Xbox, snatched three songs from *The Fine Art Of Original Sin* without permission. The theft was settled out of court in 2006.

Ironically, "The Six Feet Under the Swindle" from the same album discarded the music industry. "We think that, yeah, the cash and the fame are readily attainable, but if you want to do it the right way, you shouldn't have to trade in your heart and soul for it," Sean said in an interview.

In 2000, shortly after finishing Ink & Dagger's third and final album and on his way to a new job, McCabe asphyxiated in an Indiana motel room. He was 27 years old.

"I saw him on the street a month before he died," Robby says. "We talked and he seemed genuinely happy for the first time. He had a new job, new girlfriend, and was getting his life together. It was like he had chased away his demons."

A few years earlier Sean named one of his fanzines *Dead By 23*. The idea was live your life to its fullest, you'll die anyway. "Growing up I had recurring dreams that Sean was gonna die," Brian says, "I'd see him be carried off on a stretcher in our childhood home. I'd look under the sink and see Sean nailed behind the plumbing, crying. I never told him, but I think Sean already knew that he wouldn't be around forever. Not that he wanted to die, he just did what he wanted to when he wanted to and there's a lot to be learned from that."

"IN THE FUTURE, MUSIC WILL BE MADE BY A MAN WITH MA-chines," Jim Morrison said in an interview. Given Frank Zappa's sonic excursions with the Synthclavier and the rise of composing DJs, the lizard king's prescience is impressive.

Jeremy Michael Ward of De Facto and The Mars Volta was kind of a man with machines. Often described as a sound manipula-tor, he sculpted the live sound of his bands using the Korg Kaoss pad (a wild touch-screen effects processor) and a small arsenal of guitar effects boxes such as delay, chorus, phaser, and echo.

But before all that Jeremy Michael Ward grew up as an adopt-ee in El Paso, Texas. He and his best friends, vocalist Cedric Bix-ler-Zavala and guitarist Omar Rodriguez-Lopez, spent their teen-age years discovering women, drugs, punk rock, prog, and dub. In 1993 Omar and Cedric began playing as At The Drive-In with Jeremy's cousin Jim Ward, Paul Hinojos, and Tony Hajjar. ATDI developed an original sound by mixing the hardcore sounds of Fugazi and Bad Brains with progressive rock and a dash of pop.

Ward occasionally ran ATDI's sound, played in punk bands, and worked as a repo man. This unusual job led to a new hobby of sorts: he collected random personal artifacts from the cars he repossessed. He was used to picking up random IDs, drugs, bul-lets, and porn mags, but one day he found a leather-bound jour-nal that changed his life. The hand-scribbled pages told the story of an adopted man's search for his parents, a quest that Jeremy identified with. Intrigued, he shared the discovery with Omar and Cedric and began weaving an intricate storyline from the journal, mixing truth and fiction.

In 1999, the trio formed De Facto as a side-gig. At the Drive-In was on the verge of indie stardom, but Omar and Cedric were

AUG. 25, 2001	OCT. 2001	FEB. 1, 2002	APR. 5, 2002
A Bahamas plane crash kills singer Aaliyah (22) and eight other passengers.	Apple launches the first generation iPod.	Pakistani extremists decapitate Wall Street Journal reporter Daniel Pearl.	Alice in Chain's Layne Staley (34) dies from a speedball.

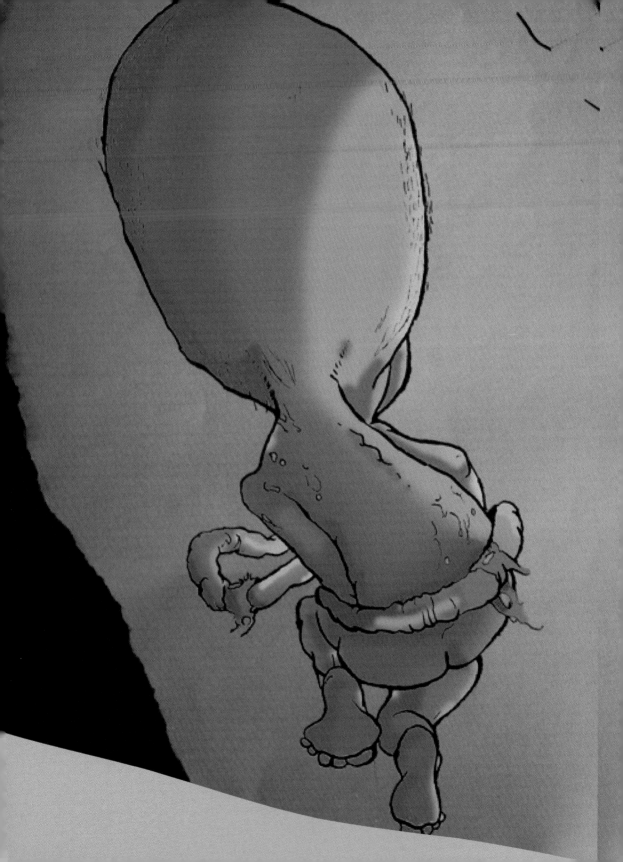

compelled to explore new artistic avenues and soon departed, ending the band in the process.

The three defecting De Factoans relocated from El Paso to the West Coast where a chance meeting with keyboardist Isaiah Owens, who at twenty-three was already a veteran of albums with Sublime, Reel Big Fish, and the Long Beach Dub Allstars, made him a fourth member.

Jeremy Ward played guitar and added sound effects and occasional voice-overs to De Facto, which offered a fresh instrumental dub sound with Brazilian elements thrown in for good measure.

Between 1999 and 2001 the band released three great albums before their sound diverged enough to justify a new project, a progressive rock band called The Mars Volta.

Jeremy Michael Ward and Omar Rodriguez-Lopez spent time recording and mixing wild sonic canvases in the studio. The duo made a limited release available on MiniDisc (the recordings were released on CD by Infrasonic Sound in 2008), and the experimental excursions show just how far Omar and Jeremy pushed the envelope.

Ward added his sound sculptures to the potpourri that is The Mars Volta—a spastic, dense, brutish, and intriguing sound, coupled with impressionistic lyrics sung in a mix of Spanish and English.

De-Loused In The Comatorium, the group's 2003 debut, received great reviews. *Q* magazine called it "An audacious, bold, and provocative artistic statement, an album that raises the bar for any rock band who aspire to re-writing the rulebook," and *Uncut* wrote, "Imagine a jam session between King Crimson, Fugazi, and '70s Miles. Now imagine it working."

Tragically Jeremy wasn't around to read those. A month before the record's release, on break from a tour with the Red Hot

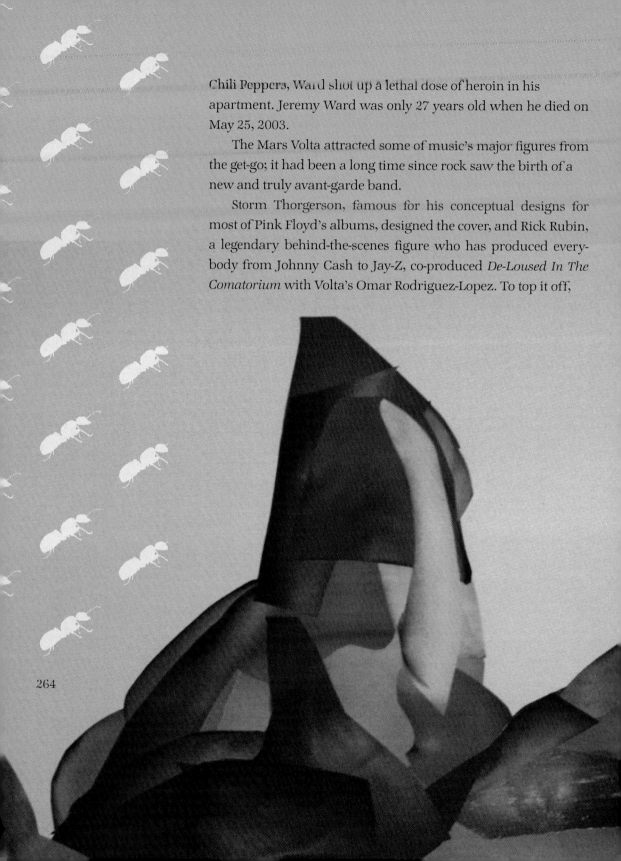

Chili Peppers, Ward shot up a lethal dose of heroin in his apartment. Jeremy Ward was only 27 years old when he died on May 25, 2003.

The Mars Volta attracted some of music's major figures from the get-go; it had been a long time since rock saw the birth of a new and truly avant-garde band.

Storm Thorgerson, famous for his conceptual designs for most of Pink Floyd's albums, designed the cover, and Rick Rubin, a legendary behind-the-scenes figure who has produced everybody from Johnny Cash to Jay-Z, co-produced *De-Loused In The Comatorium* with Volta's Omar Rodriguez-Lopez. To top it off,

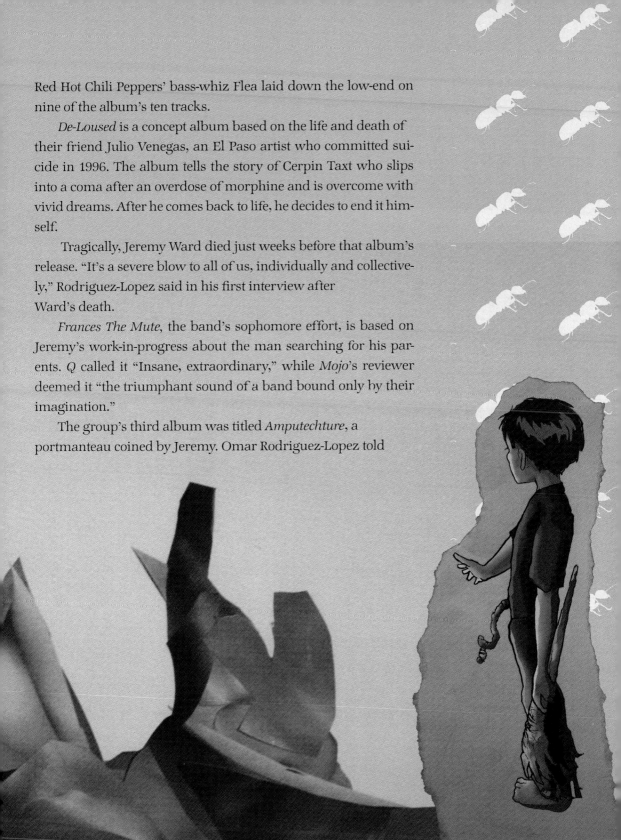

Red Hot Chili Peppers' bass-whiz Flea laid down the low-end on nine of the album's ten tracks.

De-Loused is a concept album based on the life and death of their friend Julio Venegas, an El Paso artist who committed suicide in 1996. The album tells the story of Cerpin Taxt who slips into a coma after an overdose of morphine and is overcome with vivid dreams. After he comes back to life, he decides to end it himself.

Tragically, Jeremy Ward died just weeks before that album's release. "It's a severe blow to all of us, individually and collectively," Rodriguez-Lopez said in his first interview after Ward's death.

Frances The Mute, the band's sophomore effort, is based on Jeremy's work-in-progress about the man searching for his parents. *Q* called it "Insane, extraordinary," while *Mojo*'s reviewer deemed it "the triumphant sound of a band bound only by their imagination."

The group's third album was titled *Amputechture*, a portmanteau coined by Jeremy. Omar Rodriguez-Lopez told

APR. 5, 2002

Actor Sean Penn places a $56,000 ad in the
Washington Post *where he challenges President Bush
to change his policies.*

FEB. 20, 2003

*A blaze from Great
White's pyrotechnics at a
Rhode Island nightclub
takes 100 lives.*

OCT. 21, 2003

*Singer-songwriter Elliot
Smith (34) stabs himself
twice in the chest
and dies.*

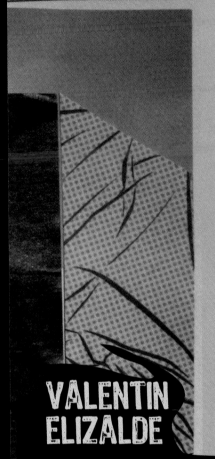

Switch magazine, "That word has been with us for a long time and we wanted to use it for something very important. For us, this third record is very important and... I don't know exactly what it does mean, but the sound of the word makes us feel good."

In an interview with Steve Appleford for the *Los Angeles City Beat* in 2005, Omar Rodriguez-Lopez said, "Obviously Jeremy didn't make it, but there was a certain point that was a big wake-up call for all of us to get our shit together. And obviously, Jeremy's death kind of sealed the fate: I understand that I can never go back now." He was referring to their liberal use of opiates, which they haven't touched since Jeremy's death.

VALENTIN ELIZALDE

The latest 27 was the popular Mexican banda music singer Valentin Elizalde who was ambushed and murdered along with his manager and driver after performing across the border from McAllen, Texas, at a fair in Reynosa, Mexico, November 25, 2006. A van followed his 2007 Chevy Suburban and once it was close its passengers pumped more than seventy bullets from semi-automatic weapons, nailing Elizalde with eight slugs. The hit was most likely related to an ongoing drug feud between the Gulf and Sinaloa cartels over smuggle routes to the US.

Shortly before his death somebody posted provocative montage on YouTube that featured photos of assassinated Gulf cartel members set to the Elizalde's hit song "A Mis Enemigos" ("To My Enemies"). Elizalde was born in the Sinaloa region and once wrote a tribute song to its leader in the style of narcocorridos, songs about the deeds of narco traffickers that resemble old folk songs about real-life rum smugglers and gangsters.

It's speculated that the killing was orchestrated by Los Zetas, a rogue group of Mexican commandos hired by the Gulf Cartel (The US Army's School of the Americas in Georgia once trained many Los Zeta officers—dangerous and well-equipped people who are now responsible hits on US soil, kidnapping DEA agents, and shoot-outs with the US Border Patrol.) According to the BBC more than 2,000 people died from Mexican drug cartel violence in 2006.

Elizalde was known as "El Gallo de Oro," the golden rooster, and released ten albums between 1998 and 2006. He was found in the backseat of the car clutching his trademark rooster pendant that he always wore on a necklace.

Elizalde was posthumously nominated for a Grammy for Best Banda Album in 2007.

ONLY REAL CELEBS ARE INVITED TO MAKE GUEST APPEAR-
ances on *The Simpsons*, and Weird Al Yankovic only parodies de
facto hits. "Smells Like Teen Spirit" received the ultimate of honors when Kurt gave Weird Al the green light to record the spoof
"Smells Like Nirvana." Curiously Weird Al is tied to an unrelated
mania surrounding the number 27.

A couple of fans noticed appearances of the number 27 in
Weird Al videos "Like A Surgeon" and "This Is the Life." Reporting for a fanzine in 1993 Pam Ritchie and Carlotta Barnes asked
Weird Al drummer Jon "Bermuda" Schwartz if there was any
significance to the number: "I asked Al, who evidently hadn't noticed before. He hesitated and said '27 is a funny number'."

Three months later, Weird Al performed near Eugene, Oregon, and his backstage trailer came randomly posted with a large
sign that read "27." Bermuda snapped a photo of Al pointing at
the sign and sent it to the editor at the *Midnight Star* fanzine. With
that the beast was officially unleashed. Fans found 27 references
in Al's earlier lyrics and in other videos. Are Weird Al's 27s a series of coincidences or a deliberate conspiracy? Aluminum is ab-
breviated "Al" in the periodic table and its atomic weight is 27...

"I suppose I used the number 27 originally because I just
thought it was a funny number or maybe it was the right number
of syllables," Weird Al said in an article published by the *Gold-
mine* fanzine in 2000. "Maybe there's a deeper meaning to it than
that, but at the time I just thought that the number seemed to
work best for different situations. ... [T]here became this kind of
whole cult based around the number 27, and people looking for
the number 27 as it would occur in my work. And I was aware
this was going on, so I would kind of feed the flames a little bit,
and from that point on, started putting the number in more con-
sciously."

27

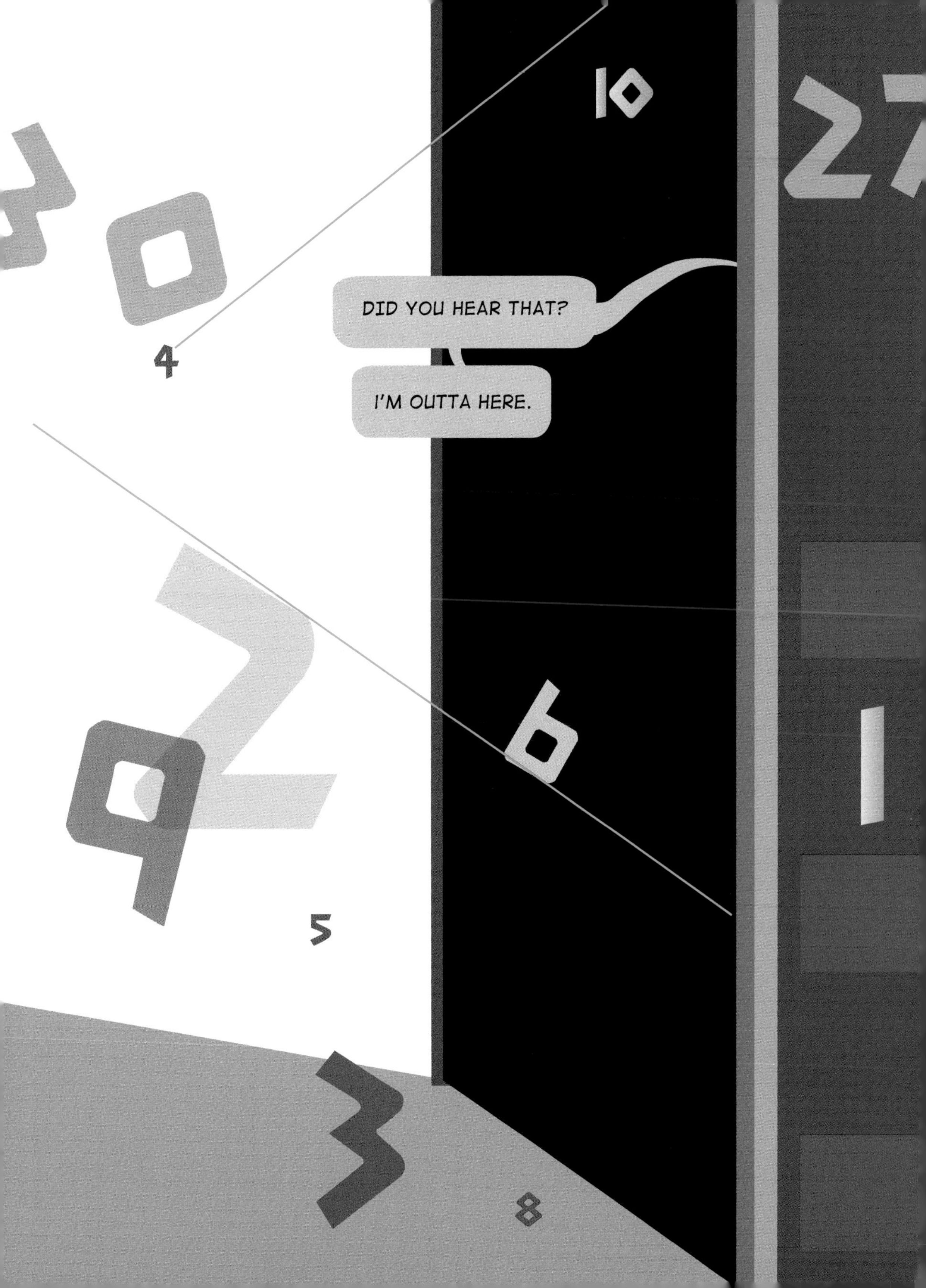
DID YOU HEAR THAT?
I'M OUTTA HERE.

PYTHAGORAS BELIEVED THAT EVERYTHING COULD BE BROKEN DOWN IN NUMBERS AND THEREFORE PREDICTED AND MEASURED IN RHYTHMIC PATTERNS.
DURING A STUDY TRIP TO BABYLON PYTHAGORAS LEARNED ABOUT THE *TETRAKTYS*, A TRIANGULAR SHAPE THAT CONSISTS OF FOUR ROWS MADE FROM TEN POINTS.

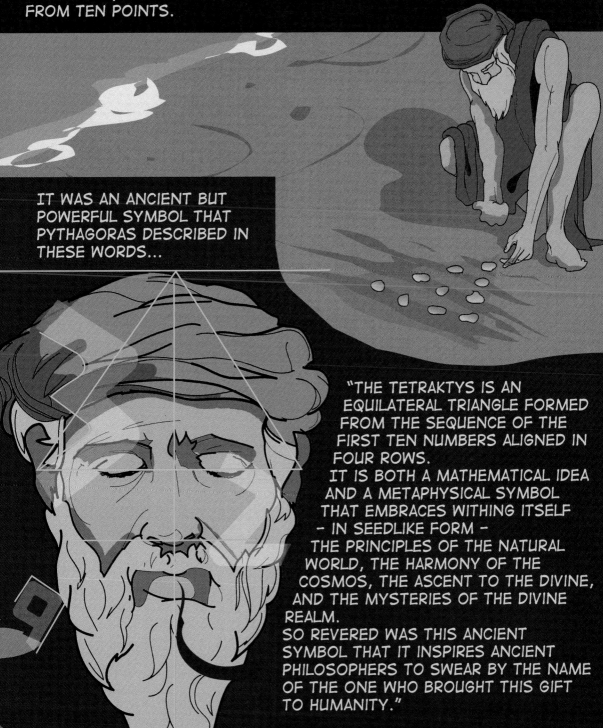

IT WAS AN ANCIENT BUT POWERFUL SYMBOL THAT PYTHAGORAS DESCRIBED IN THESE WORDS...

"THE TETRAKTYS IS AN EQUILATERAL TRIANGLE FORMED FROM THE SEQUENCE OF THE FIRST TEN NUMBERS ALIGNED IN FOUR ROWS.
IT IS BOTH A MATHEMATICAL IDEA AND A METAPHYSICAL SYMBOL THAT EMBRACES WITHING ITSELF
- IN SEEDLIKE FORM -
THE PRINCIPLES OF THE NATURAL WORLD, THE HARMONY OF THE COSMOS, THE ASCENT TO THE DIVINE, AND THE MYSTERIES OF THE DIVINE REALM.
SO REVERED WAS THIS ANCIENT SYMBOL THAT IT INSPIRES ANCIENT PHILOSOPHERS TO SWEAR BY THE NAME OF THE ONE WHO BROUGHT THIS GIFT TO HUMANITY."

HE PREACHED A STRICT WAY OF LIFE AND LED HIS DISCIPLES DEEP INTO VEGETARIANISM,

STRICT RITUALS,

AND SELF-DISCIPLINE THAT BEGAN WITH THREE LONG YEARS OF SILENCE BY THOSE WHO WERE INITIATED TO THE SECRETS OF THE FOUR — THE POWERFUL *TETRAKTYS*.

ADD THE FIRST FOUR NUMBERS 1, 2, 3, 4

AND YOU END UP WITH THE DIVINE LAST NUMBER OF THE SEQUENCE.

THERE ARE FOUR ELEMENTS

EARTH

AIR

FIRE

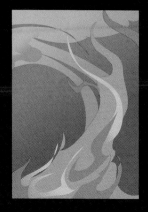

WATER

FOUR SEASONS,

SUMMER

FALL

WINTER

SPRING

SEE, *TETRAKTYS* MEANT FOUR IN GREEK.

KABBALISTS USED THE SYMBOL, ROMAN CATHOLIC BISHOPS' COAT OF ARMS FEATURE TWO *TETRAKTYS*, AND TAROT READERS OFTEN LAY DOWN TEN CARDS IN THE SAME TRIANGULAR FASHION.

IN AN OLD STORY PYTHAGORAS WALKED PAST A BLACKSMITH
SHOP AND REALIZED THAT THE PITCH OF THE RED HOT METAL
BEING HAMMERED ON THE ANVIL DEPENDED ON THE WEIGHT OF
THE HAMMERHEAD.

AFTER THIS EPIPHANY HE CONDUCTED VARIOUS EXPERIMENTS
AND CAME TO A MUSICAL LAW THAT FIT PERFECTLY WITHIN THE
REVERED *TETRAKTYS*.

THE MAGIC OF MUSICAL SCALES WAS NOW QUANTIFIABLE:
DOUBLE THE WEIGHT OR TENSION FOR AN OCTAVE (A RATIO OF 2:1),
THE RATIO 4:3 CREATED A MUSICAL FOURTH,
AND 3:2 A MUSICAL FIFTH.
THE NEXT WHOLE TONE IS FOUND IN THE 8:9 RATIO,
ITS OCTAVE 2:1 OF THAT AND SO ON.

IN SIXTEENTH-CENTURY ITALY, LUTE PLAYER AND MUSICAL THEORIST VINCENZO GALILEI CORRECTED PYTHAGORAS' HARMONIC LAWS AFTER HE EXPERIMENTED WITH THE PHYSICAL RELATIONSHIP BETWEEN STRING TENSION, PITCH, AND MATHEMATICAL CONSTRUCTION OF THE LUTE. HIS SON, THE FAMOUS GALILEO GALILEI, FOLLOWED IN HIS FATHER'S FOOTSTEPS AND CHANGED THE WORLD BY DEMONSTRATING THAT

VIRTUALLY EVERY PHYSICAL PHENOMENON COULD BE QUANTIFIED BY MATHEMATICS.

KNOW HOW TO TUNE THIS BUGGER??? I'VE BEEN PLAYIN' FOR YEARS AND YEARS AND STILL HAVEN'T QUITE GOT IT...

A CENTURY AND A HALF AFTER PYTHAGORAS' DEATH, PLATO, HIMSELF A PYTHAGOREAN, DERIVED SOMETHING NEW FROM THE *TETRAKTYS*, WHICH HE WROTE ABOUT IN *TIMAEUS*.

THE ONE (CALL HIM/HER/IT/DIVINITY/CREATOR, GOD OR WHATEVER YOU LIKE) CREATED THE COSMIC SOUL AS A PROJECTION OF HIMSELF USING TWO STRIPS OF NUMBERS.

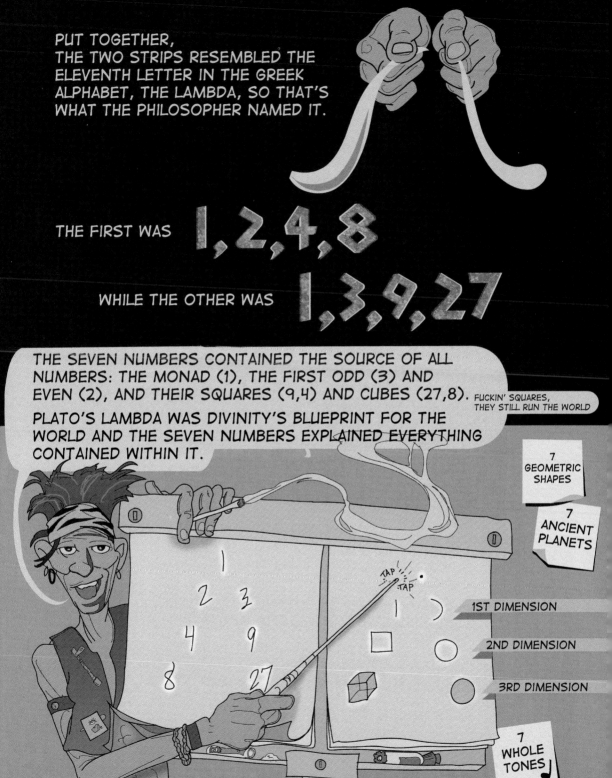

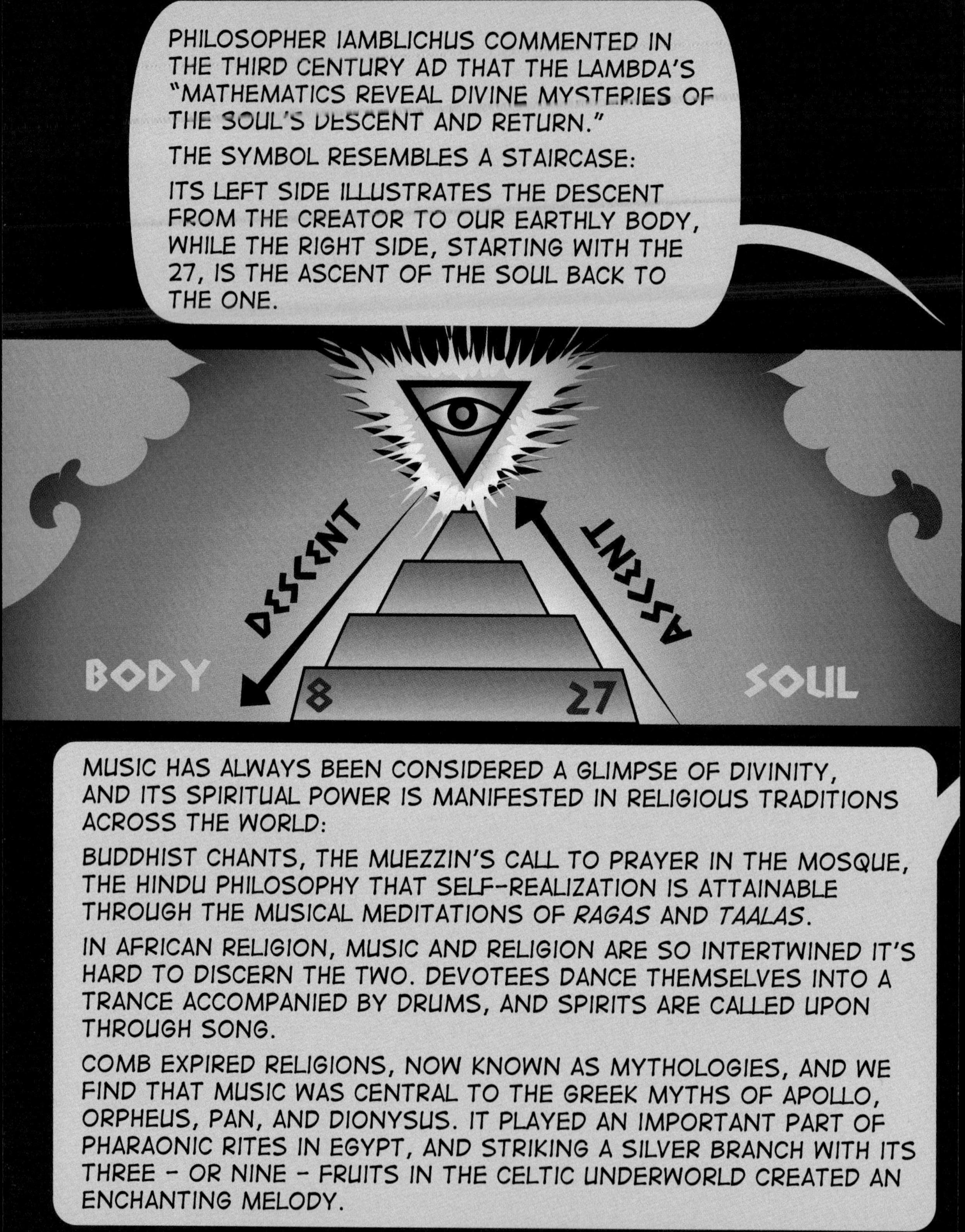

PHILOSOPHER IAMBLICHUS COMMENTED IN THE THIRD CENTURY AD THAT THE LAMBDA'S "MATHEMATICS REVEAL DIVINE MYSTERIES OF THE SOUL'S DESCENT AND RETURN."

THE SYMBOL RESEMBLES A STAIRCASE:

ITS LEFT SIDE ILLUSTRATES THE DESCENT FROM THE CREATOR TO OUR EARTHLY BODY, WHILE THE RIGHT SIDE, STARTING WITH THE 27, IS THE ASCENT OF THE SOUL BACK TO THE ONE.

DESCENT

ASCENT

BODY

SOUL

8

27

MUSIC HAS ALWAYS BEEN CONSIDERED A GLIMPSE OF DIVINITY, AND ITS SPIRITUAL POWER IS MANIFESTED IN RELIGIOUS TRADITIONS ACROSS THE WORLD:

BUDDHIST CHANTS, THE MUEZZIN'S CALL TO PRAYER IN THE MOSQUE, THE HINDU PHILOSOPHY THAT SELF-REALIZATION IS ATTAINABLE THROUGH THE MUSICAL MEDITATIONS OF *RAGAS* AND *TAALAS*.

IN AFRICAN RELIGION, MUSIC AND RELIGION ARE SO INTERTWINED IT'S HARD TO DISCERN THE TWO. DEVOTEES DANCE THEMSELVES INTO A TRANCE ACCOMPANIED BY DRUMS, AND SPIRITS ARE CALLED UPON THROUGH SONG.

COMB EXPIRED RELIGIONS, NOW KNOWN AS MYTHOLOGIES, AND WE FIND THAT MUSIC WAS CENTRAL TO THE GREEK MYTHS OF APOLLO, ORPHEUS, PAN, AND DIONYSUS. IT PLAYED AN IMPORTANT PART OF PHARAONIC RITES IN EGYPT, AND STRIKING A SILVER BRANCH WITH ITS THREE - OR NINE - FRUITS IN THE CELTIC UNDERWORLD CREATED AN ENCHANTING MELODY.

In 1969 the Beatles were still the most popular band in the world, but the fab four were busy squabbling and charting out individual courses. Ironically, they recorded John Lennon's "Come Together" that summer at Abbey Road Studios.

It's difficult to pinpoint the exact origin of *Paul is Dead*, but during that fall an urban legend grew among college kids scattered across various Midwest campuses that Paul McCartney was dead and that he was replaced by a look-alike. Stoned inquisitive minds soon found clues supporting the theory in song lyrics, on album covers, and by spinning certain songs backwards.

In the middle of October an on-air caller named Tom Zarski provided enough clues to convince Detroit DJ Russ Gibb to play the *White Album*'s "Revolution 9" backwards. Like Zarski promised, Gibb heard the words "Turn me on, dead man" in place of the chorus.

One of Gibb's listeners was a student journalist at the University of Michigan named Fred LaBour. Coincidentally he was assigned to review the Beatles' latest disc for the student newspaper. Inspired by the clues he had just learned about, LaBour spiced up the *Abbey Road* review with additional clues that he made up. It was meant in good fun, but people everywhere—even mainstream newspapers and newsweeklies—took his words literally.

Paul came out of seclusion and posed for a cover for *Newsweek* to prove that he was still alive, but the conspiracy had already taken a life of its own that will linger for as long as the Beatles' music.

A few clues are found on the iconic *Abbey Road* cover. One of those is the license plate on a white VW bug that's parked in background. The plate reads "281F," which is interpreted as "28 IF," the age Paul would've been *if* he was still alive. McCartney was born June 18, 1942, and *Abbey Road* was released in the UK September 26, 1969, which made him 27, not 28.

DEC. 13, 2003	APR. 22, 2004	AUG. 13, 2004	DEC. 26, 2004
US forces capture Saddam Hussein.	NFL player Pat Tillman (27) dies from friendly fire in Iraq.	Hurricane Charley kills 27 people in Florida.	Tsunamis in the Indian Ocean kills more that 225,000 people in 11 countries.

TO MANY MUSICIANS, 27 IS A CURSED AGE THAT THEY HOPE TO OULIVE. COUN-TRY artist Gretchen Wilson wears a dog tag with a 27 embossed on it, and she explains that it was "a number that just kind of showed up around the time that I got my record deal and "Redneck Woman" was first coming out on radio. It's a number that has just stayed with me ever since then. I don't know what it is or what it means. It just seems like now it's sort of a guiding light for me. If I go too long without seeing a 27, sometimes I feel like I might want to re-think the path that I'm on."

John Lennon was also intrigued with nine, his guiding number. This is not an ex-haustive list, but consider this:

He was born October 9 (as was his son Sean). Lennon took and failed nine General Certificate of Education exams (the equivalent of an American high school proficiency test). Brian Epstein first saw the Beatles November 9, 1961. Beatles signed their record contract May 9, 1962. Lennon penned songs titled "Revolution 9," "One After 909," and "No. 9 Dream." He first met Yoko Ono November 9, 1966. When John was shot and killed the evening of December 8, 1980, it was already December 9 in his hometown of Liver-pool.

Author Robert Rosen writes that after Lennon discovered *Cheiro's Book of Numbers* he consulted it incessantly. The Beatle recognized himself in Cheiro's explanations:

> *"Number 9 persons are fighters in all they attempt in life. They usually have dif-ficult times in their early years but generally are in the end successful by their grit, strong will and determination. They are hasty in temper, impulsive, independent, and desire to be their own masters."*

The book also made him alert to the significance of 9's multiples:

> *"The number nine is the only number that when multiplied by any number al-ways reproduces itself* [i.e. 9x5=45; 4+5=9]. *The number 9 is an emblem of matter that can never be destroyed."*

Lennon quickly found those multiples in other parts of his life; Yoko's birthday is February 18, Paul McCartney's is June 18, and Lennon received his green card July 27 after a drawn-out legal battle. The couple's New York City apartment was at West 72nd Street (9 x 8).

JULY 2, 2005

Live 8: Ten concurrent concerts takes place across the world in support of the "Make Poverty History" campaign.

Another obsessor was Bryan Ottoson, guitarist with the alternative metal band American Head Charge, who tattooed "333" on the back of his neck to represent the synchronicity of his life's events that seemingly happened in threes. He said he looked at the time every day at 3:33 p.m. and 3:33 a.m. inexplicably and without fail. Bryan died April 19, 2005, from an accidental prescription-drug overdose in the tour bus almost three years to the date after he joined the band. But the significance of threes didn't end with Ottoson's death. Brian Ottoson was 27 when he died (a factor of three) and the band cancelled three shows following his death.

While Ottoson is one of the last in the line of thirty-four 27s, it's interesting that another curse, if you want to call it that, preoccupied a different breed of musicians much like The 27s do today.

Born January 27, 1756, the famous classical composer Wolfgang Amadeus Mozart wrote twenty-seven numbered piano concertos. The premiere of *No. 27* was Mozart's last performance—he died of fever nine months later—and the piece paved way for the grandiose sound that the great composers favored in the nineteenth century. **The most famous of this wild-coifed crop was Ludwig van Beethoven, and his death three years after completing his last symphony seeded a mortal fear among composers that followed. It's known as the Curse Of the Ninth.**

Beethoven's Ninth premiered in 1824 and is perhaps the most famous classical piece ever written. The European Union voted to use one of the movements as its anthem, and if you've seen Stanley Kubrick's *A Clockwork Orange* you might recall that it's Alex's favorite composition.

JACK WHITE

Jack White of the White Stripes obsesses over the number three. Most of the band's sound, stage décor, record names, and liner notes can be broken down in threes. "Red, white and black is the most powerful color combination of all time," Mr. White says, "from a Coca-Cola can to a Nazi banner." Remember White's car accident on his 28th birthday? His left index finger broke in three places and was fixed with three tiny screws.

In 1979, Sony and Phillips met to discuss the size of the then-new compact disc. Phillips suggested a diameter of 11.5 centimeters, which was capable of storing sixty minutes of music, but Sony's vice-president Norio Ohga disagreed. He insisted that his favorite performance of Beethoven's Ninth, which happened to be the slowest version in the archives, should fit on a single disc. Convinced, Phillips decided to bump the CD's diameter to twelve centimeters so it would hold all seventy-four minutes of the Ninth.

This last symphony was written after Beethoven had gone deaf and was (and still is) regarded as such a masterpiece by critics and composers alike that nobody thought it could be topped. Nevertheless, it soon became a necessary goal that subsequent composers' Ninths were grand, crowning achievements.

Early in the twentieth century, composer Gustav Mahler was plagued by the series of eerie coincidences, starting with Beethoven's death in 1827. Franz Schubert completed his Ninth symphony and died. He was only thirty-one and was buried next to Beethoven, his idol. Fellow Austrian Anton Bruckner was old and frail when he sat down to write his Ninth in 1891. The symphony's first three movements were completed three years later, but he died while sketching out the finale, which was meant as a deference to Beethoven's Ninth. The Czech composer Antonín Dvořák followed. He completed his grand Ninth and died in 1904.

Beethoven's legacy fascinated Mahler immensely, but the events that had transpired since the master's death weighed heavily. Not only was he worried about making a Ninth that could stack up to his idol's, but he was also genuinely scared that he would die in the process. To beat the curse he didn't number the symphony that followed his Eighth—he named it instead. This clever decoy boosted his confidence that he had escaped the *Curse*

AMERICAN HEAD CHARGE

American Head Charge is an industrial/alternative/nü metal band akin to Slipknot and System of a Down. The group's self-released debut album caught the attention of Rick Rubin, who signed and produced *The War of Art* in 2001. By then the group was a supporting act on Ozzfest and the Pledge of Allegiance tour with Slipknot and others. In April of the following year guitarist Dave Rogers quit and Bryan Ottoson was invited to join. Less than 24 hours later Ottoson landed in Los Angeles to play guitar on the "Just So You Know" music video.

Over the next couple of years, three of the band members drifted out to the deep end with drug use. After rehab stints and a few new faces on board the band recorded *The Feeding*, which Bryan co-wrote ten out of twelve tracks for. The album was released in early '05, but disaster struck a few months later when Bryan was found cold on the bus. The night before, he downed a few drinks after a gig, popped penicillin and a pain med he was prescribed for strep throat, and went to bed in a bunk on the bus. They found the 27 year-old dead the following afternoon in North Carolina. His death was ruled an accidental prescription drug overdose.

Despite powerful live shows, AHC never made as good a name for themselves as some of their nü metal peers. Nevertheless, tracks from *The Feeding* (2005) have popped up here and there in popular entertainment. "Leave Me Alone" was featured on an episode of HBO's *Entourage*, while "Loyalty" was included in the multi-platform video-game *NHL 06*.

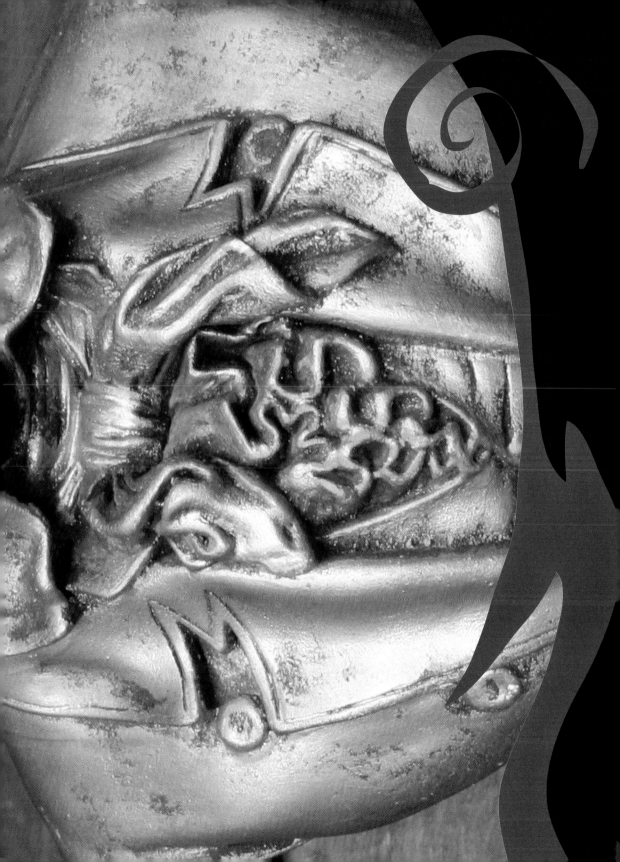

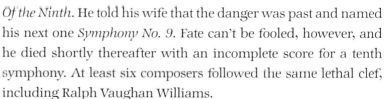

ALEXANDRE LEVY

Brazilian composer Alexandre Levy spent most of his life in São Paulo where he pioneered a fusion of classical composition with Brazil's popular folk music and rhythms. Levy died prematurely at 27 and Levy's hometown grants a prestigious award in his name.

Of the Ninth. He told his wife that the danger was past and named his next one *Symphony No. 9*. Fate can't be fooled, however, and he died shortly thereafter with an incomplete score for a tenth symphony. At least six composers followed the same lethal clef, including Ralph Vaughan Williams.

"It seems that the Ninth is a limit. He who wants to go beyond it must pass away. It seems as if something might be imparted to us in the Tenth which we ought not yet to know, for which we are not ready. Those who have written a Ninth stood too near to the hereafter," Austrian-American composer Arnold Schoenberg wrote in an essay about Mahler.

NIRVANA'S METAPHORICAL THRESHOLD TO THE HEREAFter was the band's performance at *MTV Unplugged*. In retrospect it was one of the most important shows of Cobain's career. He insisted that the MTV set would have to look different than it usually did. The network fought the idea, but eventually had to budge.

Kurt wanted stargazer lilies, black candles, and a crystal chandelier—mood setters usually reserved for funerals. To go with the theme, most of Kurt's song selections were dirges, and more than a third mentioned death.

Kurt was terrified of the acoustic format and entered the stage pale as a ghost. He was used to projecting his anger through 12 inch speakers, not an acoustic guitar. Although he stomped the overdrive pedal for David Bowie's "The Man Who Sold the World," the acoustic arrangements served his songs well. For many people the performance and subsequent live album demonstrated his songs' sensitivity, vulnerability, and emotion.

Nirvana closed the set with "Where Did You Sleep Last Night," a country blues traditional attributed to Kurt's favorite blues artist Leadbelly. The tune dates back to the 1870s, and bluegrass and country artists such as Bill Monroe, Peter Rowan, Merle Travis, and Gene Clark have played it. Pigpen and the Dead recorded it as "In the Pines" on an early demo, and Dolly Parton included it on *Heartsongs*, released the same year as Nirvana's *Unplugged*. "The song has been handed down through many generations of my family," Parton explained in an interview. On the surface it seems odd that the King of Grunge would perform an old folk standard, but the song's dark lyrics about love and decapitation fit Cobain's persona. Not only that, he screamed that last line like he meant it: *"I'll shiver the whole night through."*

Less than five months later he faced the barrel of the shotgun and pulled the trigger. Courtney wasn't present at Kurt's public vigil, but she offered a taped spiel where she read from Kurt's suicide note and added commentary. She prefaced the last sentence by saying, "Don't remember this because this is a fuckin' lie." It read, *"It's better to burn out than to fade away,"* a line from Neil

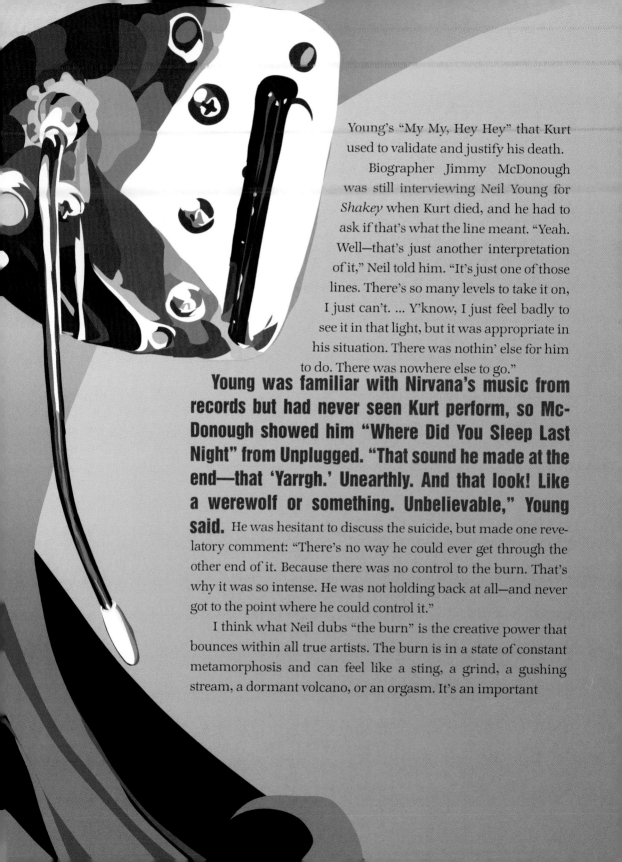

Young's "My My, Hey Hey" that Kurt used to validate and justify his death.

Biographer Jimmy McDonough was still interviewing Neil Young for *Shakey* when Kurt died, and he had to ask if that's what the line meant. "Yeah. Well—that's just another interpretation of it," Neil told him. "It's just one of those lines. There's so many levels to take it on, I just can't. ... Y'know, I just feel badly to see it in that light, but it was appropriate in his situation. There was nothin' else for him to do. There was nowhere else to go."

Young was familiar with Nirvana's music from records but had never seen Kurt perform, so Mc-Donough showed him "Where Did You Sleep Last Night" from Unplugged. "That sound he made at the end—that 'Yarrgh.' Unearthly. And that look! Like a werewolf or something. Unbelievable," Young said. He was hesitant to discuss the suicide, but made one revelatory comment: "There's no way he could ever get through the other end of it. Because there was no control to the burn. That's why it was so intense. He was not holding back at all—and never got to the point where he could control it."

I think what Neil dubs "the burn" is the creative power that bounces within all true artists. The burn is in a state of constant metamorphosis and can feel like a sting, a grind, a gushing stream, a dormant volcano, or an orgasm. It's an important

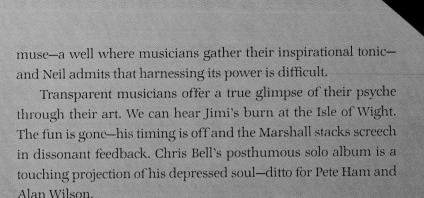

muse—a well where musicians gather their inspirational tonic—and Neil admits that harnessing its power is difficult.

Transparent musicians offer a true glimpse of their psyche through their art. We can hear Jimi's burn at the Isle of Wight. The fun is gone—his timing is off and the Marshall stacks screech in dissonant feedback. Chris Bell's posthumous solo album is a touching projection of his depressed soul—ditto for Pete Ham and Alan Wilson.

Nietzsche called the burn a Dionysian reaction, and The 27s used it to compose, record, and perform music that added new veins to the organism of rock & roll. Some are thick arteries while others are mere trickles. Brian Jones. Jimi Hendrix. Janis Joplin. Jim Morrison. Kurt Cobain. Strong associations appear from merely reading their names. Jimi once said he wanted to lead a big band, and in a profound way he got what he asked for. He has written and conducted by example for pretty much every rock band since he took London by storm.

The big five's instant impact hasn't been replicated by the rest of The 27s, but that's of little importance to the greater story. D. Boon and the Minutemen were important to fans in the American hardcore scene. The trio showed that it was possible to make songs and tour without industry sponsorship and stadium engagements. Their "our band could be your life" philosophy

inspired an infant Red Hot Chili Peppers, R.E.M.'s Michael Stipe, Sublime's Brad Nowell, and many more.

Then there are 27s who, like vintage wine, get better with age. Artists are frequently misunderstood, and it can take time before their influence manifests. Take the Stooges, who expanded on the Stones' dirtiness. Compare "I Wanna Be Your Dog" to "I Wanna Be Your Man." At the tail end of the sixties the unrefined garage sound was abandoned until the reactionary Stooges added crude chaos and über-fuzzy guitars to the shambles of early rock. People literally laughed at the music and lack of musicianship, but were transfixed by Iggy's outrageous stage antics. The proto-punkers remained a freakish anomaly until the Ramones united in their love of the Stooges and popularized punk. In a few decades the Stooges went from being the wart of rock to having its three early records on *Rolling Stone*'s Top 500 Albums of All Time. Not bad, huh?

Similarly, power pop picked up where the Beatles left off, but Big Star and Badfinger were oddballs too. Saccharine harmonies and tight rock arrangements weren't nearly as

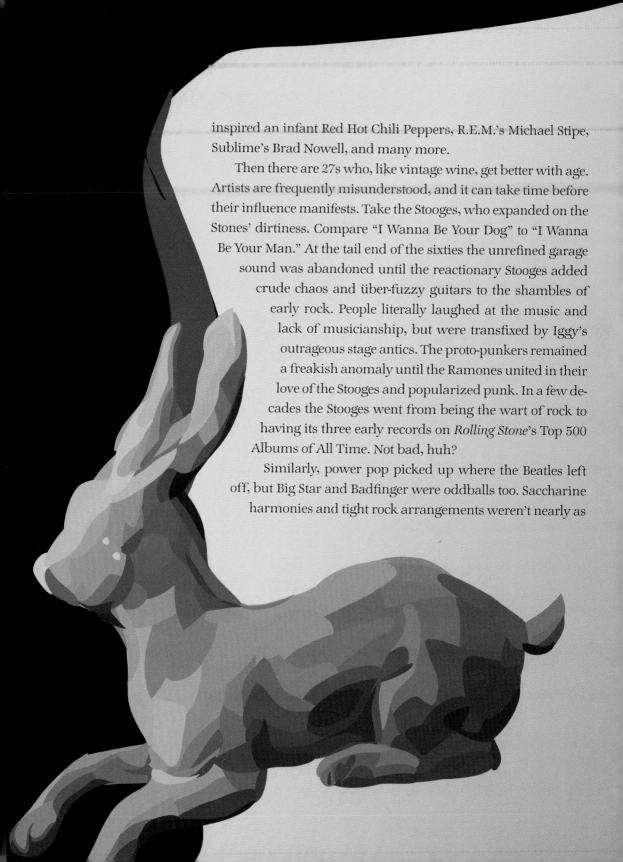

cool as misogynic stadium rock. Yet away from the flattering spotlight they produced a sound that paved way for Cheap Trick, The Bangles, The Smithereens, Teenage Fanclub, The Posies, Matthew Sweet, and others.

Bear in mind that influencing other musicians can take years or even decades, so it's difficult to determine how important Sean McCabe, Jeremy Ward or Brian Ottoson will be five or ten years from now. It all depends on how they are remembered by fans and musicians, but if The Mars Volta's explosive popularity is any indication, Jeremy Ward might very well become increasingly revered.

Rock's thickest artery is without doubt the blues as it nourishes every other sub-genre with its music and/or lyrical themes of love, suffering and sudden fortune. Its undisputed leader, at least in the eyes of rockers, is Robert Johnson.

He lived without limousine success and appears naked in his suffering, mysterious and enigmatic. His desperate, depressing, short, magnificent and creative life epitomizes the bruise worn by all 27s. Brian's blues. Jimi's blues. Jim's blues. Janis's blues. Gary's blues. Dyke's blues. Jeremy's blues. Alan's blues. Chris's blues. D.'s blues. Mia's blues. Tah's blues. Kurt's blues. Jeremy's blues. And so on.

"People, whether they know it or not, like their blues singers miserable," Janis told rock critic and biographer David Dalton. "Maybe my audience can enjoy my music more if they think I'm destroying myself." Cue Amy Winehouse.

A glance in the rearview mirror shows just how habitually drawn we are to tragedies. Theatre sprung from this art form in ancient Greece. Fast-forward to a famous play written in late six-

teenth century England: *Romeo and Juliet* is the greatest love story of all time because the lovers take their own lives to be together forever. Janis was right: we are drawn to miserable blues singers, desperate lovers, hopelessly addicted rock stars, mobster bosses, clever drug lords, and intelligent killers—any time beauty is coupled with tragedy. It's an unbeatable combination that the sensationalist press knows how to cover, and it's a tradition that runs like a bloody river from the gladiators in Roman coliseums to the glossy celeb weeklies of today. Death and celebrity have always fascinated mankind.

If somebody collected the causes of rock star deaths and placed them in a hat, The 27s would run the gamut: a couple of car and plane crashes, heroin overdoses, over-abused livers, cancer and disease, a possible drowning, a disappearance, murder, drive-by and assassination, strychnine, monoxide poisoning, suicide by hanging, an equestrian accident, and gobbling liberally from rock star accoutrements and then choking while sleeping it off in a comatose state.

It's no wonder that the deaths of young artists receive attention and continue to fascinate even decades after they're gone. The world keeps spinning, but the works and personas of these creative souls remain as definite as the stoic gravestones commemorating their lives. **The 27s will never release a string of strung-out records, play sponsored reunion tours, or become world activists with White House meetings.**

"There are glints of beauty and bedrock of joy that come shining through from time to precious time to remind anyone who cares to see that there is something higher and larger than ourselves," legendary rock critic Lester Bangs once wrote.

The 27s were still young when they died for their art and ideals—a prerequisite for that iconic status. They will always be on the top of their game, or at least near it. Yet we can't help but wonder what they would've sounded like if they hadn't died when they did. Would Pete Ham have retired from touring to a studio cabin in the woods where he'd write pop hits for a new crop of stars? Would Jesse Belvin have been a black counterpoint to Frank Sinatra? What would Hendrix sound like? Acoustic folk blues? Jazz-rock fusion a la Miles Davis? Sweaty disco-funk or MIDI guitar surrealism? In the end it doesn't matter because The 27s were never dealt cards for the later rounds. They did what they could in 27 short years and left music cherished by millions around the world.

Rock is ruthless; it's an art controlled by a few industry heavies where success is measured by record sales. Rock is big business where an original sound isn't enough to triumph and platinum sales don't necessarily equal money. And even those who do find financial success aren't home free. Soon the brutal realities that are glued to fame become evident. The sex. The drugs. Long nights. Recording. Endless touring. The lack of stability. The press. The pressures.

The 27s epitomize rock, bound by strong passions, ingenious music, and incredible fame scarred by cutthroat tribulations, death, and disillusion. They're connected by their age, three to the third power, divinity multiplied by itself. Lester Bangs wrote, "It may be time, in spite of all indications to the contrary from the exterior society, to begin thinking in terms of heroes again, of love instead of hate, of energy instead of violence, of strength instead of cruelty, of action instead of reaction."

the WRONG way

The day following Cobain's death, *Seattle Times* ran a four-column wide photo that showed parts of his dead body as seen through the window. The paper had cropped what was left of his head and splattered brains, but one of his legs, a black Converse All-Stars sneaker, and parts of his torso were visible in all its gory glory. The photo proved too much for fans and the public. It was a rare case that pained our collective voyeurism, enough for us to object in unison, "*Show some respect for krissakes!*" Or was it simply that we didn't want to see just *how* tragically our hero-rock-star died?

As music fans most of us fall victim to the glorification of rock star culture—sex, drugs, and rock & roll—but we don't want to see them comatose with a needle in the arm, passed out with a white-rimmed bloody nose, or their body mutilated after a traffic accident. We'll save that kind of voyeurism for the *real* heroin addicts on inner-city streets and the random accidents we can slow down to see.

"If the word death were absent from our vocabulary," celebrated writer Arthur Koestler wrote six years before he committed suicide, "our great works of literature would have remained unwritten, pyramids and cathedrals would not exist, nor works of religious art—and all art is of religious or magic origin. The pathology and creativity of the human mind are two sides of the same medal, coined by the same mint master." Real artists wear that medal every day, and we expect them to. Their job is to dazzle, baffle, inspire, and create empathy and disgust. And bear in mind that it's an ungrateful task that eats away the soul of its creator.

Aldous Huxley once wrote, "After silence, that which comes nearest to expressing the inexpressible is music." Music holds a divine power. It has the ability to bring back memories of youthful summers, can lift spirits to incredible highs, provide comfort during lows, make you laugh, smile, cry, dance, reflect, meditate, focus, or lose yourself to Dionysic ecstasy. The 27s have provided that cultural and emotional soundtrack ever since Robert Johnson was poisoned in 1938.

Three years ago we sat in a Chicago bar down the street from the fabled Chess recording studio and decided to create this book about The 27s. On the surface they're all connected by their deaths, but we wanted the book to be a celebration of their lives and legacies. It's a strange oxymoron that these fantastic people are dead, yet keep on giving, inspiring, and almost... well, still living. Don't fall in the trap of emphasizing *it's better to burn out than to fade away*. The line that matters isn't found in the first verse, it's in the last:

"Hey hey, my my / rock and roll can never die."

Thanks for the music.

SELECTED SOURCES

Ambrose, Joe. *Gimme Danger: The Story of Iggy Pop.* London: Omnibus Press, 2002.

Albertson, Chris. *Bessie.* New Haven: Yale University Press, rev. and ex. ed., 2003.

Azerrad, Michael. *Our Band Could Be Your Life: Scenes from the American Indie Underground 1981-1991.* New York: Back Bay Books, 2001.

———. *Come as You Are: The Story of Nirvana.* New York: Doubleday, 1994.

Bangs, Lester. *Psychotic Reactions and Carburetor Dung: The Work of a Legendary Critic: Rock 'N' Roll as Literature and Literature as Rock 'N' Roll.* New York: Anchor Books, 1988.

Bellis, Mark A., Tom Hennell, Clare Lushey, Karen Hughes, Karen Tocque, and John R. Ashton. *Elvis to Eminem: quantifying the price of fame through early mortality of European and North American rock and pop stars.* Journal of Epidemiology and Community Health 2007; 61:896-901.

Brite, Poppy Z. Courtney *Love: The Real Story.* New York: Simon & Shuster, 1997.

Brown, Geoff. *The Life of James Brown.* London: Omnibus Press, 2008.

Bynoe, Yvonne. *Encyclopedia of Rap and Hip Hop Culture.* Westport, Connecticut: Greenwood Press, 2005.

Charles, Ray. *Brother Ray: Ray Charles' Own Story.* New York: Da Capo Press, 1978.

Cheiro. *Cheiro's Book of Numbers.* New York: Arco Publishing, 1980.

Clayson, Alan. *Brian Jones.* London: Sanctuary Publishing Ltd., 2003.

Cobain, Kurt. *Kurt Cobain Journals.* New York: Riverhead Books, 2002.

Cooper, Mark. *Liverpool Explodes.* London: Sidgwick & Jackson, 1982.

FEB. 22, 2006	MAR. 25, 2006	JUNE 2006	AUG. 19, 2006	JAN. 1, 2007
The Apples iTunes Store sells its 1,000,000,000[th] music track.	Downtown LA is crowded with 500,000 people protesting a proposed crackdown on illegal immigration.	The Western press reports on "Zirzamin 27," Iran's covert nuclear project.	Reggae icon Joseph Hill dies after leading Culture for 27 years.	After the inclusion of Romania and Bulgaria, the European Union now numbers 27 members.

Cope, Julian. *Head-On: Memories of the Liverpool Punk-scene and the story of The Teardrop Explodes (1976-82)*. London: Thorsons, 1999.

———. *Repossessed: Shamanic Depressions in Tamworth & London (1983-89)*. London: Thorsons, 1999.

Courrier, Kevin. *Dangerous Kitchen: The Subversive World of Zappa*. ECW Press, 2002.

Cross, Charles R. *Room Full of Mirrors: A Biography of Jimi Hendrix*. New York: Hyperion, 2005.

———. *Heavier Than Heaven: A Biography of Kurt Cobain*. New York: Hyperion, 2001.

Dalton, David. *Piece of My Heart: A Portrait of Janis Joplin*. New York: Da Capo Press, 1991.

Davis, Stephen. *Jim Morrison: Life, Death, Legend*. New York: Gotham Books, 2004.

De la Parra, Fito. *Living the Blues*. Self-published, 1999.

Densmore, John. *Riders on the Storm: My Life With Jim Morrison and the Doors*. New York: Delacorte Press, 1990.

Dodd, David. *The Complete Annotated Grateful Dead Lyrics*. New York: Free Press, 2005.

Dyson, Michael Eric. *Mercy, Mercy Me: The Art, Loves and Demons of Marvin Gaye*. New York: Basic Civitas Books, 2004.

Echols, Alice. *Scars of Sweet Paradise: The Life and Times of Janis Joplin*. New York: Henry Holt and Company, 1999.

Evans, David. *Tommy Johnson*. London: Studio Vista, 1971.

Faithfull, Marianne, and David Dalton. *Faithfull: An Autobiography*. New York: Little, Brown and Company, 1994.

Friedman, Myra. *Buried Alive: The Biography of Janis Joplin*. New York: Bantam Books, 1974.

Gans, David, and Peter Simon. *Playing in the Band: An Oral and Visual Portrait of the Grateful Dead*. New York: St. Martin's Griffin, July 1996.

Getz, Michael M., and John R. Dwork. *The Deadhead's Taping Compendium Volume I*. New York: Henry Holt and Company, 1998.

Gordon, Robert. *Can't Be Satisfied: The Life and Times of Muddy Waters.* New York: Little, Brown and Company, 2002.

Gribin, Dr. Anthony J., and Dr. Matthew M. Schiff. *The Complete Book of Doo-Wop.* Iola, Wisconsin: Krause Publications, 2000.

Guralnick, Peter. *Dream Boogie: The Triumph of Sam Cooke.* New York: Little, Brown and Company, 2005.

Gysin, Brion. Ed. Jason Weiss. *Back In No Time: The Brion Gysin Reader.* Middletown, Connecticut: Wesleyan University Press, 2001.

Halperin, Ian, and Max Wallace. *Who Killed Kurt Cobain? The Mysterious Death of an Icon.* New York: Citadel Press, 2000.

Holzman, Jac, and Gavan Daws. *Follow the Music: The life and high times of Elektra Records in the great years of American pop culture.* Santa Monica, California: FirstMedia Books, 2000.

Hopkins, Jerry, and Daniel Sugerman. *No One Here Gets Out Alive.* New York: Warner Books, 1980.

James, Etta, and David Ritz. *Rage to Survive: The Etta James Story.* New York: Villard Books, 1995.

Johnson, James Weldon. *The Autobiography of an Ex-Colored Man.* Boston: Sherman, French & Co., 1912.

Jovanovic, Rob. *Big Star: The Short Life, Painful death, and Unexpected Resurrection of the Kings of Power Pop.* Chicago: Chicago Review Press, 2005.

Manzarek, Ray. *Light My Fire: My Life with the Doors.* New York: Putnam, 1998.

Matovina, Dan. *Without You: The Tragic Story of Badfinger.* San Mateo, California: Frances Glover Books, 2000.

McDonough, Jimmy. *Shakey: Neil Young's Biography.* New York: Random House, 2002.

McNally, Dennis. *A Long Strange Trip: The Inside History of the Grateful Dead.* New York: Broadway Books, 2002.

McStravick, Summer, and John Roos. *Blues-Rock Explosion.* Mission Viejo: Old Goat Publishing, 2001.

Mitchell, Mitch, and John Platt. *The Hendrix Experience.* New York: Da Capo Press, 1998.

Morrison, Jim. *The American Night.* New York: Vintage, 1991.

———. *Wilderness: The Lost Writings of Jim Morrison.* New York: Vintage, 1989.

Murray, Charles Shaw. *Boogie Man.* New York: St. Martin Press, 2000.

Nietzsche, Friedrich. *The Basic Writings of Nietzsche.* Trans. Walter Kaufmann. New York: The Modern Library, 2000.

Obrecht, Jas. *The Men Who Made The Music.* San Francisco: Miller Freeman Books, 1993.

Patterson, Gary R. *The Walrus Was Paul: The Great Beatle Death Clues.* New York: Fireside, 1998.

Price, Simon. *Everything (A Book About Manic Street Preachers).* London: Virgin Books, 1999.

Scully, Rock, and David Dalton. *Living with the Dead: twenty years on the bus with Garcia and the Grateful Dead.* New York: Little, Brown and Co., 1996.

Shapiro, Peter. *The Rough Guide to Hip-Hop.* 2nd ed. London: Rough Guides Ltd., 2005.

Smitherman, Geneva. *Talkin' and Testifying: The Language of Black America.* Boston: Houghton Mifflin Company, 1977.

Szatmary, David P. *Rockin' in Time: A Social History of Rock-and-Roll.* Upper Saddle River: Prentice-Hall, 2004.

Rolling Stone. *Rolling Stone Cover to Cover: The First 40 Years.* New York: Bondi Digital Publishing, 2007.

Tate, Greg. *Midnight Lightning: Jimi Hendrix and the Black Experience.* Chicago: Lawrence Hill Books, 2003.

Thompson, Dave. *Cream—The World's First Supergroup.* London: Virgin Books Ltd., 2005.

True, Everett. *The White Stripes and the Sound of Mutant Blues.* London: Omnibus Press, 2004.

Trynka, Paul. *Iggy Pop: Open Up and Bleed.* New York: Broadway Books, 2007.

Vincent, Rickey. *Funk: The Music, The People, and The Rhythm of The One.* New York: St. Martin's Griffin, 1996.

Wallace, Max, and Ian Halperin. *Love & Death: The Murder of Kurt Cobain.* New York: Simon & Schuster, 2004.

Wyman, Bill, and Ray Coleman. *Stone Alone.* New York: Viking, 1990.

307

FEB. 14, 2008

A 27 year-old cowardly shot 21 people, then himself, at Northern Illinois University.

JULY 21, 2008

Baltimore radio DJ K-Swift (29), a.k.a. Khia Edgerton, dies from a head injury in her pool.

AUG. 27, 2008

Blogger Kevin Cogill (27) arrested for posting nine unreleased Guns n' Roses songs.

SIGNIFICANT INTERVIEWS

Ed Berlin, Jesse Belvin Jr., Todd Baptista, Mick Box, Joshua Brown, Rich Cason, John Dixon, Ken Hensley, Nick Kollerstrom, Brian McCabe, Elaine "Spanky" McFarlane, Skip Taylor, Robby Redcheeks, Tito Rogers, Rob Tillett, Sonja Wagner (nee Gindl), Mike Watt.

MAGAZINES & NEWSPAPERS

BBC, Blues & Rhythm, Circus, Crawdaddy!, Creem, Down Beat, Guitar Player, Guitar World, The Los Angeles Times, Melody Maker, Mojo, New Musical Express, The New York Times, Playboy, Rolling Stone, Smash Hits, Time, The Wire.

WEBSITES

BlindOwl.net, Daveyd.com, Furious.com/perfect, GaryThain.com, Google.com/video, MetaCritic.com, RicheyEdwards.net, Secondhandsongs.com, YouTube.com, Wikipedia.com.

Visit The27s.com
for limited edition merch and more.